# Stir It Up

# Stir It Up

## *Home Economics in American Culture*

Megan J. Elias

UNIVERSITY OF PENNSYLVANIA PRESS

PHILADELPHIA

Published by
University of Pennsylvania Press
Philadelphia, Pennsylvania 19104–4112

Printed in the United States of America on acid-free paper

10  9  8  7  6  5  4  3  2  1

Library of Congress Cataloging-in-Publication Data
Elias, Megan J.
    Stir it up : home economics in American culture / Megan J. Elias.
        p. cm.
    Includes bibliographical references and index.
    ISBN 978-0-8122-4079-5 (alk. paper)
    1. Home economics—United States—History—20th century.   2. Women—United States—Social conditions—20th century.   I. Title.
TX23.E45   2008
392.30973'0904—dc22                                             2008006000

*For Diana Vincent-Daviss (1943–1993)*

# CONTENTS

# Introduction

IN 2003, a high school student in Glens Falls, New York, told a reporter that he would take a home economics class only if he were "real, real hungry."[1] A little more than sixty years earlier, in the popular movie *The Best Years of Our Lives*, screenwriter Robert Sherwood offered a different perspective on the subject. In this 1946 movie, an army sergeant returns home from World War II to find that his family has learned to manage without him. His daughter, Peggy, remarks that a class in domestic science at the local college has enabled her to take over the housekeeping after the family's servant left. In both 2003 and 1946, learning home economics was presented as an emergency measure, but in Sherwood's screenplay the topic served a heroic purpose while in the case of the Glens Falls high school student, it is a joke.

To better understand the meaning of home economics in American culture and society today, it is important to examine its origins and history over the past century. Contrary to the popular myth that "home ec" was born in the conformist culture of the 1950s, home economics began as an organized social movement at the end of the nineteenth century. It encompassed several interconnected and sometimes contradictory agendas, but can loosely be described as a movement to professionalize domestic work and domestic space. Leaders of the home economics movement advocated studying the home, using both physical and social sciences. Based on this research, they would discover and propagate the best methods for performing work. In addition and no less significantly, they hoped to create new professions that were connected to the elements of home life and imagined that women in particular would be drawn to these professions, creating new opportunities outside the home. Though the earliest home economists saw theirs as a rigorously scientific pursuit to put work in the home on par with other forms of paid labor, because women had traditionally performed this work, the proposed reforms would affect women's status in society and thus had much wider implications.

Because of the work of this first generation of home economists, by the end of World War II, Americans had accepted the idea that domestic space could be a site for social change, even for heroism on a small scale. Over the next fifty years that possibility evaporated as American popular culture, most intensely in the 1950s, emphasized the domestic sphere as a place where social changes did not occur—a space safe from all the upheavals of modern life. The only changes that Americans were encouraged to adopt at home during the 1950s were technological advances. A new toaster was always welcome, but new gender roles were not.

Simultaneous to the development of home economics as a field of academic inquiry, corporate producers of household goods—everything from macaroni to scouring powder—were establishing themselves as authorities on all things domestic. While female academics of the 1930s attempted to convince college girls that each woman was principal investigator in her own laboratory, Campbell's and Crisco and the makers of linoleum were tempting them to cede all responsibility for household science to corporations. Starting in the 1920s, corporations hired home economists to publicize their products, redirecting the legitimacy that these academics had created for themselves to increase profits. On the one hand this cooptation created more professional opportunities for women, particularly in business, but on the other hand it tossed aside the field's original message of women's liberation through control of the domestic environment. And in the final analysis, corporations won out over academics, commodifying lifestyles so that home economics in popular culture became product-focused rather than an intellectual movement.

This book is more than simply an institutional history; it places home economics in cultural context. It begins with an overview of the rise of home economics in higher education and then focuses on two shifts in American thinking about the subject. The first shift began in the 1920s and occurred gradually as corporations took over the domestic expertise that home economists had carved out for themselves. The second shift occurred in the 1950s when home economics largely lost the cultural authority that leaders in the field had struggled to attain. During this era, home economics became associated with dead-end high school classes for girls. Both of these shifts involved changes in popular thinking about women's roles and about domestic life.

Although home economics no longer exists as a unified movement, many of the issues its pioneers raised remain contested in the twenty-first century. Certainly the central issue of how to establish equality of authority between consumers and producers of goods remains with us, particularly in relation to food. A 2006 study found, for example, that although a majority of Americans say that they would prefer to eat healthful food, they continue to buy the larger and more fatty meals offered to them by fast-food restaurants. In this case some of the messages of home economics have been absorbed into the culture, but others, such as the power of the consumer to change the market, have not.[2]

The problem of how to value our domestic lives in relation to work for money outside the home also continues to vex American women and, increasingly, American men as well. In a nation constantly bombarded with exhortations to put "family values" above all else, there is a simultaneous push to succeed financially at all costs. These two messages are often experienced as incompatible. Indeed, at the end of the twentieth century even male government officials frequently offered the (albeit suspect) excuse that they wanted "to spend more time with family" as a reason for leaving office. In the first six years of the twenty-first century, a new focus on motherhood has produced countless web logs, guidebooks, and manifestos about what it means to care for children in modern America. And, as marriage and adoption laws are challenged and expanded, Americans experience deep conflicts over what the term "family" can mean.[3]

At the same time, persistent and growing fascination with the domestic environment as a site for change and personal transformation creates seemingly endless markets for television shows about homes, domestic-themed magazines, and domestic product lines. While Americans seem for the most part uninterested in the kind of education for and about home life that home economists of the first half of the twentieth century proposed, they exhibit a voracious appetite for the commodity of home, purveyed to them by producers of foodstuffs, house wares, television shows, magazines, and books. Home economics helped to create this market, and for this it deserves our attention no less than for the fact that it simultaneously offered strategies to resist this same powerful trend.

## Home Economics Before the Home Economics Movement

Since the late eighteenth century, American women have had access to domestic manuals and have thus been able to rely on strangers for advice on how to manage their own homes. Early domestic manuals focused particularly on how to prepare foods and how to care for sick family members but also offered advice on laundry and house cleaning. The great majority of women, however, would have learned household duties and skills not from books but from female relatives, usually mothers. This was true both because most Americans could not afford to own books and because until the end of the nineteenth century, American culture did not favor experts or value expertise.

Until the era of professional specialization that began after the Civil War, most Americans trusted experience over analysis, particularly in matters relating to the household and to agricultural production. This began to change after 1862, when the Morrill Land-Grant Colleges Act established universities in each state in which rural men could be trained in the newest methods of farming or engineering. As the Land-Grant universities grew, some also began offering courses for rural women, bringing to them new ideas about how to perform housework. Home economics—the rationalization and professionalization of housework—grew out of these early courses.

Before the advent of home economics, however, the American home passed through several important changes. Some of these were material changes, and others were changes in social and cultural attitudes toward homes and women. Beginning in the 1820s, mass production of textiles removed spinning and weaving from most homes, and the emerging market in affordable consumer goods gave women new roles as shoppers and consumers for their families. Simultaneously, new national ideals began to focus on woman's role as first teacher of children. Particularly in the northeast there emerged a call for women to receive a basic education so that their sons might have better role models as they grew into full and virtuous citizenship. Even as women were gaining access to basic education in topics traditionally considered male, they were also encouraged to think of their lives within the home as sacred and the work they performed there as vital to society. This ideal, generally known as the cult of domesticity, identified woman's highest calling as thoughtful wife and mother. As material production retreated more and more rapidly from the home, women acquired new roles as spiritual guardians and also as consumers of mass-produced goods. By necessity these ideals, propagated in popular fiction and women's magazines, applied only to the middle and upper middle class, but such women were supposed to serve as models for all women.

An 1850 story in the popular magazine *Godey's Lady's Book* updated the tale of the country mouse and the city mouse, presenting a comparison between two female cousins that reduced morality to shopping habits. The two cousins of "Furnishing; or Two Ways of Commencing Life" were both engaged to be married and were making all of the major purchases for their new households. Anne lived in a rural town and had significantly less money to spend than her cousin, Adelaide, who was wealthy and urban. Both had been well educated, but only Anne prayed and attended church regularly. On shopping trips in the city where Anne was visiting her cousin, Adelaide spent extravagantly while Anne delighted in thrift and modesty, valuing utility above all else in her "furnishings." Although the author did not present the story as an analysis of the emerging market economy, the fact that the young women had so many choices and that they could shop for them reflected a new era of commodified domesticity. Within three years, Adelaide's husband went bankrupt, largely through his wife's improvident spending, and left for California without her. Anne's family meanwhile flourished, although in a respectably modest way. The author's reduction of two women to their decorating styles allowed the story to serve two purposes simultaneously as education and entertainment. Anne's piety, though not overtly emphasized in the story, hinted at the sanctification of the modest housewife that was to find full expression in Catharine Beecher's *The American Woman's Home*.[4]

Catharine Beecher was the most famous proponent of the ideal of woman as household saint and was also the first popular writer to suggest that the home should be run on business principles. Her 1869 *The American Woman's Home*, which she wrote with her famous sister, the novelist Harriet Beecher Stowe, offered readers not just household hints but a whole new philosophy of home management based in her own devout Christianity. Beecher defined home, family, and woman together, arguing, "The family state then, is the aptest earthly illustration of the heavenly kingdom, and in it woman is its chief minister. Her great mission is self-denial, in training its members to self-sacrificing labors for the ignorant and weak."[5] Beecher argued that it was unreasonable to expect women to fulfill this sacred mission without the proper training, which she offered in her book. She also claimed that once young women acquired this training and came to think of themselves as professionals within the home, the status of housekeeper would no longer be ranked among menial occupations but would be "as much desired and respected as are the most honored professions of men." It was quite clear that even when this glorious day arrived, however, Beecher did not expect men to desire that desirable position. In Beecher's universe, women and men existed in separate but equally valued and interdependent spheres.[6]

Catharine Beecher

Beecher's book is important as the first attempt to claim professional status for homemaking. She also, like the home economists who would form their movement later in the century, presented herself to the reading public as an authority on household matters. Unlike the home economists to come, however, she located her authority in experience, not study, having helped to raise her twelve younger siblings. This was a common strategy for writers about domestic issues in this time period, as evidenced by a story that appeared in *Arthur's Home Magazine* the year after the Beecher sisters published their guidebook. In this story, an elderly aunt advised a niece on the care of her first child, who suffered from colic. The niece, who claimed spiritedly that she would not take criticism from any other source, made an exception for her aunt because the woman had helped to raise her.[7] Taking her aunt's advice, she cured her baby.

The story offered readers potentially useful information but presented it as ancient wisdom rather than as something new. The magazine editors could assume an audience of young women who, in this era of western migration, urbanization, and privatization of family life, would not have as much casual access to the knowledge of older women as they would have had in early periods. The aunt in the story stands in for the absent aunts and mothers of the readers, bringing information that they can trust because it is delivered by a female authority who gained her expertise through experience.

Beecher's approach to domestic knowledge was novel and apparently very popular. *The American Woman's Home* became one of the best sellers of the century. The book's popularity stemmed from the fact that Beecher incorporated old and new ideas about women's ideal role in society, thereby providing her readers with reassurance as well as rethinking. On the one hand she celebrated traditional gender divisions, conflating woman with home and man with the world, but on the other she argued that women should be understood to be professionals, although always within their proper sphere. The book covered many of the topics that home economics would later embrace, such as sanitation, interior design, and health, but also included a focus on religion that would be absent from the later movement.

Building on the great success of Beecher's guidebook as well as on the growth of the middle class, a new market in domestic manuals and household science courses emerged in the 1870s. Women such as Mary Lincoln and Maria Parloa opened cooking schools and prepared advice manuals that could help middle-class women manage homes that were larger and in many ways different from those that their mothers had presided over. More stuff and

*Late 20c not 1st time ✓ teaching from*
*Moms → daughters*
*— w. expans.*
*— indust.*
*— new households*

more space, more display and less production marked the modern home as
different from that of earlier generations. Middle-class women also spent less
time actually doing and more time managing others in the performance of ✓
household tasks. Manuals that instructed them in proper methods as well as
schools to train staff promised to ease the transition from one kind of home
to another.

Home economics emerged at the end of the nineteenth century in re- ✗
sponse to and because of many changes occurring both at the level of material
culture and practices and in the more abstract realm of gender ideology and
thinking about the home. A new social discourse was emerging, known loosely
as progressivism, which privileged scientific explanations and demanded social
reform. As the industrial revolution took hold of the American economy and
as mass production, alienation, and urbanization appeared to be unstoppable
trends, Americans looked for solutions that could soften the effects of change
without slowing down the engines of progress.

In 1893 some of the trends toward home economics education came together at the Columbian Exposition in Chicago. There, as part of Massachusetts's contribution to the fair, Ellen Richards and Mary Hinman Abel offered
visitors a model kitchen designed along the same lines as the New England
Kitchen, a kitchen and restaurant they had established earlier in Boston.
Richards was a chemist and Abel was a self-taught nutritionist. Set up in a free-
standing cottage, the kitchen was designed to demonstrate "the application of
science to the preparation of food." The walls of the kitchen were decorated
with "mottoes" related to the home economics philosophy. Among these inspi-
rational sayings, which many visitors wrote down, were anonymous witticisms
such as "There are three companions with whom you should keep on good
terms—your wife, your stomach, and your conscience," and Oliver Wendell
Holmes's culinary aesthetic: "Plain food is quite good enough for me."[8]

Workers in the kitchen sold food to fair-goers, partly as a way to recoup
costs of the exhibit but mostly in order to introduce a wider American public
to the kind of wholesome low-cost meals that Richards and Abel believed
would improve national health and wealth. There is no way of knowing
whether they were successful in making the distinction between lunch and lesson real to their audience, but visitors were particularly eager to take home the
pamphlets prepared for them. In these pamphlets, published as a set subtitled
"Plain Words about Food," Richards, Abel, and seven other writers presented ✓
work that was eclectic in its approach, ranging from Richards's own simple
advice on "Good Food for Little Money" to physiologist R. H. Chittenden's

*Ellen Richards + Mary Hinman*
*Abel*

discussion of "the Digestibility of Proteid Foods," to Abel's "King Palate," a fable about how King Palate's kingdom, plagued with imps such as dyspepsia, was rescued by a knight known as Knowledge.⁹ The ideals that Abel and Richards showcased in Chicago were the founding principles of a national movement six years later.

## The Movement Begins

The first organized meeting of home economists occurred in Lake Placid, New York, in 1899, where the nine women and one man in attendance outlined a plan to bring together developing trends in education that were related but not yet overtly connected. The group called itself the Lake Placid Conference on Home Economics and met annually until 1909 when it became the American Home Economics Association (AHEA). An invitation went out in 1899 to gather "those most interested in home science, or household economics" in the belief that "the time was ripe for some united action" on their part.¹⁰

What brought the group together in 1899 was a perceived need to win public recognition for this diverse work as both interrelated and important. The two main topics presented for consideration at the first meeting were the development of professional training for leadership in the movement and the question of how home economics could assist the average woman at her housework. As defined at the gathering, leadership meant gaining access to academic communities on the same footing as other fields. Thus the leaders would have to be people with university training in relevant subjects. The question of how to help the nonacademic woman could potentially be solved, at least for those with the financial means and the interest, by the creation of college and university courses in home economics.

Describing the general tenor of the first conference, one of the participants might also have been describing the group's vision for the field itself: "It was evident that those in attendance were women capable of seeing something outside their own routine work and of recognizing the importance of work done by others."¹¹ In attempting to change not only processes but also attitudes toward processes, home economists wanted to free women from the stigma of women's work. Partly this would be accomplished by rationalizing women's labor—making less of it in the process—and partly by assigning it greater value. This created a dynamic paradox that the movement was never fully able to reconcile: if women's work was innately valuable, why attempt to replace so much of it with new technologies or for-hire services? Like the visionaries who historian Dolores Hayden terms "domestic feminists," home economists located the source of female oppression in their socioeconomic role—their labor.[12]

However, although many among the first generation of home economists were suffragists, they did not explicitly argue that freedom from toil was freedom from male oppression. Although they talked about women as victims, they never talked about men as involved in the forces that oppressed women. Liberation was from circumstances. Indeed, home economists argued that the forces of modern industrial capitalism—which, if not mastered, had the potential to oppress women—also oppressed men. Everyone lost out if the home remained pre-modern.

From its earliest stages, then, the movement included both activist and analytic agendas. Some looked forward to the day when the elements of home life—food, clothing, family relationships—would be recognized as fit topics for academic research. They envisioned this research as the exclusive realm of university-trained women who would be socially accepted as professionals. Others dreamed of a nation of perfectly efficient households run by women trained to the task and completely fulfilled in their work. The two ideas were not mutually exclusive, but emphasis on the second could tend to undermine the first. Although the first vision was achieved to a great degree, through the establishment of such fields as nutrition, interior design, and child development, it is the second that captured the popular attention and which, because it failed, gave the movement its reputation for a certain reactionary irrelevance.

## Home Economists Among the Progressives

Librarian and reformer Melvil Dewey, founder of the Dewey Decimal System, opened the second Lake Placid Conference on Home Economics, in 1900, with the encouraging statement, "Every great movement has been started by a few earnest people; a score of the right ones will do more effective work than a great mass meeting." Their numbers might still be small, he told his friends, but their impact would not be. Dewey asserted the group's identity here as an elite one with responsibilities to the masses, a shared idea among the various reform groups that fell under the umbrella of the progressive movement at the turn of the twentieth century.[13]

The ascendance of science in the academy and the reorganization of higher education were integral to the emergence of all of the progressive reform groups, home economics among them. In the forty years after the Civil War, American higher education experienced profound changes. The first colleges in America had provided general preparation for the ministry and the few other existing professions. Graduates were supposed to emerge with a deeper appreciation for culture, which was largely defined as the products of European thought. Beginning during the Civil War, with the establishment of the Land-Grant colleges, and continuing through the end of the century, new institutions were founded on a new model, pioneered in Germany. The German model stressed research and science over classics and religion. This shift included the introduction of new topics to higher education, such as psychology, economics, and engineering, which dealt directly with issues of the contemporary world. Graduates of these universities were supposed to become problem-solvers and innovators.

The new model rose alongside and in response to the emergence of the industrial economy. Changes in technology and the increasing diversification of world markets seemed to demand new kinds of education. Indeed, many of the new universities received large grants from men who had made their fortunes in industry and who were deeply invested in the production of a managerial class trained to their own specifications. Although the main goal of the new universities was to strengthen the economy and thus the nation, however, some graduates believed they had a responsibility to apply the new methods to fight the less pleasant results of modernization. Where generations before had accepted that poverty and inequality existed as part of God's mysterious plan, these young people were trained to look at the world in terms of hypotheses and proofs. They acquired the environmentalist perspective that looked to the social environment for both explanations and solutions. Furthermore, the universities themselves were steadily expanding to include new fields of study, many of which were concerned directly with human experience. As a group of home economists noted in 1903, there was a "general elasticity in educational curricula at the present time," which might allow their subject to find a home in higher education.[14]

Simultaneous to the rise of the research university, women's educational opportunities expanded. Some of the new universities, notably the Land-Grant institutions, admitted female students, first to Normal (teacher training) schools, but soon also to liberal arts and science curricula. Female students at research universities, as well as those attending the growing numbers of women's colleges, often experienced a sense of loss on graduation when they found that despite their education, most professions remained closed to their gender. Among the frustrated, a small group turned their talents to the solution of social problems, in the process creating new professions for themselves, notably in social work and the many subfields of home economics.

Ellen Richards, founding figure of home economics, embodied many of the changes of the era. An 1870 graduate of Vassar College, she found no way to apply her interest in chemistry until she was admitted to the recently opened Massachusetts Institute of Technology. Because MIT was so young and the kind of education it offered so new, it had not had time to establish a tradition of exclusion before Richards applied. The first woman to graduate from MIT, she focused her scientific attention on the urban environment, studying water and air qualities in Boston. Richards envisioned home economics as "euthenics," the sister science of eugenics. Where eugenics bred the perfect individual, euthenics would supply the ideal environment. This particular vision for the movement did not catch on, but the central idea that social problems, including the drudgery of the housewife, could be solved through scientific research did endure.[15]

Like other reformers of the time, home economists both relied on human ingenuity to solve social problems and focused early on the scientific management of wasted energy. Frederick Taylor, the most famous scientific manager, studied workers to help employers get the highest levels of productivity in the least amount of time. Taylor and other scientific managers like Frank and Lillian Gilbreth introduced the idea that a standard of efficiency was achievable in any workplace through the implementation of systems. Taylor's most influential idea was that there was "one best way" to perform any task.

Home economists came to this idea contemporaneously, claiming that wasted labor kept American women shackled to the past while they might move briskly into the future if their labor were systematized. Indeed, Lillian Gilbreth systematized her own home life, a story made famous in the memoir *Cheaper by the Dozen*, written by two of the Gilbreth's twelve children. Following "best" business practices, the Gilbreths instituted family meetings, workflow charts, and bidding for preferred household tasks. For their part, home economists conducted motion studies of domestic labor, encouraged the use of pedometers by housekeepers (to count, and thus eventually save steps), and advocated redesign of kitchens to reflect the physical individuality of the women who used them. Isabel Bevier of the University of Illinois even wore a pedometer herself at work, both indicating an obsession with efficiency and reflecting the movement's campaign to make women think of home as work space.

Because the home had not been engineered as the workplace had, home economists argued, it was rife with potential dangers, including malnutrition, poison, disease, exhaustion, poverty, waste, family conflict, and boredom. As antidotes, they offered nutrition, bacteriology, interior design, scientific management, household economics, conservation, and developmental psychology. Home economists repeatedly identified "drudgery" as their nemesis, arguing that women's work in the home could be made both easier and more interesting and that society at large would then recognize its value.

The movement was fully committed to the new managerial society and to the applications of scientific principles in place of folkways in most situations. But home economists also held onto the past, or an idealized vision of it, in that they advocated a home-centered world, in which the lures of the market were never stronger than the ties of family and place. In fact, they saw these connections as potentially strengthened through the application of managerial and scientific principles to the domestic sphere. Theirs was a nostalgic modernism, one that sought to correct the weaknesses in traditional life so that its strengths—moderation, community focus, an organic design aesthetic—could be made all the stronger. Despite the difference in intended audience, however, there was much overlap between the settlement house movement, social work, and home economics, particularly at the University of Chicago, where Sophonisba Breckenridge was a member of the Department of Household Administration in 1920 when she helped to create the university's Graduate School of Social Service Administration.

Although it has been a common perception that women interested in the sciences were sidelined into home economics, personal correspondence of these leaders reveals women who were enthusiastic about the field that they were themselves creating, rather than frustrated at being pushed into a field created by men to neutralize women's presence in the academy. In December 1917, Sarah Arnold, dean of Simmons College and founder of the home economics department there, wrote to Martha Van Rensselaer, co-chair of home economics at Cornell, "I have had no chance to tell you how much I have appreciated being with you and Miss Rose in this big and earnest piece of work. It certainly calls for our utmost devotion and our utmost wisdom. I am thankful to be marching with you."[16] In 1917, Arnold would have been referring specifically to home economists' work in food conservation during the

First World War, but it is easy to hear her praise for the larger mission that the three women, pioneers in their field shared.

## Heroines for a New Age?

The disconnect that often occurred between how home economists viewed their movement and how the larger society viewed them says much about their effectiveness in changing attitudes toward work in the home. During its first twenty years, the movement and its leaders were generally portrayed positively in the popular press. New courses in colleges and high schools were newsworthy events, and although there was often a tone of surprise in these articles, they generally did not offer criticism. A writer in the Fort Wayne, Indiana, *Morning Journal Gazette* noted in 1901, that although "many women in all ages have shown ingenuity in preparing food . . . Mrs. Ellen Richards, who has charge of the laboratory of sanitary science at [MIT,] has attacked the food problem on the more practical grounds. . . . A chemist rather than a caterer, she has sought the broad scientific principles upon which the economic sustenance of the human race depends." And in this work, she had acquired not just cooking techniques but "the authority that always results sooner or later from exact knowledge."[17] Differentiating Richards from the generation of women before her, the author presented her as a heroine for a new age.

Another article from that same year, however, exhibited ambivalence toward a movement that advocated raising the status of domestic work. "Learning Home Arts" described the recent opening of the Department of Domestic Arts at Teachers College, Columbia. Admitting that the program came into being because of a real and increasing demand for "dieticians, visiting nurses, managers of institutions," the author nonetheless focused on the easily mocked material of cooks in academia. In a nutrition class described in the article, students prepared a meal as their final exam. Professors assessed their work by eating it. Those who failed, the author explained, "must repeat the course as the digestion of the Faculty does not permit of deficiency examinations."[18]

In early responses to home economics, writers seem to have been more interested in the shorter-lived branch of the movement that focused on training domestic workers and in educating the urban poor. Thus an article from 1907 described a school for housekeeping set up in "a tenement of the better class" by the League for Home Economics to train women who may have started working for wages as early as age fourteen and had therefore not experienced the traditional middle-class girl's apprenticeship in housework at her mother's knee. The school was praised as a way of helping the working poor make the most of their scarce resources by teaching wives how to budget and manage a household. This branch of the movement, closely related to settlement houses and social work, did not represent the most influential version of the movement, that which attempted to revalue domestic work and issues as public and professional.

Even writers who admired the work of the movement tended to support the idea that its sole aim was to create perfect wives. In some cases, home economists, who, especially in the early years, did not share one standard training or philosophy, helped spread this message. In 1903, when the School of Domestic Arts and Sciences opened in Chicago, "a young man peeped into the school" and asked, "do you furnish wives here?" Mrs. Lynden Evans, who was chair of the committee that ran the school, as well as editor of the *Chicago Times* "Domestic Science" column, reported, "We told him no," but also went on to describe the school as one that would "furnish young women with the necessaries for becoming good wives."[19]

Vehement criticism of the movement in the popular press was rare but tended to come from a feminist perspective. Martha Bruere, an active suffragist, Vassar graduate, and, ironically, writer of books on household efficiency, attacked the movement as being stuck in a pre-feminist past. "Of all the inconsequent recommendations for the general instruction of girls, none is so recklessly handed about as the advice to teach them domestic science," she complained in 1916. Arguing that it had once been a proper part of women's education, Bruere explained, "as women's opportunities broadened it was dropt." There was, she felt, no need for individual women to learn housekeeping when public services and private enterprise were increasingly able to fill in for traditionally domestic chores such as butter churning and bread making.[20]

Marion Talbot of the University of Chicago had anticipated and addressed this criticism much earlier. In 1902, in a paper prepared for the third Lake Placid Conference, Talbot agreed that simply to remake the university so that it trained women students for domestic life would "be as disappointing as it would be futile. . . . There are probably at least as many women who sigh for a knowledge of the classics or of philosophy as who think their college course should have taught them how to make bread or deal with incompetent servants." She continued by articulating what she believed to be the larger social value of the movement: "Home economics must always be regarded in the light of its relation to the general social system, that men and

women are alike concerned in understanding the processes, activities, obligations and opportunities which make the home and the family effective parts
of the social fabric."[21]

Commenting on Talbot's words, home economics educator Alice Peloubet
Norton returned the discussion to the idea that American women were being
left behind by modernity. She insisted that home economics was "the best subject yet found to teach power over things. It is humiliating to be conquered by
things." Women needed to take the reins and use modern technology and
knowledge to bolster rather than undercut traditional practices and virtues.[22]

A writer in the *Chicago Tribune*, one of the few to attack home economics
on the grounds of class bias, seemed to respond directly to Talbot and Norton's
heroic description of their field, suggesting that the systems that home economists proposed for running households were themselves luxuries to many
Americans. Noting that the poor lived according to budgets because they had
no other choice, the writer further argued that those who did not have to
budget never would and in fact "do not care to free themselves from the 'dom-
inance of things' . . . and they care nothing for proteids or carbohydrates." The
average American did not feel humiliated to be "conquered" by things; rather
she or he eagerly courted the sensation. In the battle between "poor weak
human nature" and "starry-eyed science," the writer sardonically concluded,
the former would always, "outside of a few alumnae in Boston," win.[23]

## "So-called Practical Studies"

The strongest criticism of the movement came not in the popular press, however, but from other academics, particularly those in private women's colleges
who felt that home economics threatened progress that had been hard to win.

Female faculty at women's colleges resisted incorporating home economics into curricula because the field seemed to advocate a pre-feminist version
of womanhood. Faculty and administrators at women's colleges like Smith
and Mount Holyoke wanted their graduates to live a life of the mind as men's
intellectual equals, rather than their well-trained helpmeets. The first course
catalog for Mount Holyoke, for example, made a clear distinction between
skill-focused education for domestic life and liberal education. "It is no part
of the design of this seminary to teach young ladies domestic work." Although the catalog acknowledged the importance of housekeeping, it insisted
that the private home was the proper venue for education in such topics.[24]

M. Carey Thomas, president of Bryn Mawr, was openly disgusted with the idea of including home economics in the curriculum at women's colleges. Declaring in 1908 "nothing more disastrous for women, or for men, can be conceived than this plan for the specialized education of women as a sex," she roundly rejected a "college curriculum of women with hygiene and sanitary drainage and domestic science and child-study and all the rest of the so-called practical studies." Thomas argued that even if most female students married, they still needed the broadest possible education in order to raise intelligent sons.[25]

In 1905, the Association of Collegiate Alumnae, which would later become the American Association of University Women, declared home economics an inappropriate topic for women's college education. Founded in 1881, the ACA was committed to making higher education for women acceptable to society at large and to forcing society to recognize that women were intellectually equal to men. Home economics did not seem to them to fit in with this project. In a statement issued in 1906, members of the group argued that although courses in "practical housekeeping" could be very useful to women after they left college, "as an applied science it has not the same educational value as courses that give liberal training." Even if most women were going to end up managing their own homes rather than pursuing careers, "our future homemakers should have the broadest liberal training upon which to base technical knowledge." In other words, the members of the ACA saw home economics as a skill set, not a field of study, and believed that these skills could be picked up quickly outside of college. What a woman learned in the liberal arts curriculum would enrich her intellectually, which was much more important in the long run than whether she could, as the old song asks, "bake a cherry pie."[26]

Pointing out that "the very women who are themselves making a successful profession of teaching [home economics]" did so "thanks mainly to their having received the sort of education they now deprecate for women in general," Mary Leal Harkness, professor of Latin at Sophie Newcomb College, warned against the spread of home economics courses. "The real result of their educational theories, if they can ever get them put into general practice," she predicted of home economists, "will be to bring both schools and women to even a lower level of the mediocrity which grows out of the effort to do too many things, and of elevating things above thoughts."[27] In an interesting reversal of Alice Peloubet Norton's claim that home economics education would free women from the tyranny of things, Harkness saw the field as mired in the material.

All of these tensions—the public's ambivalence toward women's roles in society, feminists' distrust of a movement that emphasized the domestic sphere, fellow academic's discomfort with the field as a profession, and home economists' own dual progressive and traditional visions of women—buffeted the movement throughout its history. Indeed, in the 1950s, when Flora Rose, dean of the College of Home Economics at Cornell, looked back at the early days of the movement she had helped to start, she recalled the establishment of the field in terms that connected that very materiality to modern feminism. Remembering how she and her partner, Martha Van Rensselaer, acquired control of their department's budget, she said, "It made a great difference in our work and everything we did. For the reason that Virginia Woolf said in a title of a book, 'We now had a room of our own and our income.' . . . It would be a wonderful thing if every woman had her own income."[28] Rose and her peers created departments "of one's own," choosing material that was at once rigorously academic and intensely personal.

*[Handwritten margin notes:]*

Enduring tensions in the move.:
1. public's ambiv. → ♀ roles
2. feminists' distrust of move. focused on domestic
3. ♀ academics discomfort w/ the field as a profession
4. paradox of home econ. view of women: progressive yet tradit.

Flora Rose, Dean of Coll. of Home Econ @ Cornell

## CHAPTER ONE

# A Department of One's Own

WHEN THE DEAN of the liberal arts college at the University of Illinois asked home economist Isabel Bevier how much credit her department was giving for bread making, she answered proudly, "Not much, because we are not baking much bread." The pronouncement expressed the ambiguities of the field. Scientifically trained home economists insisted both that bread baking was an intellectually worthy pursuit and that they were not doing it. Their status lay in the nuance. They were not baking bread but studying it (sometimes while it was being baked), a distinction that it would be easy enough for their peers in other departments to mock long before the days when social history and cultural studies emerged to recognize the ordinary stuff of daily life as meaningful in a larger context.[1]

Bevier recalled another episode early in her career when a superintendent of the university, whose two daughters were students there, accosted her to complain about the course descriptions for her department. He stopped her in a hallway to say, "'Do you know you haven't the word cooking in that catalog once?'" Bevier replied, "Oh that is because cooking is not all that we do with food. Some we freeze, some we dry, some we just wash and eat raw. I wanted a chance for a large liberty for my work in food so I said 'selection and preparation,' which covers much more nearly what I want to do."[2]

Whereas the liberal arts dean had sneered at Bevier because he did not think bread making was rigorous enough for the academy, this trustee felt that she was being too scientific. Both men mistook the movement's motives by believing that Bevier would be teaching young women to cook. To one man this seemed inappropriate and to the other entirely proper. What Bevier

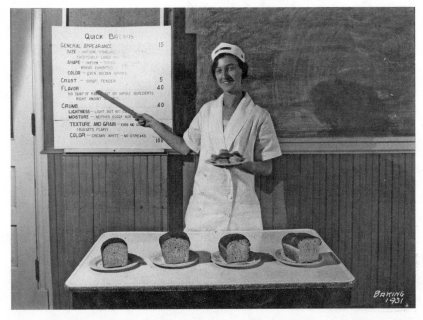

Figure 1. A University of Kentucky food science student demonstrates different ways of preparing bread, 1931. University of Kentucky Archives, 1998ua:001:021:0005.

tried to explain to them both was that she did not emphasize the practical over the abstract in methodology, only in subject matter. Her students would learn to approach the material of daily lives—bread, cloth, air—both as physical and social scientists. Whether they ever learned to cook their parents a nice meal was beside the point.

Bevier was certainly not alone in the difficulties she experienced establishing her department. The two extremes of criticism—that the field was too practical or that it was too abstract—were familiar to most of the movement's pioneers and continued to haunt the field into the 1960s. Flora Rose recalled her first ten years at the Cornell University: "My complaint about the educators who were here at Cornell at the time, the people in Education, [was] that they always spoke about Home Economics in terms of bound buttonholes and pumpkin pies—as if that constituted Home Ec—and of course that was very irritating to those of us who saw something beyond that."[3]

When Martha Van Rensselaer was hired to develop a home economics department at Cornell she also encountered skepticism from her faculty colleagues. Lacking a bachelor's degree and any significant training in science,

she set out to create her own major and earn her degree, modeling the education she hoped soon to provide others. When a male bacteriology professor
asked her why she wanted to take his course, she replied, "I would like to
learn about the bacteriology of the dishcloth so that I may explain to farm
women the importance of its cleanliness." To which the bacteriologist replied,
"Oh, they do not need to learn about bacteria. Teach them to keep the dishcloth clean because it is *nicer* that way."[4]

For Van Rensselaer, budding home economist, there was nothing nice
about a dishcloth unless the woman using it understood and applied to it the
scientific principles of cleanliness. The anecdote became one of the foundation
legends of the movement, reminding home economists of the resistance they
had encountered, not just to the establishment of their field but also to the
idea that women could benefit from advanced understanding in any context.
Expressing another common theme of the movement, Van Rensselaer's response supported the idea that knowledge led to a sense of mastery that in turn
led to improved work habits. If a woman knew what she was doing and why it
mattered, she would be less likely to experience it as drudgery and more likely
to do it well.

The bacteriology professor perhaps feared a loss of status if the applications of his science were presented as so very practical. Home economists
looked for the intersection of the mundane and the theoretical as the place to
establish their authority, while most academics derived their sense of importance from establishing levels of expertise beyond the reach of the uninitiated.
And in 2008, when American supermarkets and drugstores overflow with
sanitizing gels and disposable sponges, it seems as if Van Rensselaer's perspective has prevailed at least to some extent.

This vision of domestic life has persisted so long because it was there, at
the level of the microbe, that home economics first took shape as an academic
field and cultural force. Bacteriology and sanitation were the foundational
courses in most of the home economics programs that emerged around 1900.

## Next to Godliness

The courses that home economists chose to adopt and adapt reflected the earliest assumptions and limitations of the movement. Most home economists
in colleges borrowed sanitation courses from their engineering schools and

bacteriology from natural science departments. Their initial centrality reflected the major influence of Ellen Richards, who had trained as a chemist and developed an interest in the home through her interest in air and water purity. In 1883, she founded a Sanitary Science Club with other members of the Association of Collegiate Alumnae and the group published a guide to household sanitation in 1887. While mindful of their manual's potential to alarm readers, Richards and her co-authors nonetheless called on "the eternal vigilance of the housekeeper" in matters of sanitation to preserve family and community health.[5] Sanitation courses considered sanitation issues within the home, exploring consequences of and suggesting solutions for poor sanitary conditions. Bacteriology approached the question of sanitation on a more basic level, exploring the living conditions of and effects on humans of bacteria. The interest in sanitation and bacteriology also reflected the social reform impulses of early leaders in the movement who, like many other progressives, focused their attention on American living conditions.

The first course that Isabel Bevier's department of home economics offered was Home Architecture and Sanitation, six lectures on the history of architecture, heating, and plumbing.[6] Her first request of the students in her department was that they step outside the boundaries of their traditional gender roles and see their sphere—the home—from the outside. Furthermore, she wanted them to take it apart, mentally, and understand all of its parts and functions. Homes were machines and they could be designed and reorganized for maximum efficiency. By making the home an academic subject, Bevier deromanticized it and woman's relation to it.

At the same time, by appropriating a course on domestic architecture and sanitation from the engineering school, Bevier re-humanized the subject. The home should be considered as a machine, but it was just as important that it also be considered in its many relationships to the human lives lived within it. When Bevier appropriated such courses, she altered their content by putting more focus on household contexts. There is no evidence, however, to suggest that she or other home economists simplified the scientific content of their courses. Women of the first generation who had trained as scientists had most often done so at coeducational institutions. As H. C. Sherman, a chemist who had worked with Isabel Bevier, remembered, there were "No hyphenated or watered-down science courses for Miss Bevier!" He credited her with setting "the stamp of sterling quality upon the new coinage and the scientific esteem in which home economics" was held.[7]

Introductory courses in chemistry, biology, and physics were usually pre-requisites to more specialized courses in the field. Home economics majors would often take these courses outside their department, alongside students in liberal arts and science majors. Later, this strict adherence to standards established by male science professors would come under attack, but for the first generation it seemed essential to achieving full acceptance in academic circles.

To begin home economics education with courses in bacteriology and sanitation was to start with a kind of emergency mentality, further supporting the need for the field. Bacteriology identified the enemies to healthful modern living, and sanitation introduced ways to combat them. The early twentieth century was when Americans first became aware of the bacteria that live among us and first began to experiment with preventive measures that are familiar to us today. National exposure to the subject in Upton Sinclair's *The Jungle* (1906) sensationalized the germ as an enemy. Sinclair argued that the way to combat the germ, in the form of unclean meats, was through a reorganization of labor and regulation of capitalist enterprise. Along with urban reformers and progressives such as Jane Addams and Florence Kelley, home economists had begun to address Sinclair's concern before *The Jungle* was even published. Urban reformers insisted on sanitary reforms in cities and industries. Home economists meanwhile argued that women, as the primary purchasers of food, must be educated so as to avoid poor-quality goods, not only because such goods were dangerous but also because they wasted money.

Florence Kelley, leader in the consumer education movement, complained that information about bacteria was not available to the average woman in a form she could use "to avoid 'buying smallpox,' as she put it, along with her new garments."[8] By drawing attention to the bacteria in ordinary life, home economists were arguing for the necessity of their field and also to the interconnectedness of branches of knowledge. While they borrowed material to establish their academic households, home economists expanded the scope of these preexisting fields.

## Square Meals

Two connected subjects that could not be borrowed from other departments were food science and nutrition. Food science is the study of the chemical nature of foodstuffs and how they react under changing conditions, including digestion. Nutritionists study the effects of food on the human body. Animal nutrition had been a regular course in the agricultural colleges that emerged in the 1860s, but when home economists attempted to introduce human nutrition to college curricula, as Isabel Bevier discovered, it was not so easily accepted. The reason for this difference, as will be discussed here, had much to do with gender ideology of the time.

Home economists saw the study of food science and human nutrition as integrally connected to the study of bacteriology and sanitation. In 1882, Ellen Richards had published *The Chemistry of Cooking and Cleaning*, an early attempt to introduce the public to concepts of nutrition and bacteriology simultaneously. Summarizing what was at that time the relatively new understanding that the world we live in is composed of combinations of a limited number of chemical elements, Richards confidently declared that "to understand something of the nature of these chemical substances and their common forms is a necessity for every housekeeper who would not be cheated of her time and money." In a sense, Richards argued, cooking and cleaning were the same kind of work, because both involved the manipulation of chemicals. The understanding of how chemicals worked, both in food and in sanitation, would be the path to purity and purity the path to strength.[9]

Although a few studies in nutrition had been conducted before the end of the nineteenth century, the field came into its own only in the early twentieth century. The term "vitamin" was coined in 1906, but researchers, both male and female, had already begun to isolate the essential elements of nutrition in mammals in the 1870s. In food science and nutrition courses, students were expected to learn to think about food as a substance that it was as important to test as to taste. Food science courses were taught in specially designed kitchen laboratories and it was standard for students to wear uniforms to indicate their status as professionals. Photographs from the turn of the century show young women in long white aprons with white caps on their heads. By the 1920s, students wore white lab coats without the white caps that had made them look like housemaids. Kitchen laboratories provided standard kitchen equipment such as stoves, ovens, and sinks, but in a scientific environment, isolating the technology of the kitchen from the home itself. Significantly, in primary and secondary school foods classes, students tended more often to wear patterned aprons and to use equipment designed for home use.

Although nutritionists and food scientists are still frequently accused of having no interest in how food tastes, palatability was never entirely ignored. Whitman Jordan, the author of a 1912 textbook, *Principles of Human*

Figure 2. Domestic science students at the University of Idaho in 1902 wore uniforms that resembled those of servants. Special Collections & Archives, University of Idaho Library. 1902

*Nutrition: A Study in Practical Dietetics*, noted that "relish for food" was essential to nutrition because when food was attractive the body responded by producing digestive enzymes. "Forced nutrition," he noted, "does not conform to the best conditions for efficient nutrition." Important as this issue was, however, as a food scientist, he did not consider it appropriate to discuss anywhere in his more than 450-page text how to make food appealing.[10]

Amy Daniels, professor of foods and nutrition at the University of Missouri and a leading pioneer in the field, described a course titled General Foods, offered at her college between 1912 and 1914 and typical of the kind of work in foods conducted at other colleges. Prerequisites for the course included organic chemistry, inorganic chemistry, botany, bacteriology, and physiology. Daniels explained, "The method of conducting the course is inductive," or what in contemporary pedagogical terminology would be termed "project-based learning."[11] Students were not given recipes to follow but were instead asked to create their own methods using their knowledge of how substances would behave in combination and under a variety of processes.

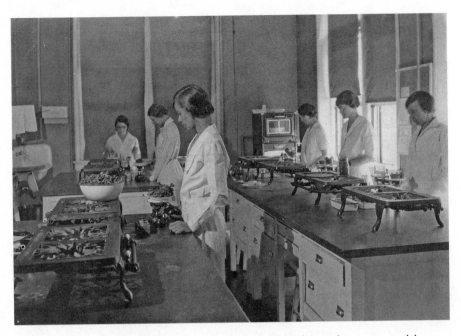

Figure 3. Students attending the University of Kentucky during the 1920s wore lab coats in the kitchen laboratory. University of Kentucky Archives, 1998ua001:021_0013. 1920s

In classroom experiments students tested the chemical makeup of food-stuffs and recorded their observations. A suggested experiment for determining the effect of acid on starch, given in the textbook *Food: Its Composition and Preparation,* was typical of the kind of work performed at the introductory level in food science laboratories: "(a) Add lemon juice to a starch solution and continue cooking. Observe the effect and explain. Divide the result in two portions. (b) test result of (a) with iodine. (c) test result of (a) with Fehling's solution. Explain."[12] A subsequent experiment required students to test the effects of digestion on starch by using their own saliva to form a compound.

Because home economists came to their interest in food from a scientific perspective that emphasized the differences between purity and contamination, and systems rather than cultures, they took a distinct approach to food that was sometimes exaggeratedly dismissive of taste. In reality the recipes they assembled for use in extension bulletins and high school classrooms were packed not with recipes for food pills or flavorless pottages but rather with much that remains appealing even to early twenty-first-century tastes. Although they took

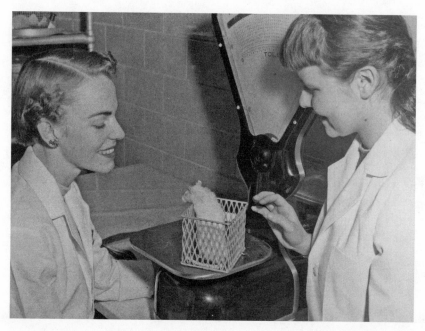

Figure 4. A student and a technical assistant in the University of Idaho Home Economics Department weigh a rat as part of a nutrition study, c. 1950. Special Collections & Archives, University of Idaho Library.

a scientific approach to food, some home economists were also interested in palatability, attempting to determine this quality through taste tests. In her collection of lessons from the Rumford Kitchen exhibit at the World's Columbian Exposition in Chicago, Ellen Richards included the motto "The palate is the Janitor, and unless he be conciliated, the most nutritious food will find no welcome," indicating that the founders of the movement were aware that they could not force feed the public for their own good.[13]

Caroline Hunt, who founded the home economics program at the University of Wisconsin, told a reporter, "There has been an unfortunate tendency among students of nutrition to underestimate the importance of palatability, individual preferences, and family customs." Correcting for this in her own work, Hunt oversaw taste tests, sometimes to the surprise of the general public. "Spectators at a pie-baking contest at the department" in 1927 "were astonished to see the judges score the pies by tasting them." A reporter explained, "They had half expected the judging to be done with scientific instruments." A member of the department pointed out that while digestion could be re-created in the laboratory and nutrition tested on lab rats, taste was one thing that only a human subject could determine.[14]

Innovative in their approach to food as research material, nutritionists were yet not culinary pioneers. Their interest was in advancing knowledge rather than pleasure. Indeed it is likely that if they had appeared to pay closer attention to taste than to chemistry, they would have opened themselves up to yet more criticism from those who thought food an inappropriate subject matter for academic study.[15]

Introducing food science and nutrition to the university as two of the core elements of the field was essential to the movement, but also problematic. The difficulty was that no matter what names home economists gave to courses in nutrition, food science and dietetics (the study of how certain diets relate to health), the public and other members of the academic community insisted on regarding these as cooking classes.

Part of the problem for critics of food science and human nutrition arose in the late nineteenth century with the emergence of spheres of expertise that were defined very broadly against fields of amateurism. Although home economists attempted to align themselves with the experts, the culture more generally classified anything to do with the kitchen and with women as amateur. Women's work in the kitchen was valued as important, sustaining, even sacred—but not professional. This distinction was crucial to a culture more and more reliant on classifications in order to understand society. Where earlier generations had been satisfied with spiritual explanations—God's will or fate—Americans at the turn of the century constantly sought to assign all of existence to categories. Thus to allow work that was traditionally performed by women to be considered professional was problematic because it destabilized established categories.

Another reason for distrust of the study of of food science and human nutrition may have been that in animal nutrition courses the issue of palate was largely considered irrelevant, whereas once home economists began to talk about people and food, the problem of the subjectivity of taste entered the discussion. This problem continues to haunt scholars interested in the emerging field of food studies who encounter resistance to the idea that food can be studied objectively as an expression of culture. Home economists were able to establish themselves as experts only as far as they were able to claim that their studies of food were objective.

Nutrition professors like Cornell's Flora Rose were hired because they had backgrounds in the "hard" sciences rather than certificates from cooking schools or experience in restaurants. Courses like Physiology of Nutrition, offered by Simmons College, Food Selection and Preparation at Cornell, or Experimental Cooking at the University of California at Berkeley, which involved "quantitative food analysis," all suggested a significant change in woman's relation to food.[16] Food science courses reversed a woman's traditional path from kitchen to table, sending her back into the kitchen as observer instead of preparing her to emerge from it with piping-hot delicious dish in hand.

When Isabel Bevier was hired to develop the home economics department at the University of Illinois, the president of the university encouraged her to emphasize the scientific over the domestic. "I don't care," he told her, "if you can cook or not . . . I want you to run your department and it will be judged by the results obtained in its laboratories and classrooms and its success by the measure of University respect obtained for it."[17] For both Bevier and her president, the battle had to be won among academics. Whether those outside the university community ever understood the field, and there is much evidence that they never did, would not ultimately matter.

In the effort to gain public acceptance, home economists often presented nutrition as a matter of social as well as personal health, claiming that the physical well-being of the nation contributed to its ethical or moral well-being. They made this claim with particular urgency during the crisis periods of the two world wars and the depression, but it has remained a constant theme. Progressive-era reformers interested in urban poverty and immigrant communities promoted the education of the urban poor in "American" foodways. That the particular cuisine that they advocated represented only one of the many different food cultures in America was not something they recognized. For these reformers, food that was most like that of northern Europe was most wholesome and therefore correct. Some home economists, however, showed more cultural sensitivity. For example, a course in the History of Housekeeping at Cornell included some education in international foodways, the instructor reasoning, "No one can run a cafeteria on a happy, profitable and logical basis, who does not know some of the food customs of the people, why the Italian is as devoted to his salad as the new Englander is to his baked beans."[18]

Urban reformer Jacob Riis expressed this ideal of "wholesome" cookery as social remedy when he said that the best way to encourage temperance in tenement neighborhoods was "a cookery school slapped down right there in the middle of the block."[19] Similarly, philanthropist Pauline Agassiz Shaw advocated giving Ellen Richards a grant "to pursue studies in the food and nutrition of workingmen and its possible relation to the question of the use of intoxicating liquors."[20] Riis and Shaw both assumed that immigrant and working-class women were partly to blame for their husband's drinking habits because they did not provide correct food for their families and they assumed that these drinking habits themselves were unhealthy. Neither considered the role of culture or of economic conditions in social drinking. Riis's language is slightly violent, suggesting that the cooking schools were to serve as a form of punishment for urban communities.

Most home economics departments did reach out to their surrounding communities, particularly through extension programs, and food was an important part of this outreach, but they attempted to work in more subtle ways than that suggested by Riis. Here the difficult issue of palatability became central. Because Americans in the early 1900s were largely uninterested in food's nutritive qualities or in the concept of "whole foods," home economists tried to develop methods of making them eat what was good for them. This problem was acknowledged in a *Journal of Home Economics* obituary for famous cooking school director and cookbook writer Maria Parloa when she died in 1909. Parloa's students, her memorialist noted admiringly, learned "how to cook in healthful, economic, and yet tempting ways." The use of "yet" here acknowledges that home economists were aware that what they offered as nutritious was often rejected as flavorless.[21]

In 1911, New York State legislators were invited to the Cornell campus as part of a project to get funding for a home economics building. Dean Liberty Hyde Bailey of the Agriculture College asked Martha Van Rensselaer and Flora Rose, co-chairs of the Department of Home Economics, to prepare a meal for them. As Rose remembered it, "We said we would be delighted to. We would always take on anything that came along." The two women prepared the meal and served it with the help of seven students. Menu selection proved all-important:

> One of the things we had was creamed cabbage. Those were the days when they smothered vegetables in white sauce—the white sauce sort of stood for home economics—but we made it really right with buttered crumbs on the top, and when we served this, the Legislator sitting next to me said, "Miss Rose, what is this delicious dish I am eating?" And I said "Well, you are eating scalloped cabbage, good old simple plain scalloped cabbage." And he said "Oh no I am not, I don't like cabbage but please give me some more." . . . And later when we asked for money for a building, he whirled round in his chair and said, "I want to vote for the woman that made me eat cabbage."[22]

The legislature allocated money for a new building. The story is interesting on several levels. The legislator knew that he ought to eat what was good for him, but needed the lure of the cream sauce and buttered breadcrumbs to do so, reflecting both the tastes of the time and the degree to which nutrition had already become something of which people were aware. Rose herself acknowledged changes in taste when she implicitly contrasted "those days" of white sauce to 1953, when she recounted the story, by which time it had become less ubiquitous. She also obliquely reflected on the role of her field in changing tastes when she said that home economics was synonymous with the sauce that made the healthy palatable. One home economics textbook writer felt that white sauce was so important she included three chapters on the substance—one on thick, one on thin, and one on medium white sauces—as well as another chapter on creamed vegetables.[23]

The story of the cabbage-eating legislator appears several times in the collected papers of the department, suggesting that members of the department found it meaningful. Although it can be read as an example of men in the university exploiting the women of the department by using them to entertain guests rather than taking them seriously as academic peers, we can also, and more interestingly, see the story as a victory for the women of the department.[24] Van Rensselaer and Rose used their own domestic skills to get what they wanted from the nondomestic world of state and academic politics. The legislator is made to look something of a fool, voting his palate rather than his convictions. As well as seeming foolish, however, he is also portrayed as a student, a successful product of the movement. He knew that the women of the department had done him a good turn nutritionally by making him enjoy cabbage, and he voted funds for a new building.

Although the early home economists show much evidence of having enjoyed food as much as any of their contemporaries and although they experimented with it scientifically, there was very little cultural experimentation. Although by the 1920s such excursions into the gently "exotic" as tamale pies, Hawaiian chicken, and lo mein were regular items in the home economics sections of women's magazines, the first generation of home economists tended to stay close to the foodways of northern Europe. Most of these women shared this ancestry, and the food they experimented with overwhelmingly reflected this heritage. The "native" cuisine of home economists can be generally described as one in which single flavors tended to be emphasized over complex layering of flavors. This was food that was not highly spiced, although spices were used, usually singly or in pairs. In her 1913 textbook for secondary school students, Emma Conley noted, "The condiments in common use are cinnamon, cloves, ginger, mustard, pepper, allspice, nutmeg." These spices Conley tellingly termed "condiments" because of their nutritional effects of aiding digestion.[25]

To twenty-first-century readers this food may seem bland, but it is important to remember that home economists who wrote recipes were attempting to provide basic rules for thinking about and preparing foods. Spicing can be a matter of individual preferences and has no direct bearing on the nutritional value of a meal, while the grail that home economists sought was one diet for all.

An important influence on the home economics cuisine came not through cultural heritage or the economists' shared commitment to the scientific method, but through the movement's early and continuing association with agricultural colleges. When the Office of Home Economics was opened in 1915 in the U.S. Department of Agriculture, home economists worked closely with agricultural experts to create recipes for crops, such as mung beans, that American farmers might usefully grow but that American consumers might not yet eagerly eat. At a government "sheep experiment station" in Idaho in 1926, for example, a variety of types of sheep were raised and slaughtered as lambs. Legs of these lambs were then shipped to the Bureau of Home Economics for recipe experimentation and palatability tests. This was done in the service of making it easier for consumers to adopt lamb into their regular diet if it should be found profitable for American sheep ranchers to produce it. A similar experiment in 1931 captured the imagination of a writer for the *Chicago Daily Tribune*, who contrasted the ordinary conditions of eating roast lamb to those experienced in the Bureau of Home Economics laboratory in Washington, D.C. "Sounds savory, doesn't it," the writer asked his readers, referring to the many slices of roast lamb consumed in the study. "But wait a moment. No mint sauce goes with the lamb. No salt; no pepper; not a bit of seasoning," and "another thing—Uncle Sam wants statistics, not adjectives. So you can't merely smack your lips and say 'Delicious.' . . . You've got to know all about the seven gradations in aroma, texture, tenderness, and flavor."[26] In the midst of a vast and deepening economic depression, such an experiment might indeed have seemed newsworthy. It was typical of writers in the popular press from any era in the movement's history, however, to become fascinated by the unexpected overlap of laboratory and kitchen that home economics so often presented.

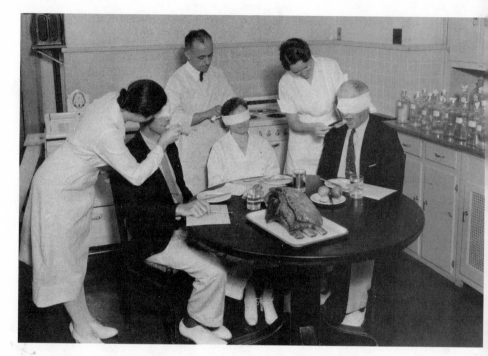

Figure 5. Employees of the U.S. Bureau of Home Economics participate in a blind taste test of roasted meat at the bureau's Beltsville, Maryland, research facility, c. 1930. National Archives and Records Administration, RG176 HE 33095C.

This cuisine of supply was not necessarily widely successful, resulting in such delicacies as a spice pie with soybean pulp featured in a New York State extension bulletin, or the soy-bran muffins designed by the U.S. Bureau of Human Nutrition and Home Economics in 1943, yet it is interesting to see that the attempt was made so early to support diversification of agriculture through diversification of the American diet.[27]

The question of what Americans will eat and what the market offers them continues to be an important issue for nutritionists. In 1897, when she was teaching at the Pennsylvania College for Women, Isabel Bevier defined a problem that seems to linger in 2006. She noted that cost and "individual taste," rather than thinking about nutrition determined how people shopped for food. "The Americans are not economical feeders," she concluded, "Too much is bought that is not valuable, too much is wasted, and too much is paid for things that could be replaced to better advantage with cheaper and better substitutes."[28] Bevier and her peers in the movement wanted to adjust American attitudes toward food, to make their relationship toward it more scientific and even more businesslike. But failed!

## Power of the Purse

In an attempt to create a nation of educated consumers, home economists conducted exhaustive studies of how Americans spent their money and how they might do so more efficiently, according to a particular understanding of efficiency. As part of the study of household economics, they devised countless budgets for households of varying sizes and classes, attempting to tailor diets to both occupation and pocketbook. The family of a factory worker was considered as a unit in which certain levels of nutrients would be required for maximum efficiency. With the proper nutrition and thrift, a family might even move up the economic ladder, into a whole new and, if they were wise, professionally designed budget.

Economics courses that were borrowed from liberal arts departments dealt with classical theories of economics. Soon, however, home economics professors began to teach a more specialized form of the subject. As John Leeds, who taught household economics at Temple University wrote in his dissertation on the subject, "Household economics is not a separate science. It is the application of the science of economics to the househol. . . . [It] deals with all those activities of the housewife, and her assistants in household work, which are concerned with the production and consumption of the commodities and services which satisfy the wants of herself, her husband and children for food, clothing, and shelter."[29]

While acquainting students with the theoretical side of economics and offering a general, and sometimes critical, picture of the U.S. economic structure, household economics courses turned students' attention to the daily, domestic practicalities of the subject. Rather than thinking about the wealth of nations, economics courses in these departments considered the household budget, from sows' ears to silk purses and everything in between. Economics, in the form of budgeting, was part of other courses in the field, too. Food science courses dealt with it, as did domestic architecture, interior decoration, and textile sciences and clothing design.

As with the study of sanitation and nutrition, home economists were not content simply to teach conditions; coursework pointed firmly toward one

correct behavior. At every opportunity teachers and writers on the topic advocated moderation and thrift. When buying a cut of meat, they urged their students to choose neither the cheapest nor the finest but to get something of
good value and make the most of it. If selecting fabric for a new suit, students
were taught to think in terms of durability first, then beauty. Indeed, home
economists considered durability a kind of beauty of its own. This message was
increasingly at odds with the emergence of consumer culture in America, valuing control of desire over the amassing of wealth. Bertha Terrill, for instance,
who created the home economics program at the University of Vermont and
was dean of women, described the value of household economics courses in
terms of behavior modification: "Effort is made to help the student differenti-
ate sharply between a haphazard existence without conscious purpose or direction and a life intelligently controlled by a consistent standard of life."[30]

Home economists in high schools, colleges, and universities taught American women to think of themselves in terms of income and budgets, subtly introducing the notion of class into the liberal arts education. As students
prepared budgets for every conceivable level of income they were implicitly
being asked to imagine themselves in the full range of economic shoes. What
would it be like to live on a workman's wages? What was the difference in
quality of life between the workman's family and the family of a professional?
Using examples from real families, home economists encouraged a kind of
class awareness through meaningful detail unlike any offered in political science, history, or economics courses at the time.

At the same time that they encouraged awareness of difference, however,
they often also preached an aspirational sameness. Helen Kinne, in her textbook *Shelter and Clothing*, asserted, "A home based on the right principle will
be *simple*. There will be simplicity of living, honesty in the expression of what
is offered in the home. No ostentation or living beyond one's means; simplicity in entertainment in offering freely of what one has to friends without
apology or explanation; simple furnishings, simple, healthful food, simple,
artistic clothing."[31] Students of the new science could achieve its goals
through living a life that ignored class politics and that emphasized internal
harmony over external perceptions.

Molly Dewson, who would later achieve fame as a Democratic Party activist and journalist, briefly taught courses in household economics at the
School of Housekeeping in Boston, part of the Women's Education and Industrial Union. The School of Housekeeping was established in 1897 and sub-
sumed by Simmons College, a vocational college for women, in 1902. Because

the field was so new, Dewson had to write her own textbook, a guide to budget making titled *The Twentieth Century Expense Book*. The book did not include budgets for families with children.[32] Like Dewson, who shared her private domestic life with another woman and did not have children, many early home economists were in the process of self-creation as a first generation of professional women, and their work often reflects their own needs in this role more strongly than the needs of the general population of women.

The courses they taught and books they wrote tended to suit and therefore subtly endorse the lifestyle of the single woman or the professional couple with few or no children as much or more than that of the larger family. A cooking course at Simmons College offered in 1917–18 was actually specifically designed for the single woman and titled Kitchenette Cookery. As part of the class, the busy students prepared and ate lunch together.[33]

Although Molly Dewson may not have intended an overt critique of women's economic roles in society, Edna Day, of the University of Missouri Department of Home Economics, clearly intended something of the kind in her introductory course for freshmen: "We take up what is probably more sociological than economic, the discussion of the fact that the work that used to be done in the home by the women is largely done in factories, and hence the home maker is not the producer in the sense that she used to be, and we discuss some of Mrs. Gilman's ideas of the wife earning money outside of the home. It is all very elementary. I do not expect much more than to set the girls to talking."[34] The removal of production from the household and the increasing importance of the housekeeper's role as consumer was a common theme in household economics, one that connected these courses to the proto-women's studies courses to be discussed later in these chapters.

Day's approach was clearly provocative. Charlotte Perkins Gilman advocated a form of women's liberation that rejected traditional ideas of motherhood as a woman's primary calling. Gilman advocated for homes in which there were no kitchens because she thought that women were unjustly chained to the domestic. The only way she could see to free them within their own homes was to make it physically impossible for them to do domestic labor. By removing kitchens and advocating public childcare, Gilman amputated limbs from the traditional notion of womanhood.

The professionalization of many elements of domestic labor potentially freed some women—those who could afford such services—to participate in public life to a greater extent than ever before. Caroline Hunt, who introduced the home economics program at the University of Wisconsin, wrote that private

industry in cooperation with municipal governments might fill in where cooperative labor arrangements had failed and thus free women for greater participation in social reform movements.[35] As they lost their roles as domestic
producers, however, women had to work actively to maintain their control of
the domestic sphere. Just because you could now buy bread already baked and
even sliced did not mean that you should abandon all knowledge of bread
making and simply buy whatever loaf advertisers succeeded in selling you.

Woman's role had shifted from producer to consumer, but was no less
great in its importance. In fact, as variety became the spice of consumerist life,
a woman needed to know more than ever before about domestic products
and processes. Furthermore, thanks to modern science (both physical and social), it was now possible for women to know more than their mothers and
grandmothers ever had about food, clothing, and shelter. A woman's choices
in the market were now informed by scientific studies of vitamins, nutrients,
and calories, as well as investigations into labor conditions and durability
studies of materials from dishwashers to handkerchiefs.

## Design for Living

One of the early difficulties in creating a unified academic field was in ensur-
ing a balance between what was considered scientific and what was considered aesthetic work. Although the public at large might have thought of art
and science as opposites, the former expressing emotion while the latter exercised reason, founders of the movement envisioned the two approaches working in harmony. Ideally, the study of the home united science and art so that
a properly trained housekeeper managed the household with techniques that
intertwined her knowledge of biochemistry and fully developed aesthetic
sense. To the general public, however, the inclusion of design courses in the
curriculum simply suggested that home economics meant sewing as well as
cooking.

Courses in design, sometimes collected under the title of Household or
Domestic Arts, included interior design and decoration as well as textile science and clothing design and construction. As the home economics movement
grew and prospered in the schools and extension services as well as in state and
national government agencies, interior design diverged from textiles and clothing, but both remained connected through the theme of curative aesthetics.
Although it is easy to see how interior design and even decoration fit in with

the general theme of home economics—the perfected home—textile science and clothing design have a less obvious and more problematic connection.

Including these courses in home economics represented a traditional connection of women with textile work. Until the Market Revolution of the 1820s, American women had been responsible for producing most of the textiles used by their families. Spinning and weaving as well as sewing and mending of all clothing and linens were central activities in women's lives. To include this work in the new, modern vision of domestic labor, then, highlighted a problem: was home economics the study of the home as a social unit (in which case, because textile and clothing production were no longer a major part of this world, they should not be included) or was it an attempt to educate women in the best methods of the kind of work they had traditionally performed? Was it bound by gender expectations, or did it have an independent social science agenda?

Home economists justified the inclusion of textile science, the cloth equivalent of food science, and clothing construction by emphasizing women's new role as consumers of the textiles that their grandmothers had once produced. The connection with women's work in the past was often reinforced with the study and recreation of historic clothing. In *Shelter and Clothing, a Textbook of the Household Arts*, Helen Kinne and Anna Cooley, home economists at Teachers College, Columbia, defined the study by offering an economic analysis of women's roles in a changing society: "Woman is the chief purchaser, and upon her rests the responsibility in household affairs of making each dollar procure full value."[36] Their textbook, which included an intriguing section on the ethics of buying underwear, argued that because women purchased textiles for their homes and clothing for their families it was imperative for them to know the most they could about the production of such things. When quality goods could not be found in the market, furthermore, home economists wanted women to have the skills to make their own.

Helen Goodrich Buttrick's textbook, published in 1924, argued that "principles of clothing selection" were more necessary than ever before because women were in the workforce in greater numbers than their mothers had been and therefore needed to know how to dress themselves for the professional world, both to appear correct and to be physically comfortable. Buttrick and other home economists emphasized a connection between textile selection, clothing design, and health. Advocating the new idea that comfort should be as important a consideration as appearance in clothing selection, they suggested simplicity and encouraged women in particular to reject the

Figure 6. Cornell University clothing design students model historical and contemporary clothing, 1940. New York State College of Home Economics Records, #23/2/749. Courtesy of the Division of Rare and Manuscript Collections, Cornell University Library.

tight bindings that had been traditional for the middle and upper classes for several centuries.[37]

Mary Schenck Woolman, professor of domestic arts at Teachers College, Columbia, and one of the pioneers of the field, argued that women ought to

know about the labor conditions under which cloth and clothing were produced in order to exert moral pressure on the industry to reform exploitive
and wasteful practices. When purchasing cloth, women should think first of
their own conditions—what were they going to use the cloth or clothing
for?—then of the conditions of labor—was the bolt of flannel produced using
safe and fair practices?—and then of the nation—was this a company that
had a good reputation for quality and labor relations? As did their colleagues
in nutrition, textile science experts urged socially conscious consumerism.[38]

Anna Cooley and Helen Kinne offered another interesting justification
for the study of design in general that was based not in economics but in an
earlier ideal of woman as spiritual guardian of the home and family: "The
house is the place where the homemaker surrounds herself with artistic and
harmonious furnishings and where she tries to work out the ideals and standards of the home that will create the real home atmosphere and bring about
the development of all members of the family. The material things of the
home express the real spirit of the family and exert an untold influence on its
moral and intellectual life."[39]

According to this philosophy, common to founders of the movement,
aesthetics substituted for religion, which had been the ennobling force in earlier domestic ideals. This elevation of style to the level of sacrament both supported and also potentially undermined the emergence of consumer culture
by claiming meaning for objects but reserving the ultimate authority over this
meaning for the person who arranged them.

Following the aesthetic philosophy of William Morris, English poet, reformer, and founder of the Arts and Crafts movement, home economists
equated the experience of beauty with psychological comfort, rather than awe
or ecstasy. As one home design textbook from 1917 informed students, "Par-
lours have long ago become unfashionable and the comfortable living room
has taken its place in the average home." A woman invented for the sake of the
textbook's narrative had "suddenly decided to reorganize . . . her home . . .
after Miss Travers, from State College, gave such a helpful talk on 'Common
Sense in Home Management.' "[40]

Of course the approved ingredients of the ideal living room—Arts and
Crafts furniture and pottery, hand-woven rugs, and Japanese prints—were
not cheap or readily available and therefore carried their own class markings.
An educated visitor to the euthenically correct living room would have been
able to read her hostess's social status just as easily as might a similarly educated visitor to a high-Victorian parlor. A visitor would have noted the

absence of thick draperies and carpets, seeing instead bright sunlight and easily swept wood floors and perhaps would have envied the way in which a
built-in bookcase and window seats reduced the number of places for dust
bunnies to gather. The woman of the house would have seemed a smart, sensible character without morbid attachments to the past or unseemly need to
show off her family's financial status.

Domestic scientists believed fervently in Morris's invitation to "have
nothing in your houses that you do not know to be useful or believe to be
beautiful," and further conflated the two, so that an object's beauty was in its
utility. This was in direct contrast to the Victorian fashion for objects chosen
for meaning. For home economists, the difference between a glass-enclosed
wreath made of the hair of dead relatives and a few dried grasses in a simple
earth tone vase was the difference between the dark ages of superstition and
the new bright future. The vase and grasses were beautiful because they performed psychic work—they soothed jangled nerves and reconnected one to
the natural world.[41]

Because most women did not think of aesthetics in terms of utility, home
economists tried to reeducate them. Bulletins from extension programs announced the new thinking while classes in domestic architecture drew students' attention to how homes were going to be used by those who lived in
them, rather than judged by those who visited them. It was not necessarily a
good thing, home economists taught, to have a big house. A big house meant
more work for the woman who lived in it and potentially more room for the
kind of clutter that detracted from a home's ability simultaneously to calm
and to energize. A modest house designed for the functions of domestic life—
food production, some textile work, and restorative relaxation—was really superior to the finest mansion. Eleanor Roosevelt acted on this philosophy in
1932 when, rather than redecorate the White House's public rooms, she reorganized its kitchen to make work easier for the staff.[42]

In order for American women to design or arrange homes and clothing
that were functional and aesthetically fulfilling (according to the sensibility of
the movement), they had to learn what a house or a blouse actually was, how
it was constructed and what relations parts had to the whole. Historical surveys were included so that students could get a sense of fashions changing
over time as technology and taste evolved. Students were encouraged to think
of themselves as potential innovators but only within the boundaries of what
their teachers considered the main functions of housing and clothing and the
legitimate range of taste.

Both clothing and housing reform were small but vital movements in America beginning in the last half of the nineteenth century. Catharine Beecher herself had been an advocate of both, encouraging women both to reject the corset and to redesign their homes. Both changes she advocated were to be made in the interest of improved circulation. Home economists involved in textile sciences and clothing design likewise advocated an aesthetic of the natural, preferring rich but not bright colors to decorative details. Good fit, good fabric, and good construction mattered above all else as utility had its own strong aesthetic appeal to this generation of innovators.[43]

A 1907 textbook on textiles and clothing explicitly connected domestic architecture and clothing. "Many of the principles governing architecture and art," the authors argued, "apply equally as well to dress. Both in architecture and dress construction should be decorated—decoration should never be purposely constructed."[44]

As with the introduction of food science and nutrition to the average woman's kitchen, clothing and interior design textbooks encouraged women to see their ordinary lives as designed and composed rather than fated or pushed along by customs and fashion. On the one hand this suggested a much greater degree of agency for women than expressed in previous gender ideals, but on the other it demanded a potentially overwhelming attention to detail. Although preaching a gospel of moderation—"all decoration should be designed to enrich, not assert"—this ideal continued a long-standing, potentially stifling tradition in which women express their identity primarily through appearances.

Domestic architecture courses taught students to see the single-family home as a work environment above all else. Ideally, the environment would be designed so that each individual could fulfill her potential, assuming that her potential was to clean, cook, care for children, and yet have enough time to keep up with current events and have a rich cultural life. Attention was given to placement of sinks, stoves, and work surfaces, both in relation to each other and in relation to the woman who would be using them. Stairs and doors should all be placed convenient to the natural movement patterns within the house. Despite the reality that most students would not have the opportunity to design their own houses, domestic architecture courses taught them to think of the home as a variable and controllable environment, something that existed to serve its users rather than the other way around.[45]

Courses in textile science and clothing design likewise aimed to empower students. Knowledge of how textiles were created and what their properties were enabled women to demand the best quality from producers while skills in clothing design and construction potentially liberated women from the dictates of fashion altogether. The woman who had no inclination to make her own clothing might still protect herself from shoddy mass-market goods by recognizing the principles of clothing construction. A minor scandal erupted in 1933 when it was discovered that the Bureau of Home Economics was spending taxpayers' money studying button placement on boys' pajamas. A writer in *Scientific American* defended the study, arguing that these tests saved women much money and time and that to protect the consumer in a world where corporate manufacturing appeared to have few checks on its greed was the least the government could do. He noted that in response to the prevalence of poorly made garments the department developed new patterns and provided them free to consumers and producers alike.[46]

More and more, as the movement grew, home economists attempted to install themselves as social authorities and experts in a powerful space between the consumer and the producer, protecting the former from the latter through the provision not just of facts but also of a fact-seeking mindset. Home economics teachers and extension agents wanted women to believe they had control over their world but they located control in the details of daily life. At the level of the inseam and the drainpipe, however, control might not ultimately appear to be so meaningful. Connections between all aspects of domestic life were often difficult to convey in meaningful ways.

## Let's Play House

All the disparate elements of the home economics course came together in household management courses. Here the abstract was set aside in the hustle-bustle of the practical. Beginning in Illinois in 1909, home economics departments began adding "practice houses" to their facilities. The practice houses were the laboratories for courses in household management. Typically, a group of students, usually more than four but less than ten, lived for a period of several weeks together in a house or apartment that had been outfitted to resemble a real home. High schools also, when funds were available, set up practice apartments, cottages, or suites of rooms, but did not live in these spaces as college students did. During their period of residence, students rotated household roles, some cooking, some cleaning, some working on budgets, some on

Figure 7. A group of home economics students in one of the home management houses at Iowa State College, Ames, Iowa, 1944. The simple, naturalistic table decorations reflect the home economics aesthetic. Library of Congress, Prints & Photographs Division, FSA-OWI Collection, LC-USW3-002813-D DLC.

decoration, and one serving as "hostess." Beyond learning household skills, students practiced actual family living.[47]

At Teachers College, Columbia, a suite of rooms decorated by the design department to resemble "any ordinary Harlem or Brooklyn flat," served as a "demonstration department." In this department, students or, as the author of an article about the program saw them, "victims" were required to "keep house on a minimum salary, eat certain prescribed foods in definite doses, walk, work, sleep according to the rule and remain contented and happy! In short, it is to be a play house for scientific grown-ups." As was typical of non-home economists who wrote about practice houses, this author found the idea amusing, especially in regard to a reaction by male faculty members. Although the author acknowledged that Teachers College was attempting to train home economics professionals, a group of "benedicts," or unmarried male professors, "weary in the search for a competent wife," had offered a scholarship of two hundred and fifty dollars a year for a student in the program, "provided that at the end of her course she marry one of their number." The winner would be determined based on "50 per cent good looks and 50 per cent ability."[48]

For those not steeped in the philosophy of the movement, the sight of young women "playing house" suggested only training for marriage. And even this kind of training was only *as* and not *more* important than beauty, that old standard by which women had long been judged. Home economics students, however, seem to have been so taken with the idea of the practice house that in 1921 students at the Michigan Agricultural College in Lansing actually raised the $1,000 needed to build their house themselves by selling lemonade, shining shoes, and, of course, performing housework.[49]

Wherever it was possible, childcare was also part of the course. Some departments, like Cornell's, made arrangements with local orphanages to temporarily adopt an infant. The child was then reared by students who worked as a group. While participating in childcare, students continued to perform other household duties as well as to attend classes and complete assignments for other courses. Motherhood, then, was experienced as compatible (more or less hectically) with intellectual and professional development. Every six weeks or so, the child would acquire a new group of "mothers." Children stayed in the practice home until a family could be found to adopt them, which apparently seldom took very long. Far from being put off by the idea of a child raised by a collective of female experts, according to scientific methods, families considered these the best possible infants. In 1928, for example, Louise Stanley, chief of the U.S. Bureau of Home Economics, looked into obtaining one of Cornell's "model babies" for a friend who was hoping to adopt a boy.[50]

An article about the practice-house baby at Oklahoma A&M University affirmed this popular notion that the experience was good for children. "David, the A and M college baby came originally from eastern Oklahoma. He might have grown up to be the town's bad boy—to develop into an alley rat, a beggar, a bandit." He was taken in by the Oklahoma Children's Home, who agreed to send him to the School of Home Economics at Oklahoma A&M. The implication of this article was that David had been rescued from a grim fate and that society had escaped his potentially destructive influence all through the help of one social agency and a group of coeds. For those who questioned the practice of cooperative child-raising, home economics journalist Katherine Glover assured them, "One naturally wonders what the effect

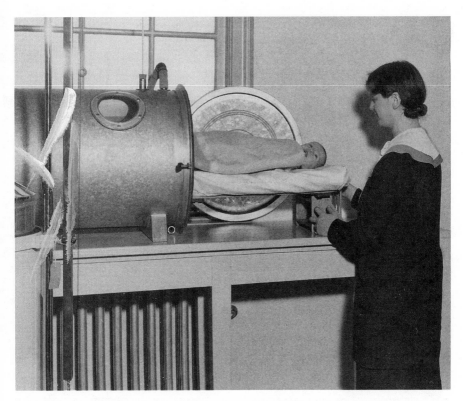

Figure 8. A Cornell student performs an unidentified test on a practice-house infant, year unknown. New York State College of Home Economics Records, #23/2/749. Courtesy of the Division of Rare and Manuscript Collections, Cornell University Library.

of composite mothering is upon the babies themselves. . . . If they miss the love of one mother, one must remember that all of these babies would in all likelihood have been institution babies." For Glover, as for young David's chronicler, it was obvious that six mothers were better than none. A writer in the *Los Angeles Times*, however, pointed out that the practice baby's mothers were not only many but temporary, noting that Nancy Lee, the practice-house baby at Penn State, "loses thirty perfectly good foster mothers" on graduation day. Returned to the hospital from which she came for a brief hiatus, Nancy was back at "work" in the college summer session.[51]

The practice baby turned out to be mockable as well as desirable. In 1928, two professors in the College of Arts and Sciences at Cornell published a poem in the *Saturday Evening Post* from the perspective of a practice baby. As a child, the professors surmised, he was blissfully happy:

> With the lips and eyes of a valentine
> and a smile from the Sunday comics;
> he was the Practice Baby in a College of Home Economics . . .
> "Oh what a lucky baby I am!"
> He often used to cry,
> "To have a hundred Mammas
> to make me hush-a-by!"

But in adulthood he felt disappointed and yearned for his earlier life,

> And now he's grown to be a man,
> and grievously he misses
> the care of his Model Mammas,
> their cuddling and their kisses;
> and oft he murmurs to himself,
> with his scowl from the Sunday comics;
> "Do they need a Practice Husband
> In the college of Home Economics?"[52]

From the point of view of these two male professors, the practice house served as a sort of harem with a baby pasha. Its primary interest lay in its abundance of motherly young women. The poets clearly mocked the notion of the practice baby while also suggesting that the field itself existed only to create perfect wives and mothers, rather than professionals in a wide range of fields. Here the practical nature of the program perhaps overshadowed the analytic.

A group of home economics students responded with a poem that concluded,

> But if *all* the practice house babies
> Came back on some future day,
> they *might* be model husbands,
> but they'd be awfully in the way![53]

Although the students conceded that it might be possible to educate men to be model husbands, they implied that even the best men, especially in a crowd, were superfluous to the functioning of a well-run home.

By "borrowing" infants for the practice house, home economists used the fruits of other women's misfortune to bolster their own professionalism. Bringing students into contact (if only obliquely) with the consequences of poverty and lack of birth control also made students more aware of the world in which they lived and especially of problems in women's lives. As self-contained a fantasy as the practice house seemed, it also had the potential to make students begin to deal with adult issues.

The practice was controversial and some colleges preferred to introduce students to child development in other ways. At Kansas State University, for example, Amy Englund, the chair of the Department of Home Economics, explained, "We do not have a child in the practice house as we believe there is a better way to teach child care and training." In 1925, when she wrote this statement, students in household management classes at her college attended "baby clinics" offered by a graduate nurse at a local hospital. In the future they hoped to open a nursery school, an enterprise that many other home economics departments became involved in. Nursery schools affiliated with home economics departments were frequented by teams of students with clipboards, and some even had two-way mirrors that allowed students to watch children behaving "naturally." Some schools had practice babies as well as nursery schools, and one little girl who had been taken in at the age of six months by the South Dakota State College home economics department was raised in the practice house and began attending the college's nursery school at age two. In 1931, she was four years old and still living at the college, presumably giving students an excellent opportunity to see how children develop.[54]

At the University of Illinois, students in the practice apartment met weekly to discuss all aspects of household management, taking the tasks of housekeeping as a cooperative, rational enterprise. A student's final grade was based not simply on how she performed household tasks, but also on "how well she analyze[d] the situations which confront[ed] the group, use[d] time to advantage for herself and others by making and following a reasonable plan, cooperate[d] . . . and develop[ed] satisfactory group relationships."[55]

The ideal homemaker, then, was one who not only managed all household work well but also could work constructively with others and, perhaps most interesting, make time for her own individual pursuits—her studies. The lessons that such experiences taught young women were strikingly at odds with traditional notions of married life. In the practice house, a woman was a member of a team, rather than solely responsible for all things domestic. She shared tasks with other people who were her equals and she always maintained outside interests, so that her entire persona was not collapsed into the domestic.

The collective spirit that made household management facilities so interesting for those who were living in them actually made them inappropriate as a "practice" houses or apartments. The homes that students would likely make as they married and had children would for the most part be solitary endeavors in which each woman performed all duties all the time. As children grew, tasks might be delegated to them, and husbands could sometimes be counted on for help around the house, but the bulk of the domestic work a woman would do would be nothing like the teamwork she had practiced at school.

The systems established in practice houses were unconscious enactments of the home life that home economists thought ought to be, rather than what was. In the ideal, domestic work was as important as work done outside the house (lectures and other schoolwork for students in the house) and it was performed by teams of equals who rotated roles. Each member of the team was also able to participate in life outside the home, ideally one that both informed her domestic work and was informed by it. This ideal of balance between home and the wider world was basic to the home economics movement yet elusive in real lives.

The model of home life found in practice houses, then, was an approximation of the cultural ideal, although home economists never mentioned this. The fact was that it was not feasible to have men living in practice houses acting like husbands. If it had been culturally acceptable for male students to take these courses, then the revolutionary notion of shared domestic labor might have been modeled within practice houses. That no female student was given the role of "husband" in these courses subtly implied that it was a nonessential role in the ideal home. In fact, academic administrators played the role of husband in that they funded these courses. Although the courses provided students with a model of home life that relied on teamwork, home economists did not educate female students in strategies for achieving true partnership with future husbands. Somehow, of their own accord, and in defiance of Western history, men would just magically accept domestic responsibilities and recognize women as their social equals.

There are many possible reasons why home economists did not follow the implications of the practice house to its logical conclusion. Very few of the movement's leaders actually lived with men and many lived in domestic partnership with other women, so that in their own daily lives the ideal had already been achieved and was therefore not a pressing issue. Another likely reason was that making such demands or pointing out the inherent inequality of separate spheres was radical and would draw the kind of outside attention that home economists did not want. In need of funding from state legislatures and acceptance by the culture at large, home economists would have been hesitant to state openly the revolutionary implications of their movement. Some may also have been afraid to draw attention to their own relationships by attacking traditional gender roles within marriage. Most likely, home economists of the first generation did not even see the implications of the practice house as a serious platform for action. They may simply have been unable to look at gender roles as alterable, much as their personal and professional lives challenged them to do so on a daily basis.[56]

## The Study of Women

As the pioneers of the movement assembled the elements of their field in curricula they were openly self-reflective, in many cases creating courses that would help students to see their own place in a larger history of thinking about and working in the home. These courses offered home economists another chance to justify their existence by allowing them to claim that the domestic environment was not static and that women's roles in society had changed over time. If this was the case, then it made sense to study these changes, partly as a way to understand larger social transformations and, more importantly, as a way to help people adjust to change. These courses, which covered such topics as the history of the family, the home economics movement itself, and women in industry, were particularly a feature of the first twenty years of the movement and express its most radical tendencies. That such courses largely disappeared by the 1940s reflects both the movement's maturation and social transformations that tended to limit the kind of implicit criticism of the status quo that these courses introduced. They are worth discussing here because they represent an attempt to expose gender role ideology as changing and changeable some sixty years before the emergence of women's studies in higher education. And this challenge comes from the last place we would expect to find it.

In 1907, Flora Rose joined the Cornell faculty and together she and Martha Van Rensselaer taught a course titled The Home, which covered the "history and evolution of the home; laws governing the home life; the home in its relation to outside factors; home-making as an occupation; correlation of

science in home economics."[57] By offering such a course they clearly intended
to make students think about women's roles in society. That the course was
taught by two women who had never been married, had no children, and were
in fact soon to move in together to establish a lifelong domestic partnership
made the course modern in ways that its instructors perhaps could not recognize. Rose and Van Rensselaer, like Dewson with her child-free budgets, were
offering an alternative to the traditional even while they were attempting to
preserve the nuclear family by modernizing it. When such women lectured on
the new career opportunities opening to women in home economics, they
served as living examples not simply of those same new career opportunities,
but of alternate lifestyles.[58]

At the University of Chicago in 1912, Sophonisba Breckenridge, a lawyer
and scholar who had earned her doctorate in political science and economics
in 1901, taught a course titled The Economic Position of Women, in which
women's economic, legal, and social status were considered from prehistory to
the present day and even into the future. Breckenridge dedicated the last three
weeks of the semester to considering "remedies" to inequality. Among these
suggested remedies were protective labor legislation, education, and "admitting
women to professions." Unflinching in her realism, Breckenridge included a
discussion of prostitution as a result of limited economic opportunities.[59]

Somewhat less progressive, George Ayers, a dean of the University of
Idaho College of Law, hoped to offer a course in law to students in the home
economics department that would be "about what a lawyer, an old friend of
the family, would say to the widow of his friend and to her daughters in case
they were likely to be situated so that they could not always see him and he
were advising them for a long time to come." Paternalistic in his perspective,
Ayers nonetheless realized that knowledge of marriage and property law could
be useful to a great number of women.

In the 1910s, Cornell offered courses taught by Blanche Evans Hazard, a
labor historian with a Ph.D. from Harvard, who appears to have been very
much interested in women's roles in society. She taught Woman in Industry,
Primitive Woman, and Woman and the State, as well as a course in the history of housekeeping. Hazard described her course on women in industry as
dealing with factory conditions, the conditions of tenement life, and occupational diseases.[60] Jessica Peixoto, a sociologist, historian, and the second
woman to receive a Ph.D. from the University of California at Berkeley,
taught two courses in the household science department there in 1909 titled
The Household as Economic Agent, and the Child and the State.[61] Isabel

Bevier of Illinois also taught courses on the history of women's education and the history of the family.

Such courses were generally simplistic in their approach to cultural history and tended to offer a triumphalist version of history in which civilization was always progressing and modern American society stood at its apex. Yet they were remarkable in that they introduced the history of ordinary life and of women and children into higher education. They were also notably progressive in the ways in which they attempted to connect the past to the present, a task with which history teachers continually struggle. For home economists, the greatest lesson these courses could provide was that of progress that students might take into their own lives. A section on the family lives of ancient cave dwellers might now seem absurd, but for the pioneers of home economics such a unit alerted female students to their own potential for change. A course like Breckenridge's went even further and explicitly laid out for students what at least one woman considered the pressing issues of the day and what they might do as citizens to shape their society.

Breckenridge, Hazard, and Peixoto represented the most maverick tendencies of the movement, in which the consideration of womanhood itself was an essential condition of the study of the home. Most others did not go so far in their attempts to understand the broader context and cultural construction of a woman's life and her labor and this approach was reserved for college courses. In the 1970s, however, these issues would return to home economics classrooms, as women's studies emerged in colleges and universities.

The interesting contrast between the lives that many home economists lived and the purported focus of their field—the life of the ordinary homemaker—became the basis for a critique of the field that emerged in the 1920s and 1930s. The critique that home economics as an academic subject was too far removed from the daily needs of most women simultaneously represented the success and failure of the movement. Much of this critique had to do with the differences between the way the subject was taught in elementary and high schools and how it was taught in colleges.

## "So Commonplace a Subject": Home Economics in the Schools

In an early attempt to educate elementary school teachers in how to teach household science, home economics teacher May Haggenbotham made a suggestion that summed up the spirit of the entire field. She suggested that teachers mentally walk students through the home, interrogating the purpose and potentials of each space. For example, she proposed, "Ask the *purpose* of the vestibule, and try to get the pupils to state what the purpose would naturally dictate as to furnishing and decorating. Have patience to draw them out. They have never thought much about so commonplace a subject."[62] The last two sentences could describe the work of home economics in general—applying thought and analysis and action to the banal.

Because they believed in the utility of their field and in its power to transform society, home economists were eager to introduce students to their topic as early in their school career as possible. Beginning in 1914, with the Smith-Lever Act, the federal government provided funding to do this, but home economics programs had already been introduced in public schools throughout the nation.

At the first Lake Placid meeting, as mentioned earlier, those gathered emphasized the need for "trained" women to lead the field. Rather than encouraging women who knew how to cook and sew to go out into the schools and pass on this knowledge, it seemed crucial to the movement's pioneers that the public persona of home economics be professional. They would supervise the training of the women who would teach the topic in schools rather than allowing this to be done in Normal schools or departments of education because they alone possessed the training to put each part of the field into context.

The introduction of home economics into primary schools and high schools can be seen as both a success and a failure according to the early ideals of the movement. It was a success in that the courses were quickly picked up and spread throughout the country, but a failure in that it ultimately had the effect of undermining home economists pretensions to cultural authority. By 1911, Sarah Comstock could write without much exaggeration in *Collier's* magazine, "Our public school systems have introduced cooking and sewing into their courses until now these subjects are taught from the Atlantic to the Pacific," yet the quality of this education remained suspect both to those who believed in its potential and to others who consistently doubted its worth.[63]

In a review of the state of the field in 1920, six home economists from a variety of backgrounds and institutions offered a harsh critique of how the topic was being handled in primary and secondary schools. The team members, who had conducted quantitative studies of elementary and secondary school courses and "a minute analysis of the textbooks used," found five major problems including focus on subject matter rather than pedagogy or learning, lack of meaningful assessment, lack of articulated study, and "vague statement of aims and outcomes."[64]

Because of a lack of high standards, careful organization, and pedagogical innovation, the authors reported with obvious irritation, "The public schools are teaching home economics as [just] so much sewing and cooking." Scientifically trained women in colleges and universities might be performing research in biochemistry or developmental psychology, but at the introductory levels the topic lacked cohesion and therefore legitimacy. Directly contrasting primary and secondary home economics education to college work, they assured readers that "again and again the student of public-school teaching can observe that emphasis is placed, not on the varied, many-sided subject matter urged by the college teacher," but upon simple skills.[65]

Contrary to the kind of criticism leveled at home economics programs in higher education—that they were too impractical—these critics found that  the field at its lower levels was dangerously pedestrian. Textbooks tended to mix the arcane with the every day in a way that might bewilder students. Often, textbook writers conflated the entire field of home economics with food preparation, limiting the potential for students to see more in it. And lessons on food preparation could veer quickly from seeming like science lessons to seeming like lunch. For example, a very early textbook, *Domestic Science and Household Arts for Use in Elementary Schools*, published in 1900 as a compendium of contemporary ideas about domestic education, offered a lesson on eggs that began very scientifically and ended on toast with a parsley garnish. Part of the pedagogical radicalism of the movement was to bring the processes of daily life into the academic setting, but the field's innovative potential might be lost on students at times like these. The frequent inclusion of lessons in table setting and etiquette also blurred the lines between science and socialization in home economics courses.[66]

Originally, home economists had argued that their topic should be added into the school curriculum, much as it had been in colleges, by using existing courses to teach more about the home. Thus a mathematics class could easily use examples from domestic life in order to make both topics—math and daily living—more accessible. Likewise science courses might just as well require experiments in edible materials as in the non-edible or to make students aware of the connections between what might be in their beaker and what could be on their plate. History and social science courses, these pioneers argued, could and should address changes in domestic life and labor for this, ultimately, was what might matter to students.

Interesting as this idea might be pedagogically and politically, however, it had major obstacles in that few teachers of traditional subjects would likely be open to the idea of re-orienting their class work toward domestic examples. Even if they had, home economists' own insistence on high standards would have required a mass reeducation of the nation's teachers to assure that they were teaching the topic correctly. And even if this logistical nightmare were achievable, there were still topics, such as nutrition, textile science, and household management, that would have to be introduced separately as well as the problem of how to emphasize the interconnectedness of the various parts.

Because of these problems, it made much more sense for home economics to be introduced as an entirely new topic and, indeed, school boards seemed happy to offer it to very young children and to older girls. Because it is not possible to teach first-grade children the basic principles of physics whether you are using bread baking as an example or not, these courses involved the simplest tasks only—cooking and sewing. Even this, according to the authors of the 1920 study, they did poorly, usually requiring small children to learn sewing, which employs fine motor skills, before cooking, which uses "grosser" motor skills and is therefore more appropriate to their age abilities. In many schools, this choice might have depended on the kind of equipment available. Hand sewing can take place in any kind of room, whereas some version of a kitchen is necessary for teaching cooking. As early as 1911, a writer in *Craftsman* magazine, generally a source sympathetic to the movement, noted that most home economics programs in schools lacked funding: "The average public high school which admits domestic science to its family of school courses, makes it the Cinderella of the group." Equipment, when available, was given poor placement, such as basement rooms and "under such conditions it is little wonder that both students and teachers of the department tend to lose caste."[67]

What writers who decried the field's low "caste" in terms of popular acceptance and its disorganization did not discuss, however, and what had tremendous impact on how the field was perceived was that home economics as a school subject was gendered from the very beginning. The argument that home economics skills and perspectives would be useful later in life and could lead to more complex course work in college was significantly undermined by the fact that the topic was generally offered only to girls. Some schools offered special home economics courses for boys, but this hardly helped to disconnect domesticity from femininity because the assumption was that boys and girls needed to know how to do different things in the home. Boys learned to make simple, "bachelor" meals, not how to feed their families every night. Sometimes they practiced home repairs or learned how to help budget the money that it was assumed they would be bringing into the home as sole breadwinner.

Particularly in the 1930s, when the devastation of the Great Depression disrupted traditional gender roles, home economics educators showed an interest in crossing gender boundaries. For three weeks in 1930, for example, male public school students in Muncie, Indiana, attended home economics courses while female students attended "industrial arts" courses. As Ella Hollenbeck, publicity chairman for the home economics department of Muncie City Schools, noted, "Boys will be boys—sometimes, and sometimes girls would be boys and boys would be girls. At least there are times when girls and women wish for the ability to do some kinds of work ordinarily done by men, and certainly all men sometimes find themselves so hungry they would gladly cook their own supper."[68] Home economics courses for boys were consistently portrayed as offering a kind of emergency training. In the event that no woman could be located, a man might have to feed himself.

A 1931 report on home economics courses for male high school students in Long Beach, California, revealed how such courses differed from those designed with female students in mind. The course was titled Family Adjustments and was given through the sociology department rather than the homemaking department because "the sociological aspects of the home rather than skills [were] emphasized." Where women were being trained to be both analysts and practitioners, men were expected to play the role of objective observer in the home.[69]

Before the course was offered, a questionnaire was sent to male students to find out what topics might interest them. Among the proposed topics were "legal points which safeguard a home," as well as the more esoteric "Man must vision the ideals he wishes to realize in family life and consciously bend his efforts toward reaching these ideals." Some topics did not directly relate to home life, such as "the names, cost, and wearing qualities of standard woolen and worsted materials used for men's suits and overcoats," suitable for the style-conscious bachelor, while others, such as "something about table etiquette, home etiquette," insisted on a new understanding of the home and workplace as linked. This linkage, evident also in the suggestion of a course in "the application of art principles to the planning and furnishing of an office or home, as knowledge of color, line, spaces, proportions, etc.," reflected the ideal prevalent among home economists of the era that the world outside the home was as much in need of domestication as the domestic was in need of modernization.

The Long Beach experiment aside, when men enrolled in home economics courses these were most often institutional management classes, a group of topics that later became the core of hotel management programs at a number of large state universities. Hotel management, with its large staffs and potential for high salaries, was seen as a male occupation. In vocational high schools, particularly in urban areas, some boys were similarly offered courses in cooking for large groups with the assumption being that they would end up working in restaurants or institutional kitchens rather than staying at home to cook for their families.

There are many potential reasons why home economists do not seem to have had much interest in making their courses coeducational from the beginning. Although they claimed that what they taught was useful for anyone, whether she or he managed a home or not, they chose the material for their field from work that had been traditionally female. Carving out a new field for female authorities, in which they could stand as not only equal to men but often as superior to them in their knowledge of this field, home economists of the first generation might well have been reluctant to share this new authority with men. And in fact, research that Margaret Rossiter has done on developments in the 1950s suggests that the pioneers had something to fear from inviting men into their field.

## "She Doesn't Know Much About Living"

During the 1930s, just as the Great Depression made it seemed to the movement's leaders that their skills were most needed, critics began to attack home economics in higher education as too abstract, not focused enough on the daily needs of the ordinary housewife. The department at Berkeley suffered such an attack from a former student. Margaret Wilkinson Bindt, who had graduated from Berkeley with a B.A. in household science in 1925 and had since married, complained to Berkeley president Benjamin Sproul that household arts and household science courses were too specialized and organized according to "a lifeless, academic approach." Bindt argued, "There is nothing which a girl, looking forward to a career of some sort, but also looking forward ultimately to marriage, can take which will give her the general orientation in this most important field."[70]

Bindt reported that many of her friends were discouraged from taking household science courses because the prerequisites were too difficult, complaining, "If one wishes to take the work offered by the department of Household Arts in Household Management, the student finds that a course in Civil Engineering is prerequisite." A survey on student attitudes toward home economics curricula collected by the *Journal of Home Economics* in 1937 echoed these sentiments. Many wanted to include "more all-round training for living . . . more practical home management house experience, more chance to develop social qualities, more training in the solution of financial problems," and, oddly, "more music appreciation." For women who had spent their entire lives trying to get away from the finishing school model of women's education, such demands must have been troubling.[71]

Agnes Fay Morgan, who was chair of the department at Berkeley, was a researcher in the field of food preparation. She remained adamant that her field was a science, not a skill set, and that her curriculum accurately reflected the prevailing wisdom of the field. Helen Thompson of the home economics department at the University of California at Los Angeles stated, "Our students want training for work. Practically none of them look forward to home making as their sole occupation." In 1939, Morgan was still defending this position. In a paper delivered to the annual meeting of the Association of State Universities and Land-Grant Colleges, Morgan called for home economics education to emphasize scientific training. She argued, "The research method . . . and the presence of research activity must infiltrate every phase of the undergraduate courses in order to ensure a supply of professional research personnel and also a fair degree of return from the effort and expense of maintaining a research program." Arguing that a strong reputation for research was essential to the status of the field, she quoted Martha Van Rensselaer, who had several years earlier written to Morgan, "I should like to assist on a research program because I think it is absolutely fundamental to home economics progress." For Morgan and for Van Rensselaer, the field's status derived from its reputation as a science and its distance from the kitchen.[72]

In the popular press, this attitude had been mocked from the movement's earliest days. In 1914, an article in *Collier's* magazine had celebrated Mrs. Anna Scott, who was "not handicapped with a degree from a school of domestic science" yet traveled through the mining communities of Pennsylvania, helping women to stretch their food budgets. Trained home economists had tried to work in this area, the author noted, "[but] the attitude of those whom they sought to benefit has been militant. Women of mature years resented the suggestions of domestic theorists." They and the author seem-ingly much preferred Scott, who identified herself as "a graduate of the college of necessity, which is unchartered." When she gave a demonstration of her methods at Teachers College, Columbia, one of the leading schools in the movement, "with fine scorn she put aside the casserole that had been left for her and the spatula that gleamed from the whitest of kitchen tables" because they were too expensive for the women she worked with. " 'Those are not the things that you will find in the kitchens in which I am working now.' She laughingly said." Home economists were derided as being out of touch with the women they claimed to serve. The author, a woman herself, had more re-spect for traditional forms of female education—the informal and anecdotal—than for the new theoretical basis for housekeeping.[73]

An article in *Household* magazine in May 1929 addressed the argument against theory. Irene Westbrook wrote a column titled "Us Brides of a Year" that discussed the issues of a first home, one without children. In May she wrote a story about a woman, Ida, who had been teaching home economics for eight years before she married Fred. Using her domestic science back-ground she announced that she would run their household on $75 a month. His family was skeptical. "Fred's going to ask you what you did with all that money at the end of the month," a sister-in-law said to her confidentially. "You've been a successful teacher, and theory is all right in the classroom but it can't work in the home."[74]

According to Westbrook, however, Ida managed very well, and ended up with savings at the end of the year. Westbrook was endorsing the idea that theory, taking a long, objective, analytical view of the situation, was the only way to run a successful home. Ida, a trained, professional home economist, had an advantage over her sister-in-law because she believed that she herself, not her husband, was the ultimate authority in the management of her home. Ida, not Fred, decided the household budget and how it should be spent. She looked at her work in the home as an extension of her previous career, not as dependent on her relationship to her husband. For Ida, theory was the in-dispensable means to practice. For Isabel Bevier, too, there was no point in simply teaching the most efficient methods of housework; what mattered was the conceptual.

In 1929, Benjamin Andrews of Teachers College noted that Bevier dis-missed early versions of home economics, taught by those who did not have academic training, as "that heaven, home, and mother kind of teaching." An-drews remembered that Bevier herself "always stood for careful preparation for scientific background and a wholesome life philosophy . . . and for facts and principles rather than emotionalism in content."

Bevier desacralized the home and the woman within it, working against Catharine Beecher's earlier philosophy in which woman, although ideally trained for her work, also existed in a semi-mystical connection to the domestic sphere.[75]

Within the ranks of home economics leaders, too, there were differing opinions on how to weight theoretical and scientific education against practical skills training. Lita Bane, Bevier's successor at Illinois, suggested that many in the field were improperly focused on abstracts. In contrast to earlier home economists, who had attempted to change the status of all women through their rationalization of women's work, Bane argued that home economics education was best tailored to the needs of the individual. Although she harkened back to the older model in her worry that the field had not made homemakers adequately aware of their social worth, she went on to declare that "the successful homemaker is not preeminently a scientist; she is an artist—proficient in the art of fine living." She acknowledged that the field had achieved a high level of academic standing, but she worried that this had blinded its leaders to the realities of women's lives. "On the natural science side," she argued, "we've done well. What are we going to do with the social sciences and art?" Having developed their work in the "hard" sciences, Bane wanted the field's leaders to turn their attention to the "softer" ones.[76]

Interestingly, Bane suggested that the reason home economists were overemphasizing the abstract and paying too little attention to women's daily lives was that so few of them had experience as adults with such lives. Including herself in a group perhaps unfit to preach to young women, Bane reasoned, "most of us are not living in the thick of present-day family life. . . . we know a few bachelor women's homes or apartments, the homes of a relative or two, and a few faculty families."[77] The only experience of family life that most home economists could refer to, then, was that of their childhoods. These experiences were of course almost useless because they predated the field. For Bane, unlike many of her peers, the single woman's home or the home that two women shared was not useful as a model. She lobbied for a redirection of effort away from scientific analysis of domestic work to a more detailed investigation of its practices.

Clara Brown, professor of home economics at the University of Minnesota, also sided with the dissatisfied Berkeley graduate, warning her peers that "we have loaded our college courses with prerequisite requirements in

physical and biological sciences and filled the student's days so full of laboratory hours that they have none of the leisure we talk so much about in which
to develop desirable personal qualities or to think about how to use what they
are learning." Brown blamed this neglect of students on the field's hunger for
status. "We have been so concerned about academic respectability—about
upholding scholastic standards, about living down the reputation among
some of our academic colleagues that home economics offered a haven for the
intellectually unfit, that we have failed to do what we should have done for
the majority of our students." She suggested that academic home economists
take more time to consider the needs and interests of their students, as well as
to study "current trends" in domestic life. Rather than striving to create researchers, Brown seemed to suggest, home economists should research their
own students and design curricula accordingly.[78]

Other home economists worried about such criticism, both internal and
external. In the *Journal of Home Economics*, Francis Zuill, head of home economics at Iowa State University, recounted, "An elderly man who is overseer of
the poor in a small Iowa community, in speaking of the relief activities of the
home economics teacher, said 'She knows her subjects, but she doesn't know
much about living.'" For many who read it, the comment must have stung. Although they had once been shunned for bringing the stuff of everyday life into
the academy, home economists were now attacked for not knowing enough
about these very things. For the many single women, and those who lived in female partnerships, the accusation that home economists did not know about
"life" might also have a deeper, more personal potential to wound.[79]

In a 1935 address, Effie Raitt, president of the AHEA, remarked, "[Home
economists tended to] emphasize the esthetic or scientific aspects but may fail
to note the economic and sociological. They are inclined to think more in
terms of the classroom and lab than of the home . . . fail to note obligations
to current problems of the life about them." Rather than calling for a new
focus on practical skills education, however, Raitt called for more emphasis
on theoretical connections between subfields and for greater opportunities for
postgraduate work. She quoted Edward Lindemann, who argued that the
new era brought about by the Depression called "for relational, rather than
analytical thinking." In home economics this would mean a shift of emphasis
to include the "soft" sciences as well as the "hard" sciences that had earned the
movement its public respect.[80]

Abby Marlatt, head of the Department of Home Economics at the University of Wisconsin, confirmed that the shift from hard to soft was under

way. In 1936, she wrote, "The emphasis of training on the applied biological sciences, applied chemistry, and applied physics is now being shifted to the economics of consumption and the psychology of group relationships not only in the home but also in the community."[81] Marlatt, like Ruth Okey at Berkeley, connected this shift to the influence of the New Deal, which focused attention on practical solutions to social problems.

In fact, although neither Raitt nor Marlatt engaged this, the hard/soft, practical/theory debate was itself a result of the work that pioneers had done in the field. It had been a constant struggle for the women of the movement to come to a point when people could accuse them of not seeing the world outside their laboratories. In a sense, the moment that the movement was criticized for being too abstract, having too little to do with women's work, was the moment it finally arrived in academia. This arrival, as is often the case with a movement, was also a departure.

CHAPTER TWO

## At Home in the World

IN 1915, the United States Department of Agriculture opened its Office of Home Economics. The office conducted studies in nutrition and subjects "pertaining to the broader field of domestic economy," including studies of how much energy women expended in daily household tasks. When plans were discussed to transform the office into a bureau of home economics within the USDA, Henry Wallace, head of the department, specified that the bureau must be directed by "a woman of executive ability, thorough scientific training, and a broad and sympathetic understanding of what is needed to make such a bureau helpful to the women of the land." Louise Stanley was selected for the position.[1]

Stanley had been head of the Department of Home Economics at the University of Missouri from 1910 to 1923. She had a doctorate in biochemistry from Yale and was a regular contributor to the *Journal of Home Economics* and an active member of the AHEA. Stanley brought the spirit of academic home economics into the arena of national projects, adding to the government's interest in supply and demand a focus on women's experiences as workers and consumers. With her appointment as chief, Stanley became the highest-paid woman in government, setting a new benchmark for women's achievement. Her appointment linked academic home economics to the funding available through government and also to the status that came with a national office.

From 1915 to 1923, Charles Langworthy had been the chief of the Office of Home Economics within the States Relations Service, which suggests that Wallace did not think the position below male dignity.[2] He seems to have felt that it was important for the movement to be led by a woman in its new phase. It was common sense in this era that that which related to the home related to women more than to men, unless it was a question of the design, construction, or physical maintenance of the structure itself. The guiding spirit of the home was assumed to be female. Wallace suggested by his action that women had an important role to play in the proposed modernization of the home. Although men like Wallace were sexist in their conflation of woman with home, they were also progressive in their belief that women and women's issues belonged in the USDA. When Stanley accepted the post, she was simultaneously assisting in the gender integration of the government and acknowledging the gender segregation of daily life. Stanley believed that the domestic lives of American women, particularly farmwomen, presented problems that were different from those faced by men and that were worthy of research and analysis. But by presenting herself as a candidate for the job she implicitly rejected the notion of separate spheres.

What is perhaps most significant about Wallace's description of the perfect applicant for the job is that he clearly believed that such a woman existed. He could be certain in this belief because the movement had created such women and widely publicized their existence. A common misperception of the home economics movement has been that men created it as a way both to "keep women in the kitchen," and to neutralize the perceived threat of women in higher education. In fact, the movement was created by and for women both to bring "scientific" methods to housekeeping and to create new careers and professional opportunities for women. These opportunities increased throughout the first ten years of the movement as hospitals hired dieticians and institutional managers with home economics degrees and corporations created "test kitchens" at women's magazines and in domestic product firms. The new authority that home economists had created for themselves became most visible, however, in times of crisis when they could emphasize the life-and-death aspects of their field. World Wars I and II and the Great Depression that occurred between them were the periods of greatest public recognition of the field as providing leadership in social reform and cultural advancement.

## Food Must Win the War

Many of the prominent home economists of the day were involved in the federal government's food conservation effort during the mobilization for World

War I. Home economists saw themselves as uniquely qualified to aid in the war effort for several reasons. Nutritionists within the movement had developed a body of knowledge about food that could be the core of a plan to organize food distribution and rationing. Home economists knew what amounts of protein, fiber, and vitamins the human body required and how to create substitutes for materials, such as wheat and meat, that would be needed by the army and consequently less available to the general public. They also had vast experience through state extension services with canning and preserving, both necessary to avoid waste during periods of dearth such as were expected to come with the war. They could take some of the hardship out of rationing, thereby making it easier for ordinary people to support mobilization and involvement in the war.

Textile scientists knew the lasting qualities of fabrics and could tell ordinary Americans what to look for if they wanted their clothes to last through potentially tough times. Most important to their own self-evaluations, however, home economists were philosophically steeped in the dogma of conservation. It was this commitment to conservation that seemed to fit home economists perfectly for the task of helping America through the privations likely to accompany war.

Because many of the leading home economists worked for state universities, by the beginning of World War I they had already developed relationships with state officials as they attempted to win funding for their departments. As already noted, Van Rensselaer and Rose of Cornell won the allegiance of legislators by serving them creamed cabbage. They also visited Albany during budget negotiations and cultivated friendships with the governor, Franklin Roosevelt, and his wife, Eleanor. Although Isabel Bevier of Illinois preferred to keep her distance from the state capitol, she kept careful watch on budget appropriations for the school and forged alliances with state officials through her work in extension services. Women who ran departments at state universities were able to enjoy the authority of state officials at times, and Van Rensselaer was adept at expanding this authority whenever possible. Agnes Fay Morgan, who was head of the Department of Household Science at the University of California at Berkeley, corresponded directly with state officials, offering the skills of her staff and students for war work.

As Elizabeth Perry notes in her biography of Democratic Party activist Belle Moskowitz, women in the 1920s were not "as powerless as their lack of public office would lead us to think. . . . [They] found creative, if unrecorded ways to exercise power." Perry terms this approach "feminine politics," a

"feminine politics"

politics that focused on ideals rather than parties and that operated through a
network of personal relationships rather than political office.[3]

The experience of helping the country mobilize for the war was one of
bonding with fellow professionals, all the while acknowledging the special position of female leadership. In the spring of 1917, the Bureau of Education issued
a call for all American women to receive home economics training. "If war
comes upon American territory," a bulletin issued by the bureau explained,
"the well-trained graduate nurse will be called to war hospitals and the ordinary
nursing of home sickness will devolve upon home women." Beyond stepping
into the shoes of professional nurses, the women of America could also perform "great services" by conserving the nation's food supply. And, true to the
home economics philosophy that attempted to place the mundane in larger
context, "Short courses in the study of the condition of national supply of
household material, needed economics, and the sociological and economic effect of women's activities should be offered." Students should see their work in
a global and historical context in order to appreciate its and their importance.[4]

By August 1917, war had come and the U.S. Congress had passed the
Food and Fuel Control Act, also known as the Lever Act, which gave the
president the authority to implement controls for the use of food and fuel. In
order to do this, President Woodrow Wilson created the U.S. Food Administration, which oversaw state and national efforts to make sure that soldiers on
the frontline were getting the supplies they needed without the rest of America suffering too harshly for it. Sacrifice was expected, but should not be
excessive. Above all, Americans should understand the conflict in which they
were engaged and their role in supporting their own army as well as their
nation's allies.

A 1918 food and nutrition textbook issued by the U.S. Food Administration provided an "Introduction to the World Food Situation," as well as a
summary of the kinds of work being conducted in the United States. so that
students could understand the urgency of their work and how it fit into a national and international context. Interestingly, this book, prepared for college
students, included descriptions of the trend towards community kitchens in
Europe both in nations allied to the U.S. and in the enemy nations Germany
and Austria. New ways of thinking about food supplies were bigger than even
geopolitical conflict.[5]

Throughout the nation, schools at all levels of education adjusted their
curricula to address the crisis. John L. Roemer, president of Lindenwood College, a two-year college for women in St. Charles, Missouri, could proudly

claim in 1917, "When the United States became involved in the great world struggle, Lindenwood College responded to the appeal to become intensely practical. . . . For the coming school year several practical courses were added, such as homemaking, which prepares young ladies to become homemakers." Just why a course in homemaking fitted a young woman to help out in war work Roemer did not make explicit, but the idea that this connection existed was prevalent and was a boon to professional home economists, particularly those in charge of college programs.[6]

By May 1918 between one and two hundred thousand female students at seven hundred colleges, universities, and Normal schools throughout the country were enrolled in courses that specifically trained them for food conservation work. Students were trained in a three-part course designed by the U.S. Food Administration to make them aware of the international food crisis, acquaint them with nutritional issues of the war and methods to conserve food, and to engage them in laboratory work. Students were expected to become leaders in their communities, and heavy emphasis was placed by the Food Administration on the responsibility that came with this new knowledge about food and war.[7]

One editorial in the *Baltimore Star* suggested that men should now be learning home economics so that the women in their lives could devote more time to war work. "The women are too busy these days," the writer explained, in a humorous tone, "to pay much attention to the plaints of their husbands, and if the men are to be cared for they must care for themselves. Let 'em learn how to darn, how to sew on buttons, to set the dough for the bread. . . . Let mother and her friends knit and sew for the soldiers." Now that women had joined the war effort, men on the home front needed to learn a little housekeeping.[8]

In an example of the kind of work that women were doing in communities across the country, high school students in the home economics department in Topeka High School in Kansas demonstrated their wheat-conserving resourcefulness in 1918 by providing their city's chamber of commerce with an all-potato dinner. Such work inspired home economics teachers to hope for more permanent alteration of the American character.[9]

Despite the massive upheaval caused by the war in Europe, home economists saw this moment as an opportunity for Americans to leave the path of heedless consumption and choose the righteous way of thrift. At the Girls Collegiate School in Los Angeles, principals Alice K. Parsons and Jeanne W. Dennen described a transformation already under way: "The war has made the most thoughtless girl pause and reflect. She is learning a little self-denial.

The constant discussion of national waste, household waste, and personal extravagance is doing an immense amount of good." Parsons and Dennen argued that economy was a lesson that must be learned, "and if the war teaches it . . . the next generation will be stronger and finer because of it."[10]

Parsons and Dennen's statement reflected a common perspective among home economists that the war was a kind of crucible from which a new, wiser America might emerge. In this belief, they were like many other progressives who saw the war as a chance to change American institutions for the better and who were mostly disappointed when the war ended and few of these promises were fulfilled.[11]

Herbert Hoover, who eagerly took up the work of chief administrator of the U.S. Food Administration, wrote that his goal in this position was to advise Americans, "Go back to simple food, simple clothes, simple pleasures. Pray hard, work hard, sleep hard and play hard. Do it all courageously and cheerfully. We have a war to win." Hoover claimed that the response of the American public was even more than he had hoped for and that in some cases people were *too* good at conservation. As an example he sited data revealing that American consumers had limited their butter and milk use so drastically that it began to affect producers adversely.[12] A writer in the *Survey* confirmed Hoover's impression of cooperation, observing, "One of the products of war is the cooperative organization of consumers. Throughout the country buying clubs, canning clubs, community gardens and kitchens are spontaneously being formed on grounds either of economy or of food conservation."[13] Yet, despite this mass enthusiasm, after the war most Americans set aside this communal spirit of thrift to follow the lures of advertising agencies into a marketplace sparkling with new consumer goods. The thrill of doing the right thing seems to have faded as soon as peace was achieved.

Evangelical as they sometimes were, home economists were occasionally able to understand that the changes they were proposing, both for wartime conservation and for postwar reform, would be neither popular nor easy. The program of a 1923 reunion of people who had worked in the Food Administration during the war included a number of satirical songs written about the very programs that home economists had designed and publicized. One titled "O.U. Hoover" described conservation efforts:

My Tuesdays are meatless,
My Wednesdays are wheatless,
   I am getting more eatless each day.

My home it is heatless,
My bed it is sheetless,
    They're all sent to the Y.M.C.A.

Another song, "When the Day Is Done," bemoaned the substitutions required to conserve meat for the troops:

I have eaten a bale
of spinach and kale
and I've never raised a row.
I have swallowed a can
of moistened bran
And I feel like an old brindle cow.[14]

Although it is unclear whether the songs were composed during or after
the crisis, it does seem certain that home economists maintained a sense of
humor about their mission. It is interesting to note that at this same meeting
home economists enjoyed a lavish reunion feast featuring such treats as
"Zephyr of Guinea Chicken," and "Fantasie aux fraises mignardises," a far cry
from the simple cuisine of the war years.[15]

## Home Away from Home

At the same time that home economists established bases for themselves on
college campuses, they were also working to get their message out to those
who did not have direct contact with colleges and universities. The beginning
of the war in Europe had coincided with the passage in 1914 of the Smith-
Lever Act, which supplied funding to states for home economics education
and extension services. In all of the state universities, home economics departments had already been taking an active role in extension services to farm
families who were also served by extension agents from the state universities'
agriculture departments. From 1914 on, however, home economists were also
given federal support to spread their teachings into the nation's public
schools. When war began, therefore, they already had a variety of programs in
place to spread the message of food conservation. Using diverse methods, they
taught Americans how to conserve food, how to preserve food, and how to

extension services to
farm families

substitute other sources of protein for milk and meat and other starches for wheat as well as how to preserve and repair cloth and clothing.[16]

Among the methods home economists used to get their message out were bulletins, farm conferences, and lecture tours. The most spectacular means used by academic home economists were the demonstration cars, specially furnished train cars that carried the home economics message throughout a state. Demonstration cars, in operation as early as 1908, arrived in small towns and parked for the day. University-trained demonstration agents, often graduate students, gave talks and demonstrations on domestic topics to audiences gathered by advance press. The more abstract and complicated experiments were left behind in the laboratory, but agents showed audiences how to use new labor-saving devices, such as the fireless cooker, and how to prepare and conserve foods.

Home economists at the University of North Carolina, which boasted "the first domestic science car ever run," removed the seats from half an ordinary passenger car and installed a kitchen with an oil stove, an icebox, a kitchen cabinet, and a "fireless cooker" in the emptied half.[17] Other schools followed this model. Cornell had two cars, one that had been emptied of half its seats and fitted with a demonstration stage, and another from which all the seats had been removed. The second car was used to bring exhibitions of household technology to farm communities.[18]

Accustomed then, by 1917, to taking their show on the road, home economists were well prepared to send agents out into the field to teach the  wartime gospels of conservation and substitution. By 1919, Cornell's home economics demonstration car had been renamed the "Victory Special," celebrating that conservation efforts had helped to win the war.[19] Even a commuter rail line, the Long Island Rail Road in New York, ran a special home demonstration train during the war that carried specialists to small towns in Long Island where they were met with enthusiastic crowds of women and girls.[20]

The war expanded public awareness of home economics, and this greater  publicity for the field helped to create new and related careers. Home economists also found places for themselves within the emerging consumer culture. Academic home economists frequently published lists of the many career opportunities that awaited their graduates. Such lists justified the training and research they were offering and let the world know that home economics was not just dedicated to creating the perfect housewife. The career lists, which expanded over the years, reflected the movement's goal "to make the whole

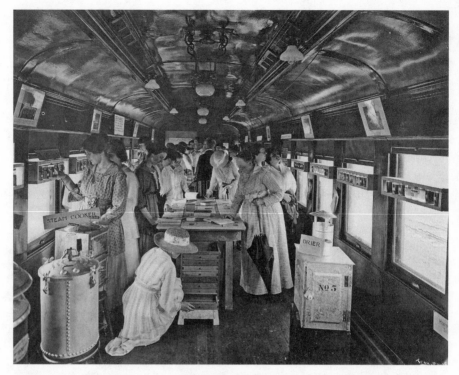

Figure 9. A demonstration train car prepared by Cornell Univeristy Home Economics Extension agents, 1918. New York State College of Home Economics Records, #23/2/749. Courtesy of the Division of Rare and Manuscript Collections, Cornell University Library.

world homelike," as the superintendent of home economics in New York City public schools phrased it.[21]

Leaders of the field eagerly imagined a world in which domestic practice and skills were applied and appreciated equally within and without the walls of the single-family home. In the interest of simplifying the lives of women who worked in the home, home economists supported the development of efficient substitutes for individual domestic labor. A good laundry, a durable pair of factory-made stockings, a nutritious lunch away from home for husband and children all seemed not just acceptable, but desirable. And what better way to ensure the quality of substitutes than to have them administered by trained home economists? If the consumer society was going to provide such services, then it was vital that the best possible quality be achieved. And simultaneously

the new market in services offered home economists the chance to make
money, achieve authority, and share their knowledge with the public.

In 1918, the annual report of the Simmons College Department of
Household Economics announced, "There is an increased desire on the part
of the students for greater specialization. This makes itself felt not so much by
way of direct expression from the students as by the eagerness with which
new specialized electives are chosen and the reluctance with which the conventional group of teaching electives is accepted."[22]

Rather than training for careers as home economics generalists who would
teach at the primary and secondary levels, students were finding themselves
drawn to specialties within the field in which they might contribute original
ideas. The field was becoming more attractive in its particulars than as a whole.
Among the opportunities for home economists besides teaching were institutional management, nutrition, dietetics, interior design, interior decoration,
textile science, clothing design, and child psychology. By 1945, a report by the
University of California listed as possible careers for home economics graduates, "home demonstration work, dietetics, institution management, laboratory
service, research, commercial production in foods, clothing, and . . . home
furnishing industries, social work, and many others."[23] In addition, it became
increasingly common for those who majored in home economics to pursue advanced degrees. Although there had been only four universities offering advanced work in home economics in 1919, by 1932, there were thirty-two
granting master's degrees and one granting a doctorate.[24]

Nutritionists and dieticians became regular staff members at institutions
such as hospitals, schools, and prisons and in the military. The home that the
public, professional world was supposed to be made to resemble was, of
course, not the home of yesterday, but the hyper-efficient and intellectualized
home of tomorrow. Home economics graduates ran cafeterias in large companies and in public and private institutions, bringing to workers, patients,
students, and inmates a modernized version of all that was potentially good
about home life. Hot, nutritious meals were provided in a setting that was
sanitary and congenial to conversation and relaxation. And while patrons ate
meals based on home economics research, they relaxed in interiors designed
by other home economists. In these environments, the visitor's spirits might
be subtly elevated by the inclusion of organic forms in decoration or a few
tasteful prints upon the walls. Home economics graduates also ran their own
businesses, opening the tearooms and lunchrooms that served working men
and women in cities and large towns.

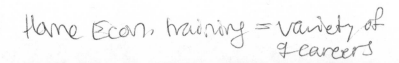

Major corporations also hired home economists to work in test kitchens and other laboratories, consulting on the creation of domestic products such as laundry powder, upholstery textiles, and electric mixers. In 1929, Marjorie Heseltine, who was director of food research at Halls Brothers Company, in New York, wrote about home economists in business. When her company wanted to send out "educational" leaflets about its products, she wrote that most of them were "prepared under the direction of a woman with home economics training." Although a "few firms" did not "consider it necessary to consult an accredited home economist," Heseltine reported that these were now in the minority.[25] She went on to say that "home economists may be surprised to learn that their very names have a certain commercial value according to their professional status."[26] Heseltine's emphasis on the "accredited" home economist and her reference to status reflect the growing sense of workers in the field that they were professionals.[27]

## Mass Media and Home Economics

For home economists, an integral part of creating and augmenting their cultural authority was finding a place for themselves in mass media. Training professionals who could go forth and work in business and in schools was not enough. American women who read magazines and newspapers or who listened to the radio could also partake in the revolution of the rationalized home.

By the end of World War I, home economists were adept at using a variety of media to spread the philosophies and practices of their movement as well as the equally important message that a new class of experts existed. They hoped that the lessons of the war—meatless and wheatless days, remade clothing, and thrift of all kinds—had transformed the nation into an audience receptive to their teaching. Heads of departments and professors as well as graduates all contributed to the growing field of home economics literature.

Many wrote for the *Journal of Home Economics*, which was started in 1909 as the official journal of the American Home Economics Association (AHEA). The journal carried technical articles on subjects such as biochemistry, nutrition, and design as well as more theoretical pieces about the mission of the field. Proceedings of each annual conference were published in the *Journal* and it contained regular reports from colleges and universities about activities in home economics departments across the nation. The *Journal* also regularly published bibliographies of literature in the field, celebrating the emergence of a body of knowledge available to all. As frequently as possible, the *Journal* printed photographs of buildings constructed for home economics departments and laboratories within buildings. Each new lab and each new building represented the field's growth as a respected entity within the academic community. The buildings were not just practical additions to the campus; they were monuments to the movement's success.

By writing for magazines, newspapers, and, beginning in the 1920s, radio shows, home economists simultaneously reached wider audiences with their messages and created new careers for women. Radio stations usually aired home economics shows early in the day so that lessons could be absorbed into that day's arrangements. For example, a casserole described after breakfast could be served for dinner that night. These shows were sometimes delivered as advice from experts and sometimes presented as narratives. Home economics programs in colleges and universities offered courses in radio and print journalism to prepare their graduates to write such shows.

Ruth Van Deman, spokeswoman for the Bureau of Home Economics, was heard weekly on the radio show *National Farm and Home Hour*. Following the bureau's lead, most academic home economics departments had their own radio shows on the college station. By 1929, Justine Hemphill was visiting the bureau twice a week to gather material for the *Housekeeper's Chat*. This radio program had begun in 1926 and by 1935 was broadcast on two hundred stations in forty-eight states and Hawaii. The purpose of the shows was "to give homemakers useful information on the scientific practice of their job."[28] KOAC, the radio station of the University of Oregon at Corvallis, broadcast a number of home economics shows, including *Hows and Whys of Housekeeping, Facts and Fancies*, which debated myths of housekeeping, and *A Half Hour in Good Taste*, on social usage, or etiquette.[29] In 1932, Cornell's radio station, WVBR, ran a series about Deborah and William Domecon (short for "Domestic Economy"), a young couple starting out in their first home and caring for their first child. The show was a sort of info-soap opera in which the young people faced down the ordinary crises of married life and learned valuable lessons about domestic management.

Like most other early radio shows, many early home economics radio shows were sponsored by corporations, particularly those selling domestic products. The listener was supposed to form what we now call "brand loyalty" because a particular company provided her with the most helpful and friendly radio companionship. Corporate home economics shows, such as the *Betty Crocker Radio Show, Aunt Jenny's Real Life Stories*, and the *Miss My-t-Fine*

*Show,* provided listeners with a mixture of materials in an attempt to both amuse the listener and advertise the product. By creating these regular, reliable moments within a woman's household routine, the show's producers and sponsors attempted to blend into listeners' lives.

Aunt Jenny's Real Life Stories, which was sponsored by Spry shortening and ran from 1937 to 1956 on Columbia, offered a unique format. The show aired at eleven o'clock in the morning, just when a homemaker might be stopping for a cup of coffee and beginning to think about what to make for dinner. In the basic format for the show, Dan, the announcer, arrived in Aunt Jenny's kitchen, where she was always cooking something that used Spry shortening. After some patter about what she was preparing—and whatever it was, Dan always wanted some—Jenny introduced a story that was continued by actors. At the end of the segment—not necessarily the end of the story, as stories ran about five shows in length—Jenny returned to her cooking. The stories that she "told" were true stories, sent in by listeners and dramatized by writers for the show. Each story was framed in terms of a problem that needed resolution, which Jenny herself eventually supplied. Because the stories were spread out over several weeks, this gave listeners the chance to puzzle over the problem and come up with their own ideas about what might be done.

Jenny, played by Edith Spencer, was a woman in late middle age with a folksy, slightly Irish accent. Her voice marked her clearly as an ordinary woman, a motherly type, in contrast to the strained "cultured" voices heard on other shows. Her advice was not that of an expert—a psychologist or home economist—but of a woman with folk wisdom and a strong no-nonsense streak to her personality. The illustration on the cover of Spry's pamphlet, *Aunt Jenny's Favorite Recipes,* reinforces this persona as Jenny uses the older term "receipt," rather than the more modern "recipe," and declares that she knows that "folks" want "*every day*" receipts that are cost effective as well as "digestible."

In an early example of what might now be called a "virtual community," Helen Powell Smith's *Let's Make a Dress* radio series joined her listeners through a common task. In a series of fifteen quarter-hour shows that aired twice a week during 1944 and 1945, Smith, who was professor of clothing design at Cornell, talked her listeners through the process of constructing a dress. Instruction booklets were sent out to accompany the show. Smith encouraged her listeners to work while they listened, creating a sense that they were participating in something like a bee, where women gathered to complete work together. In reality, as a questionnaire was able to determine, the majority of the audience listened alone.[30]

Figure 10. Radio personality Aunt Jenny was featured in a cookbook sponsored by Spry shortening. Jenny emphasized the ordinariness of her recipes as well as their "digestibility." Collection of the author.

Figure 11. Helen Powell Smith broadcasts an episode of her radio show *Let's Make a Dress*, 1944. New York State College of Home Economics Records, #23/2/749. Courtesy of the Division of Rare and Manuscript Collections, Cornell University Library.

Once the series and the dresses were complete, the radio station and state extension service sponsored a "rally" for listeners at which they met to show off their work and to meet other women who had shared their experience. In 1948, Smith wrote that the rallies gave listeners a chance "to show their dresses and extension workers to meet their radio friends, check results and interests, and stimulate cooperation with other homemaking programs." Remote cooperation might lead to more direct group work, such as canning parties or conservation drives.[31]

Smith also noted that the shows helped connect women who were remote not just from the radio studio, but from other women. "An almost blind girl," she wrote, "made her first dress and modeled it at the rally." By privileging sound over sight, the show gave this woman access to a world she had previously been shut out of. Another testimonial Smith offered was that of a "shut-in" who used the lessons in the show to make clothes for family members—her daughter and granddaughter. Although she herself, for reasons physical or possibly psychological, could not leave the house, her work, in the form of the radio dress, could go forth on the backs of the women of her family. These stories give a sense too that Smith thought of her show as one with the potential to work as a kind of occupational therapy. Radio could reach out in a way that went beyond both education and entertainment.[32]

Home economists who did not have corporate sponsorship also attempted to get their message across through a mixture of fact and fiction. The New York City Home Economics Association, for instance, aired two shows featuring the characters Mrs. Mead and Mrs. Bradford, who shared home economics information with the audience through their own scripted-to-be-casual conversations. In one incarnation of the show, in 1936, the two women were neighbors in an apartment building in the city. Mrs. Mead, the older of the two, had "had the advice and help of a nutritionist while her three children were growing up." Poor Mrs. Bradford had not, so Mrs. Mead stepped in to help her. Mrs. Mead was an interesting creation, combining two kinds of expertise. On the one hand, she represented a traditional kind of expert, not the professionally trained kind but the experienced elder. On the other hand, she had been educated by a professional herself and could now pass this knowledge on to a new generation. As a character, she was probably designed to make listeners feel that they were not being talked down to but were instead being taken into a peer's confidence. Mrs. Bradford on the other hand, had trouble with her eighteen month old and she wasn't going to pretend otherwise. Instead, she would share her troubles with Mrs. Mead and the listeners. Mrs. Mead then passed on the wisdom she had previously received when she was in this position herself.[33]

Early to recognize the selling power of a trained expert, magazines also began hiring staff home economists in the 1920s. Magazines like *Good Housekeeping* built test kitchens and printed the sensible advice of domestic experts on everything from scouring powder to squash casserole to sibling rivalry. In 1908, Theodore Dreiser, editor of *The Delineator*, wrote to Isabel Bevier in Illinois to ask if she would like to write an article for that magazine or for *The Designer* or *New Idea*, two other magazines he edited. *The Delineator* was a woman's magazine that combined fiction with fashion and domestic advice. Dreiser wrote that Bevier had been recommended to him as "someone who is interested in the sociological progress of America, and particularly in matters which concern the development and well-being of the oncoming generation of Americans." Dreiser particularly wanted Bevier to write about the practice house at the University of Illinois. He wanted information about a specific project under way in her department, but also recognized her appeal to the public as an authoritative voice on issues of modern life.[34] No record of her reply exists. When she did write for magazines, however, Bevier tended to write about her own department as Dreiser had suggested. Such articles legitimated the movement as newsworthy and possessed of its own history. Martha Van Rensselaer, of Cornell, later took up the position of home economist at *The Delineator*, supplying regular columns on household matters.

Women's magazines began to call their test kitchens "institutes" of home economics and to adopt the professional tone of academics. *Household* magazine's institute, the Searchlight, was located in a single-family home, "directed" by Harriet Allard and her staff, who performed tests on household products and recommended to *Household*'s readers only those of which they approved. The women who created recipes or designed ideal rooms for magazines were presented to readers as trained specialists, rather than ordinary women willing to share their own secrets acquired through experience. Magazine home economists were understood to be career women rather than friendly neighbors.[35]

Perhaps dearest to the hearts of home economists were the extension bulletins produced by university agricultural extension services. In these bulletins, they were experts on all they addressed. They did not have to compete with advertising or fiction or share their authority with women not trained in home economics. Rural families formed the main audience for extension bulletins. Home economists focused much of their attention on farmwomen, partly because farm women lived in the least "modern" conditions of any women and partly, perhaps, because the farm still seemed idyllic to them. Many Americans were nervous about the modern era, troubled by the growth of cities and the very trend toward the scientific that many simultaneously embraced and advocated. If the farm home could be enlightened without being ruined, then it might offer a meaningful alternative to the troubling new urban lifestyle of (presumed) anonymity and dissociation from production and nature. More pragmatically, too, the interest in farm homes came from the movement's early foundation and continued funding as the sister (or perhaps wife) to agricultural education.

In the homes of farmwomen, home economists faced much less competition than they did in the homes of urban women. Urban women were exposed to more advertising, to shops full of the latest goods, to more print media, and simply to more women leading more varied lives than were rural women. Whether the home economist arrived in a rural community through her words in a bulletin or in person as a demonstration agent, her authority experienced fewer challenges than it might have in a city. This did not, however,

make rural women any more likely than urban women to accept home economists' self-appointed authority.

Although college and university home economists tended to live a life
much more urban than rural, they often maintained an active nostalgia for
rural lifestyles. And yet, because they themselves were "new women," they
could not simply accept the ways of country people, feeling compelled to
change these ways in order to make them conform to their own ideas of what
was "modern."[36] These modern ways, however, were actually far from neu-
trally defined. They were circumscribed by the values of a very small subset of
American culture—urban, educated, politically liberal, and following the
Arts and Crafts aesthetic. Because the approach was so unilateral, rather than
collaborative, it had the potential to denigrate the lives of the uninitiated,
farmwomen, particularly.

Because home economists styled themselves as experts in a field that was
supposed to have no experts—a field in which each woman was supposed by
her very nature to be adept—they often seemed to overturn the only authority ever granted to women. Although newspapers routinely advertised the
work of home economists as having a positive effect in rural communities,
and while audiences for demonstrations and extension bulletins were generally large in rural communities, there was still an inherent tension between
the bringers and receivers of knowledge. A home economist arrived in a
woman's community and told her that everything she and her revered ancestors had ever done was incorrect. Not only was it incorrect, but also by continuing to do things in the old way, women were actually a drag on society,
keeping it stuck in the dark ages, rather than moving it forward as business
leaders and scientists were doing.

The agents who visited farm communities were often quite young. Extension work took women away from home regularly and so was not ideal for
more mature or married women, although agents did come from all ages and
marital statuses. Some extension agents were students working their way
through home economics programs and the temptation to claim total authority must have been great. In an article about the home economics programs of
Kansas State University, a farmer was quoted as saying, "These fool colleges
have always got a lot of high-falutin' notions about better living. We're living
better than our fathers did." Although the farmer may well have been invented for the sake of the narrative, in which his wife wins him over to the
program by being prettier and a better cook because of it, his attitude was
surely typical of the movement's rural critics.[37]

In an article titled "The Extensionized Farm Woman," Anna Gilbert gave the perspective of the extension agent's audience. Although Gilbert admitted that food preservation work done during the war was admirable she thought that it was no longer cost effective in the postwar economy. Reminding home economists, "One must become farm-minded to see the reason for many customs in farm homes," she called attention to real differences in the lives of agents and their audience: "We wonder why the extension workers do not realize that our life scheme is entirely different from that of city women. The surveys and reports emphasize the divergence of our life from that in a city as if we should use that as our standard. There should be two separate and distinct standards, for our conditions must necessarily be different."[38]

Home economists, for example, constantly encouraged women to make their own clothes, while Gilbert thought that if they could see the kinds of clothes farm women made "they would go away with a devout wish that what had been done might have been left undone."[39] With mass production of clothing increasing constantly, Gilbert saw no real reason for women to continue to make their own clothes. That this article was published in the *Journal of Home Economics* indicates that home economists had at least some interest in knowing how to relate to their audience and some awareness that they might be perceived as out of touch.[40]

Far from worrying that extension agents would condescend to farmwomen, A. R. Mann, dean of the New York State College of Agriculture at Cornell, worried that they might be inappropriately swayed by their audience. He called for a close relationship between researchers in universities and extension agents so that the latter could be "careful as to facts" and mindful of academic standards, so as not to "become a mere advocate of class or partisan views or be carried away by temporary moods or prejudices of those with whom she must constantly deal."[41] From Mann's perspective, home economists were in danger of getting too close to their subjects, not too distant from them.

## Home for Sale

Another force, stronger by far than resentful farmwomen, rose to challenge the authority of home economists in the 1920s. The rise of consumer culture at first seemed to offer unique opportunities to spread the word, but home economists soon found that it obscured their authority and even co-opted the very rhetoric that defined the movement.

Around 1900, producers of consumer goods began to use advertising and market research to create markets for items. Advertising began to feature not simply claims of effectiveness and desirability, but of a product's powers to transform its user's lifestyle. Indeed the notion of lifestyle began to emerge during this period in advertising. Instead of simply announcing that a washing powder, for instance, did the job, pictures and text began to claim that using it would create a happier, more harmonious, perhaps even more exciting life for the woman who used it to wash her dishes. Advertisers of domestic goods began to play with ideas of class mobility and glamour.

Many of the first generation of home economists might have reluctantly agreed with historian William Leach's assessment that corporations created a "culture of desire that confused the good life with goods."[42] Theirs, however, was a conflicted position. The home economists both helped to create important aspects of consumer society, such as the "expert," and resisted the manipulation of desire to cloud notions of necessity. Home economists also had their own very specific notion of the good life to sell to the American public, one in which subtlety, utility, and moderation were the organizing principles and operative virtues. This vision was in conflict with the emerging consumer culture at many points. The movement was part of a cultural and social shift that valued the individual as an actor in society and as such often broadcast the same message that advertisers of consumer products did: your choice as an individual is all-important. At the same time, however, home economists also advocated group awareness of consumers so that they could protect themselves from the wiles of producers. They wanted to create educated consumers who could control the market, a tricky proposition in a free market economy. And, while celebrating the average housewife who could think for herself, they continued to insist on their own ultimate authority on all issues domestic. Difficulties for the ethical soundness of this position rapidly emerged when corporations began to hire women with home economics training to market products.

Commercial producers of domestic goods were all too happy, it seems, to adopt strategies devised by home economists to spread their own, more self-interested messages. By 1928 they were making inroads on the traditional territory of the extension agent, not just by sending salesmen door to door, but by actually replacing state-funded extension agents in at least one region. In this year, the Western District Federation of Women's Bureaus in New York State complained to the state organization, "the lack of specialists' help from the college is becoming serious and that we are having to take advantage more and more of commercial demonstrations to hold the interest of the membership."[43] If the state extension agency could not afford to send a representative out to western New York to bring them the latest methods in laundry or canning, private enterprise would be happy to fill their time with what amounted to advertising.

Even within the halls of college home economics departments, where objectivity was presumed to reign, the professional's relationship with the corporation was never clear. Manufacturers supplied goods to home economics laboratories at reduced prices and many times for free. Goods included everything from ovens to yeast to sewing machine needles. Professors assigned students to work with these materials, producing analyses of each dish or dishwasher as well as performing tasks directly connected to course work. A student, then, took on the tasks of the movement's ideal woman—she observed her world with a critical eye. The kitchen was not merely a natural extension of her own self, but also a collection of goods produced in a market, each one vying for her approval.[44]

Isabel Bevier wrote to the Ideal Manufacturing Company of Detroit in 1909 to ask if they produced a stove with glass doors. She was obviously interested in making it possible for students to observe foods in the process of cooking, something that was not possible with the heavy iron doors of stoves of the time. A representative of the company wrote back to explain that they did not have such an item, stating, "We cannot say that we are satisfied that an oven with a glass in the door is practical. As a matter of fact we don't think so. However, there is plenty of room for improvement along the lines you mention."[45] Bevier, of course, was ahead of her time, but the exchange is also important because it reflects the sense that home economics leaders had of themselves as innovators.

Earlier in 1909, Bevier wrote to the American Vacuum Cleaner Company to set them straight on how manufacturers should expect to deal with home economists. The company had refused her request for a sample of their product. Bevier responded to the company, "Either you are not in the habit of doing business with state universities or you do not wish your cleaner placed in a position where it may have the benefit of being called to the attention of hundreds of intelligent women." Patiently explaining the advantages she could offer the company, she noted that there were not only 175 students in the department, but also "constant visitors in the department." In January alone, she wrote, she could expect to have one hundred such visitors to the housekeeping department. If any doubt remained, she assured the company that they would only be doing "what hundreds of other firms have done."[46] She then listed some of the discounts and gifts that the department had received from other manufacturers.

By suggesting that the company had not done business with other state universities, Bevier was reflecting that, by 1909, it had become a common practice for companies to supply departments with their goods. She offered the department as a showcase for the vacuum, suggesting that American Vacuum Cleaner Company would receive free advertising for its product, although she did not offer to endorse the product overtly. In fact, what she was saying was that the vacuum would be tested in the department's practice house and if it performed well, a wider audience would notice this performance. She already had a sense of her department as a source of authority for women of the state. The practice house would be something like the city on a hill, an example to all the many who would be looking to the university for just such guidance. She was offering the company a chance to provide the vacuum on the hill. She suggested, also, that home economists wielded such authority that the vacuum company would find it needed them even more than they needed it.[47]

In 1908, the American School of Home Economics, a correspondence school based in Chicago, published a bulletin titled "The Modern Home: Money and Labor Saving Appliances." The title made explicit the movement's belief that the ideal home could, to a degree, be bought. An educated woman would be able to choose the correct tools for her work and, ideally, markets would respond to both her knowledge and her needs in order to present her with "modern" products.

Manufacturers themselves solicited professional home economists—those on faculty and those who wrote for magazines—to endorse their products, seldom with the desired results. Academic home economists seem to have felt a sacred trust to remain neutral and skeptical publicly. When Standard Brands Inc. gave money to Agnes Fay Morgan, head of home economics at the University of California at Berkeley, to perform experiments on their bread they accepted her requirement that "her name and connection would not be given any publicity."[48]

Attempting to achieve cultural authority for themselves and their movement, leaders did not want their fortunes tied to specific products. As much as they welcomed free samples and discounts, they needed to be seen as independent, objective researchers and analysts. This was not simply a question of pride, but also an attempt to lead by example. Home economists shared a mission to make women aware of their power as consumers. They strove to teach American women to be ever skeptical of the claims of advertisers and to demand the best possible products from manufacturers. In Bevier's case this meant asking for something that had not even been invented yet.

The eagerness with which corporations attempted to attach the names of "real" home economists to their products created new opportunities for women who could serve as liaisons between women and mass producers of domestic goods. Sarah Splint a publicity agent who once attempted (unsuccessfully) to get Van Rensselaer's endorsement for Knox gelatin, was evidence of the rapidity with which the movement had established itself as a source of cultural authority. She and her business partner, Elizabeth Scott, opened an agency in New York City that they described as "a modern and essential service for advertising agents and manufacturers of women's products." The point seems to have been to connect the people who wanted to market goods to female consumers with women who could write about these goods in women's magazines. Splint seems to have been a freelance writer and editor on domestic issues. She wrote cookbooks and household management books for Crisco and served as the food editor at *McCall's* magazine during the 1930s. As consultants, Splint and Scott thereby supplied manufacturers with advertising, which was not free—they collected fees themselves—but which did not have the look of advertising.[49]

Splint's more famous peer Christine Frederick became a national authority on the homemaker as consumer, consulting with advertising firms on how to reach women consumers most effectively. In 1929, she published *Selling Mrs. Consumer*, "a manual for advertisers and manufacturers," because she believed that "the trinity of 'consumer/distributor/producer' had helped raise the standard of living for all Americans." Frederick wrote for women's magazines and turned her own home into an experiment station, complete with rationalized test kitchen. Although she had not trained in home economics, she, like Splint and Scott, represented the early success of the movement, which made it possible for women to have careers in business by presenting themselves as links to female consumers. Frederick, however, had more allegiance to business than to women, encouraging faith in advertising and denigrating the intellect of ordinary women, rather than agitating for higher standards of truth in the field or helping to create more skeptical consumers. Because of an uneasy relationship with business interests, home economists were not always in harmony with the professional women their field had helped to create.[50]

In 1934, Dan Gerber of the National Association of Advertisers commented that of the advertising firms he had surveyed, "Every organization heard from expressed satisfaction with its home economics department . . . and quite a number were able to cite specific examples of increased sales directly traceable to it." He saw the corporate home economist's role in the new economy as "the position of ambassador and liaison officer to the housewife, first to interpret her needs and then to assist in the development of plans and methods for gaining her attention and confidence." Gerber did not actually offer to meet the housewife's needs. That was the goal of academic home economics. The advertiser's interest was in finding out how to speak to homemakers in a language that they would respond to.[51]

That advertising agencies were using trained home economists rather than psychologists to interpret between women and business represented a brief moment in the history of both fields when home economists were the recognized authorities on women's lives, at least in relation to consumer culture. Gerber reinforced this understanding when he wrote, "I confess that one very worth-while product was actually crammed right down my throat by the head of our home economics department. I still think it was rather underhanded—she finally won me by enlisting the aid of my wife." Although Gerber gives home economists credit for being experts on women and their patterns of consumption, he deflates their authority in his final comment by suggesting it all comes down to the kind of female power that men have insisted women wielded for centuries—personal, nonpolitical, and emphatically unorganized. Yet in the end it is because the home economist spoke "woman" that she was able to communicate with Gerber, through his wife, some information that he eventually found profitable. It is implied that the fault was partly in Gerber himself, who did not yet consistently listen to women as experts.[52]

At the same moment that manufacturers were offering home economists roles as authorities, they were already co-opting them. As Katherine Parkin finds, companies like Campbell's picked up on the liberationist rhetoric of the era in order to sell more soup. A 1919 Campbell's soup advertisement addressed to homemakers acknowledged, "You probably know a great deal more about diet and food-values than your grandmother knew. Every intelligent housewife studies these questions now-a-days."[53] Although Parkin does not make the connection to the home economics movement, Campbell's was clearly referring to the new rhetoric of modern domesticity. The ad spoke to young women who had taken home economics courses in high school, at least, if not in college. It recognized that women had been offered a new way to think about themselves in their homes—as experts.[54]

The company tried to sell its soup as a marker of modern domesticity—
freedom from the traditional task of making soup from scratch. Parkin notes,
too, that Campbell's emphasized the cleanliness and efficiency of its kitchens,
even going so far as to imply that the corporate kitchens could produce better
soup than could a home kitchen. This claim also depended on women's exposure to the idea that some household tasks could actually be done better outside the home.

For academic home economists it was a mixed blessing that huge corporations had invested in kitchen and textile laboratories and begun hiring women
with home economics degrees. The creation of these roles meant more jobs and
higher salaries for their graduates, which created more justification for their departments to exist. Clearly they were not just training women to be housewives,
but were actually expanding the opportunities available for women in business
and supplying the corporate world with trained workers. But in contrast, these
corporate home economists did not enjoy the perfect freedom of the university
laboratory. They had to endorse the products of their employer. Although they
would have had a role in creating these products, they would have had to col-
laborate with corporate marketing agents, who might have had limited interest
in nutrition. For such a woman to be known as a home economist both bolstered the field's authority, by making it a legitimate occupation with social authority, but it also weakened the field by abandoning many of its core values.

The public's acceptance of the industrial expert easily expanded to include domestic experts. As a group, however, Americans were not as willing
to accept the more radical messages of the movement, including its aesthetic
and its emphasis on moderation. Consumer culture itself battled handily
against old ideas of modest living by providing goods at all prices that promised to make consumers feel like members of the affluent classes. Fashion out-
ran consumer education without much of a contest and throughout the 1920s
Americans spent their money on an increasing variety and number of consumer goods. As they bought their way into debt, they trusted their impulses
far more freely than the words of any domestic scientist speaking from the
cool of an academic laboratory.

## Milkorno to the Rescue

When the Great Depression struck in 1929, home economists were probably
among the least surprised or alarmed people in the nation. Although the years

since the war had been a period of growth and positive publicity for the movement, the lessons of conservation and rational living that had been so celebrated during World War I were clearly being disregarded. In 1931, an editorial in the *Journal of Home Economics* mused on the field's prescience. In 1930, writers in the *Journal* had commented on the "anomaly between the idea of thrift and the prevalent business philosophy that prosperity depended upon free spending." By 1931, "the advocates of wise spending [were] no longer like prophets crying in the wilderness, but [were] in general favor as public speakers and teachers."[55]

The Depression, horrible as it was, gave home economists another chance to convince Americans that radical new thinking about the domestic environment was the only way for ordinary women and men to exert control over their own lives. Or, as the *Journal* editorial put it, "for this slight beneficent breath of the ill wind, let the upholders of old-fashioned thrift give heartfelt thanks."[56]

In 1920, Martha Van Rensselaer had commented on the changing relationship of Americans to the commodities their society produced. Writing to Mrs. George Hewitt, president of the New York State Federation of Women's Clubs, to offer some ideas of subjects that the clubs might want to discuss, she suggested, "The psychological moment has only just arrived to accomplish anything so far as education of the spender is concerned. People have run away from thrift without knowing what kind of beast was pursuing them. They are interested in the cost of living and if it is called something beside thrift they are interested in means of spending an income."[57]

She was writing to Hewitt, hoping to involve other women because she believed it was up to women of the nation to adjust spending habits so that labor would be concentrated in the production of essentials.[58] Van Rensselaer thought that if the gospel of moderation could be spread it might combat what she saw as the problems of consumer culture—wastefulness and lack of control.

In a letter to Van Rensselaer in 1928, Louise Stanley, head of the Bureau of Home Economics, wrote, "Many products are now being supplied to the home in quantities and in forms which add unnecessarily to their price." By studying and publicizing this problem, home economists could make a real contribution to society, altering the functions of the consumer economy. She believed, "If there were better understanding of the factors which may be charged to marketing and distribution costs, it would be possible to shift demand accordingly."[59] Both women clearly saw the interests of consumers and of the national economy pitted against the interests of producers. Both believed that consumers could and must be educated to take greater control of the market.

In a pamphlet, "Thrift Program 1921–22," prepared by a number of cooperating federal agencies, this ideal of home economics was set out in terms that almost anticipated the Depression. Noting that "most of us know too little about" personal, local, and national economics, the pamphlet rallied the American woman to "put her personal and household affairs on such a business-like basis that every penny possible may be saved and that her money may be used to the best purpose for herself and her country's welfare."[60]

To remedy the common lack of knowledge, the pamphlet suggested that women's clubs offer courses on banks, the federal reserve, taxation, bonds, the IRS, thrift for children, investment strategies, and "women and the law." This would be a course in "simple legal transactions which occur in every day life and which every woman should know."[61]

When the feared collapse did finally occur, home economists were quick to respond, resurrecting many strategies used during the war and employing martial metaphors to encourage communal spirit. One of the more interesting responses came in the form of a new foodstuff, Milkorno, which represented an attempt to use techniques developed by marketing and advertising professionals to sell Americans not luxury goods but health itself. In 1933, nutritionists at Cornell first served Milkorno, a substance they had invented to help needy families stretch budgets without sacrificing nourishment. Milkorno was equal parts corn meal and skim milk with one part salt for each part of the other ingredients. It was used as a polenta-like porridge or sweetened with raisins for dessert and could be added to ground meats as a stretcher. Milkorno was served to Eleanor Roosevelt and other dignitaries in attendance at the annual "Farm and Home" week at Cornell in 1933, and in the same year, Roosevelt served Milkorno at the White House to publicize it.[62]

The following year, Cornell introduced Milkwheato and then Milkoato. The Cornell Research Foundation, which had the rights to the whole Milk-ô family, licensed them in 1934 for use by the public. As one newspaper noted, manufacturers could now produce them "in sufficient volume to feed millions of relief agency beneficiaries."[63] According to a Cornell press release in 1934, the Federal Surplus Products Corporation purchased twenty-five million pounds of Milkwheato for use in relief. Because the products could be used as substitutes for flour in baking and provided a milk supplement for families who might not have been able to afford milk, they could be very useful. Between November

1933 and May 1934, the residents of Fitchburg, Massachusetts received 880 pounds of Milkwheato as part of their federal emergency relief supplies. In Hammond, Indiana, Anna Hart offered her neighbors a recipe for ginger Milk-wheato cookies to make the best of hard times.[64]

Home economists expected the use of substitutions to be valued and exploited long past the crisis of the Depression. For researchers at Cornell's laboratories, the Depression had framed the question—how can starch be stretched and costly protein delivered in one product?—but it did not fore-close the options for the answers. It seems likely, however, that because they were introduced as a response to the Depression, Milkorno and its siblings became associated in the public imagination with hardship rather than with modernity. They were not regarded as the foods of tomorrow, but rather as the foods of shame, and as quickly as consumers could return to the old ways, they did.

Even before she made the bold move of serving Milkorno at the White House, Eleanor Roosevelt had already publicly adopted home economics phi-losophy and practices. In 1932, she published *It's Up to the Women,* her guide to Depression living. The book relied on budgets prepared by Flora Rose of Cornell and went beyond emergency measures to provide a commentary on class in America and to advocate moderation as a way of life. Roosevelt sug-gested that the homes that were more likely to retain their solidarity in crisis were those in which women had been accustomed to work. She employed the rhetoric of tradition-based and idealized "woman power." Remembering her grandmother's words, "You are a girl and I expect you to be more sensible and more thoughtful than your brothers," she modernized the sentiment. With-out returning to earlier ideals of women as deputy husbands, she argued, "women, whether subtly or vociferously, have always been a tremendous power in the destiny of the world." And now, when, because of suffrage, more women were "holding important positions and receiving recognition and earning the respect of the men," she wrote, "it seems more than ever that in this crisis, 'It's Up to the Women!'"[65]

Although home economists saw the Depression as a moment for domestic experts and visionaries to shine, Roosevelt took the notion one step further and suggested that now was the moment for women to prove their true worth in society. Just as suffragists had partly won the vote through the strengths of women's contributions during World War I, women might achieve higher sta-tus in society through their leadership in dealing with the current crisis. At the same time, Roosevelt's call to the women of the nation also reinforced older gender ideology that held that men and women had different talents and particularly that women's strengths were most often found in the domestic sphere. Like her friends in the home economics movement, Roosevelt accepted the connection between women and the home as natural, rather than culturally constructed. Roosevelt's feminism, indeed the feminism of the era, was complex, rooted as much in the past as it was inspired by visions of the future.

Alert to her power as national role model, Roosevelt introduced thrift into the White House. In 1933, a Washington, D.C., newspaper reported that the Roosevelts would lunch on a "low cost menu," designed at Cornell's School of Home Economics by Flora Rose. The menu included "hot stuffed eggs with tomato sauce, mashed potatoes, prune pudding, brown bread and coffee." Eleanor Roosevelt had committed to using a week's worth of the menus as a model for cash-strapped housewives. Lest anyone worry that the nation's culinary reputation would suffer, the cheap meals were only to be served "when no guests are present."[66] The announcement was a home economist's dream come true. The movement had gained access to the most important kitchen in the country and its message was being spread by one of the most famous women of the century. The meal itself was a model of conservation. By substituting eggs for meat, brown bread (made with rye flour, cornmeal, and graham flour) for white, and dried fruit for fresh, the menu saved money while providing important protein, fiber, and vitamins.

Convincing Eleanor Roosevelt to model conservation menus was important not just because she was the president's wife, but also because she was a member of the elite. If a balanced and thrifty meal was good enough for one of America's first families (who also happened to be the "first family") then it would surely be good enough not just for the struggling poor but also for the ambitious middle class and even the wealthy. In order for the messages of nutrition and frugality to spread, they must be phrased in such a way as to overcome the power of fashion. Despite Roosevelt's drawing the line at serving economy meals to foreign dignitaries, her public use of the recipes made home economics an affair of state.

By early 1933, as the *Journal of Home Economics* confidently announced, "There is every indication that alert, progressive home economists everywhere are alive to the demands and opportunities of the situation." Home economists were indeed involved in many projects to alleviate the suffering of the Depression. Activities they engaged in included consulting with state agencies to create budgets and dietaries, offering free classes to adults, preparing pamphlets on conservation, making lunch for students, teaching students to make lunch for relief project workers, helping families to plant subsistence gardens and leading groups in remodeling old clothes and making new clothing, underwear, and table linen from feed sacks. They were also combating the tendencies that had led to the Depression by teaming up with department stores to create window displays of "inexpensive but satisfactory toys" for children. They were working in every venue not just to meet demands, but also to reduce desires.[67]

The 1930 White House Conference on the Child and the Home, called by President Herbert Hoover, had brought many home economists to Washington where they gained greater insight into how the government functioned while enjoying national visibility as experts. Because the Depression had already begun, many of the findings and recommendations of this conference did not have the impact they might have in more prosperous times, but the gathering had certainly increased the movement's cohesion and sense of national importance. When the severity of the depression became clear, home economists hoped to parlay their authority into opportunities to rescue the nation from itself.

As Sophonisba Breckenridge, a University of Chicago professor of household administration, noted, the Depression was the field's best advertisement.[68] She wrote, "In spite of a vivid appreciation of the disaster resulting from the depression, it must still be a source of the greatest satisfaction that we are facing a future in which the outlines of domestic, social, and economic security can be discovered." She claimed that many of the social reforms of the New Deal might well have come about through the agitation of home economists without the intervention of the crash, but that the Depression might equally well have occurred without the "ray of comfort" that was home economics.[69]

Joining forces with the Works Progress Administration, home economists even seemed capable of solving once and for all "the servant problem." In Los Angeles the WPA opened a school for housekeeping that one writer in the *Los Angeles Times* found "eminently practical" as there was a shortage of domestic workers, "ironical in the face of the number of women on relief" and "complicated by the incompetence and inexperience of available women." The author, sounding very much of the employer class herself, was excited to learn that in the school, which had (appropriately) been set up in a mansion loaned for the purpose, there was also a nursery. Some of the students, it seemed, had small children, but rather than let them get in the way, "these [were] used for teaching the women how to care for a baby . . . and a good deal

Figure 12. WPA poster advertising household training, 1936–40. Library of Congress, Works Projects Administration Poster Collection, LC-USZC2-5404 DLC.

of child psychology."[70] These were lessons that both author and teachers might have hoped would last past the current emergency.

## The Era of Adjustment

Home economists mobilized against the privation of the period, but not necessarily against its lessons. In 1933 Annette Herr, a home economics teacher, claimed that because of the Depression, "the education work in home economics [was] due to become one of the most important activities carried on in the interest of society."[71] Although the field had been important before the crash, Mary Sweeney wrote in 1932, it had become somewhat caught up in the rise of consumer culture, for "in the years when wages and incomes were steadily rising, standards of living could be progressively improved by additions to income." In other words, Americans could buy their way into the modern era simply by acquiring (so-called) labor-saving devices. The crash brought this blithe progress to an end and revealed the field's true potential: "Today the situation is entirely changed. At present people are coming to realize that improvement or even maintenance of standards of living will depend upon increased maintenance of scientific information and the application of trained managing ability."[72] Herr and Sweeney both saw the Depression not as a temporary setback but as a permanent change in the American economy. As such, it required an adjustment in thinking about economic life in general.

Reflecting on "the opportunities and responsibilities of home economics in the present situation," Frances Swain encouraged home economists "to do [their] part in an education which shall prevent a recurrence of such periods of uncontrolled spending as [they] saw in 1929–1930 and the following road of leanness."[73] For her part, Swain insisted that consumer education was the key to national economic stability, but also that this would not be meaningful or effective without public attention to the conditions of labor. Supply and demand must be analyzed and understood publicly if destructive cycles were to be avoided in the future.

The field flourished in this period not simply because its practitioners saw the chance to be heroic in response to the Depression, but also because the 1930s were an era of international interest in the rationalization of social life, for better and for worse. In 1931, I. Thomas Hopkins of Teachers College, Columbia, declared that home economics education now faced "the greatest opportunity of its whole history." In an era of "adjustment," Hopkins warned, it would succeed only if it offered youth a vision of "new home in a new social life—constructive, pragmatic, dynamic." His language was that of a futurist, perhaps even a collectivist, striving to remake society along lines inspired by industry.[74]

The term "adjustment" reflected a vision of modern life in which massive social changes swirled around ordinary people and threatened to engulf them unless they made adjustments to their traditional ways of living. Progress was always nipping at one's heels, always a force to be reckoned with. Men and women had to learn not to hold their ground but instead to think of themselves almost as processes, ever changing in adjustment to the continuous changes of their era. In the same 1931 article, Hopkins predicted, "The decline in the importance of academic subjects, the increase in emphasis upon the education of the whole individual, upon conscious adjustments to changing social life, and the dependence of society upon the home for biological and social purposes are hopeful signs." Home economics, in Hopkins's vision, was part of a movement that led away from education that focused on learning about the past to a new education that prepared individuals to negotiate the future.[75]

In fact, the changes in education that he predicted had already begun in the wake of World War I. The era during and immediately after the war saw a shift away from traditional ideals of education to a more vocational approach. Most of the elite colleges dropped their classics requirements, and, with the larger state universities, emphasized social sciences and invested in a wider range of engineering courses. The postwar world was one to be analyzed, designed, and managed.[76]

In thinking about this future, home economists were alert to the international context of their movement. The month after Hopkins' article was published in the *Journal of Home Economics* another article in the same journal remarked, "Judging from the literature and correspondence that come our way, Germany is the country in which there is the greatest development of interest in household efficiency as an essential factor in national efficiency and hence as an essential item in the educational program." The article went on to note that the German government was encouraging interest in domestic science through the National Board for Scientific Management and that there was a large market in serious journals and magazines for women on domestic subjects.[77]

In 1934, Anna M. Cooley, a writer for the *Journal* who had attended the fifth International Congress of Home Economics in Berlin, reported back glowingly to her colleagues. The congress, hosted by the Third Reich, was held "In a beautiful room in a beautiful building. . . . it was decorated with swastika flags, palms and flowers and presented a gay scene with five hundred delegates assembled," she wrote, "One is very conscious in Germany today of the united effort of all women working under the Reich for a better Germany."[78] That Cooley considered swastikas no more sinister than any other element of flower arrangement represented the common perspective of the era, in which the full implications of national socialism in Germany had yet to be understood. Her interest in the closeness with which German women and their government seemed to be working was perhaps a point of envy.

This interest in the German model, in which home economics projects were well supported by the state, reflects that the field was amenable to centralized governmental programs. American home economists would have hoped to be part of a large-scale federally directed rationalization of social life, complete with revaluation of female gender roles. What actually happened in Germany under Hitler was a reactionary return to imagined traditional gender roles. The trinity of "Kinder, Kuchen, Kirche" made a woman's kitchen a holy place, but also a prison. The domestic was valued as essential to society, but was understood as adhering only to private homes and as the only legitimate option for women.[79]

The Nazi regime removed women from the sphere of paid labor in order to support their belief in the home as haven. A Nazi song celebrated German women's domestic labor in a way that limited other possibilities for them:

We want to have wives again,
Not playthings decorated with trifles.
No Woman in a foreign land has
The German wife and mother's gifts.[80]

State-sponsored interest in home economics, if it did not pick up on the liberationist possibilities of the movement, could condemn women to a very limited life. Communism in the Soviet Union, in contrast, did seem to fulfill some of the goals of the movement, as it institutionalized formerly private domestic functions. Cooperative living and public nurseries were both ideas that American home economists had advocated. Indeed, both were recreated by academic home economists on college campuses in the form of practice houses and the nursery schools that allowed home economics students to observe and care for the children of working women.

## "Learn to Live": World War II and Postwar Planning

When World War II began in Europe, home economists were already fully mobilized because of their work fighting the effects of the Depression. It was a simple matter to continue canning programs and thrift demonstrations under the new banner of support for the Allied powers and, when America entered the war in 1941, national defense and unity. Although this was the period when many of the movement's pioneers died or retired, the spirit of their work continued through the war. New media like radio and, thanks to the New Deal, new agencies like the Women's Bureau existed now to spread the message of conservation. Home economists had helped to shape these outlets over the years since World War I. The home economics editor of the *Los Angeles Times* noted that technology offered new opportunities when she suggested that the ability to freeze food at home meant that "any time is fruitcake time for a soldier overseas." Whether the cake was to be eaten or used as a weapon the writer left to the soldier's discretion.[81]

Home economists also attempted to adopt methods developed by commercial media to get their message across, even borrowing something from the makers of girlie pictures. Ruth Van Deman, who was press secretary for the Bureau of Home Economics and appeared regularly on the bureau's radio show, explained in 1944, "We're also taking a leaf from 'Life' and the other picture magazines. They're demonstrating every week that people will learn by picture what they won't read in type." In the interest of teaching canning to nonreaders, the bureau had "prepared pin-up pictures, not of canning beauties, but of competent hands washing and packing food, adjusting tops, handling cans and canner the right way." While American soldiers were being inspired by Betty Grable, their wives at home could get turned on to conservation by an attractive photograph of another woman's "competent hands."[82]

Among new techniques for wartime conservation, older methods also flourished. Meatless days and recipes featuring "substitutions" reappeared in government pamphlets and local campaigns. American housewives were told they had a vital role to play in winning the war and should consider themselves soldiers on the home front. While many women might go off to work in the defense industries, just as many others were needed at home, preserving and conserving foodstuffs and simultaneously preserving traditional gender roles in a crisis-wracked world.[83]

Government-issued posters addressed women specifically as household managers, asking them to take part in conservation programs. As part of conservation, women were asked to save all used cooking fats in cans and turn them in so that the government could use them to make glycerin for bullets.

A 1943 poster took the form of a plaintive letter from "Joe" in the South Pacific to "Mom" in which he begged her to save her fats and turn them in: "it's the best way you can help me keep firing."[84] Home economists, through extension work and their conservation work in World War I and the Depression, had created the dialogue between ordinary women and outside interests (whether civilian, corporate, or military) about what went on in their kitchens that allowed a poster like this one to seem like a viable strategy.

Newspapers throughout the country reported regularly on the work of local home economics clubs and extension programs, reflecting the great extent to which the field had been accepted as part of American life, particularly as an aid in times of crisis. As mentioned in the introduction to this book, it was a course in home economics that enabled one character in *The Best Years of Our Lives*, probably the most famous and well-loved movie about the home front, to manage when her family's servant quit during the war.

Home economist Ivol Spafford painted a portrait of the home economics teacher as super-heroine in the *School Review* in 1943. Urging reorganization of home economics education in primary and secondary schools, she argued that home economics teachers generally had a solid background in science and so could be used to fill in for the many male science teachers who left schools to serve in the military. In addition, home economics being a field closely concerned with human development and relationships, teachers in this field would be in great demand helping children adjust to the dislocations of wartime. And for all those young women marrying soldiers in a hurry, no one had more to offer than their high school home economics teacher.[85]

Home economics educators took the war as another opportunity to valorize their field and help their students to see opportunities for heroism. A letter from the acting assistant director of home economics at Cornell addressed students in June of 1941, six months into American involvement in the war, reflecting on unusual elements of the previous semester's curriculum: "We have spent some time during the spring months in the College helping you try to 'get straight' on those values which you believe to be important in a democratic society." Once "straight," students were offered opportunities to become involved with local volunteer efforts and to continue to reflect on "the ways in which each woman may strengthen herself to meet the demands of her country in this time of emergency."[86] The war was going to make women of these students as well as call on them to develop political consciousness.

Along with the note, the college included a "Statement of Belief" that it hoped students would adopt, underscoring the common theme that this was an ideological war, different from World War I. The statement called on students to stay physically and intellectually fit during the summer months and to watch out for "evidences" in their own communities of "changes in attitudes, population, economic factors (price changes, wage changes); types, hours, and conditions of employment; recreational outlets; available commodities, and other factors which affect home and community living." Part spy, part anthropologist, the home economics student was asked to immerse herself in the life of her community in order to keep it stable. She was clearly supposed to watch out for and turn in anyone who cheated on her rations or participated in the black market, but she was also encouraged to begin thinking of "democracy" as something in need of her protection. Although it was not until after the war that democracy was ubiquitously set in apposition to communism, early warnings like this set the stage for that dichotomy.[87]

As Cornell's "Statement of Belief" suggests, for all the continuity between the work of the depression and the war, home economists saw something different in the second conflict. Although many had hoped that the Depression might serve as a correction, the war was more often presented in their writing as the dawn of a better era for American culture and for the field itself. They were not alone in focusing early on the postwar world; books and articles about "postwar reconstruction" began appearing as early as January 1942 offering the reading public a mixture of anxiety and optimism that carried over into the culture of the Cold War era.

Alvin Hansen of the National Resources Planning Board issued a pamphlet in January 1942 in which he warned, "A military victory for the democracies is not enough. If the victorious democracies muddle through another decade of economic frustration and mass unemployment, we may expect social disintegration and, sooner or later, another international conflagration." His statement seems to have been especially meaningful to home economists, as it was reprinted in the *Journal of Home Economics* in April. It is easy to see why they would have found it inspiring, as Hansen locates power to shape the postwar world positively in the ordinary consumer, arguing, "Every cent expended, private and public, becomes income for members of our own society. Costs and income are just opposite sides of the same shield. We can afford as high a standard of living as we are able to produce."[88] Intelligent consumption, gaining the upper hand over material life, had long been a goal of home economists.

Mildred Swift, chair of the home economics department at the University of Nevada, Reno, also looked toward the future, remarking in 1943, "Modern education is changing and we no longer study only the three R's." Her department had just introduced a home economics certificate program in the interests of educating the many young women who were planning to marry immediately after graduation and who were "looking forward to becoming good companions to their husbands, good mothers and good citizens." More professionally focused programs would also be offered, but for those who were not going to work outside the home, the university had decided to provide special training.[89]

Swift predicted a transition toward education for living, which she described in distinctly gendered but also enthusiastic terms: "We need to know the pleasure of flowers for Sunday dinners, how to buy for ourselves and our families, how to plan outdoor fireplaces and patios. We need to learn how to live!"[90] The world that awaited Americans after the war was not, apparently, going to be governed by thrift and moderation, but rather by joyous consumption of material goods and financial comfort. As Hansen had argued, Americans would be as rich as they wanted to be. Although the Depression had seen families crowding together into smaller homes to save money and share labor, the postwar family would spill out onto their patio for a barbecue, luxuriating in space and leisure.

This new vision of American life as one of bounty and the new interest in large-scale planning to keep it this way profoundly shaped American culture in the postwar years, changing the very landscape of "home." The home economics movement's attempts to be part of this new America critically altered the movement's course, shifting it from a movement of social reform to a field that largely complemented changes already under way and beyond its control.

CHAPTER THREE

# Future Homemakers of America

In September 1959, Nikita Khrushchev appeared unexpectedly in a home economics classroom in Ames, Iowa. Two months earlier, the Soviet premier had engaged Richard Nixon in the now famous "kitchen debate" in Moscow. There, the two men had briefly argued in a model kitchen over whether American consumer culture could really give women what they wanted. Now Khrushchev found himself in another kind of American kitchen, a food sciences laboratory at Iowa State College. What he said and how it was reported in the popular press reveal not only Khrushchev's perspective on home economics, but, more importantly, popular perceptions of the field in this era.[1]

Writers for the *New York Times* and the Associated Press reported that the meeting between Khrushchev and the students was amiable. The premier "looked on with a quizzical smile at girls learning how to wash and iron and cook. 'We don't have such schools,' he remarked. 'Our mothers have to teach that.' After wishing the girls success in finding husbands, he left with a compliment. 'I don't know how you feed your people,' he said, 'but you are very nice girls.'"[2]

Although it is doubtful that the students were learning to wash, iron, and cook all in the same room at the same time, the writer defined the field  by the popular assumption that it was general housework. Khrushchev's comments also reinforced two common beliefs about the work, that it was traditional female knowledge and that in the end it did not matter so much what the students' skills were as long as they were "very nice girls." Like the previously mentioned Columbia professors who offered a home economics scholarship and marriage proposal to a young woman based half on skills

Figure 13. When Nikita Khrushchev made his surprise appearance at the Iowa
State College Department of Home Economics, he would have encountered a classroom like this one, photographed during a food preparation class in 1942. Library
of Congress, Prints & Photographs Division, FSA-OWI Collection, LC-USW3-
002673-D DLC.

and half on looks, this article fifty years later reflected the enduring assumption that woman's most important quality was physical and social attractive-
ness to men.

*Newsweek*'s version of the encounter was more detailed (or perhaps em-
bellished), and showed a more contentious Khrushchev. Repeating the premier's statement "our mothers have to teach that," the writer clarified, "By
'that' he meant home economics, academic dialect for, among other things,
cooking and changing diapers." This again was a typical critique of the field,
that it was pretentious to claim academic standing for what were really the
most basic female skills.[3]

The Soviet leader engaged in a brief dialogue with the dean of the College of Home Economics, Dr. Helen LeBaron. As he challenged her work, she

responded with pride, and the reporter took a few more opportunities to make fun of the field:

> Suppose a man marries one of these girls, Khrushchev wondered (as has many another man), "how can he check on her knowledge and efficiency?"
> "If she graduates from Iowa State, she is bound to be efficient," replied Dr. Helen R. LeBaron. . . . Khrushchev was not to be put off. "Suppose she is a graduate and she doesn't know how to cook pancakes?" he asked, sniffing the unmistakable odor of burning pancakes. "I think," he added, turning to the girls, "when you get married you'll settle that question better with your husband without the help of the dean."[4]

In fact, as LeBaron could have told him, most home economics programs offered courses in family relationships and developmental psychology precisely so that students could in a sense answer such problems with the help of the dean. Education for family living was a major priority in education during the 1950s.

Although "the girls giggled at this sally," the writer reported, he had hit upon something important: "Khrushchev poked his thumb into a tender spot because most of the girls at Iowa State are there not for the 'challenge of getting straight As in advanced wifemanship,' but because the 'famous' sex ratio was 4 to 1."[5] In other words, they did not need to study to become wives, because it was statistically bound to happen to them whatever they majored in. It had of course been one of the recurring justifications for the movement that no matter what career path a woman chose, she would always, whether single or married, need to know how to care for a home.

Where other reporters had lumped together washing, cooking, and ironing, the reporter for *Newsweek* had the students making pancakes and not very well at that. It is again unlikely that this is what was happening in the classroom, but it would give the readers a homey sense of the students as sweet amateurs. Although reporters following Khrushchev's visit to the United States tended to portray him as both blustering and doctrinaire, when the topic was home economics, writers seemed to agree with him that there was something adorably silly about this branch of American education. As the *Newsweek* writer noted, "In an age when man is reaching toward the cosmos, half of American institutions that admit women offer home economics courses." Home economists' early attempts to sell their field as the key to modernity had apparently failed, not just for one writer, but also for the culture at large.

Although nutritionists with degrees in home economics designed the foods that traveled with astronauts "toward the cosmos," the field seemed to most people more and more like a quaint school for wives. Indeed, one administrator of home economics education admitted, "I guess we did too good a job teaching women to be homemakers," resulting in a shortage of qualified applicants for professional positions in the field.[6] This shortage in trained home economists due to marriage had existed at least since 1950, when Dr. Opal T. Rhodes, director of home economics education at Indiana University in Pennsylvania, had presented data showing not only that home economists married in greater numbers and more quickly than any other group of female college graduates, leaving paying jobs when they did so, but also that their marriages lasted longer than anyone else's. While one in five marriages nationwide ended in divorce at the time, only one in six hundred marriages to home economists did.[7]

Home economists found themselves in an odd situation, having done "too good a job" of training women for wifehood and not a good enough job convincing everyone else that housework was a serious profession. For the most part what happened was beyond the control of home economists, involving major shifts in the economic, political, and social life of the nation such as the Cold War, the baby boom, the emergence of television as a dominating force in culture, the GI Bill, and suburbanization. How home economists responded to these changes, however, did help to shape the future of the field and how the public perceived it.

## Postwar Anxiety and Home Economics

Postwar America, as many historians have noted, was a nation awash in anxiety. Sometimes portrayed as an era of consensus, it can more usefully be understood as a time of desperate search for consensus. Emerging from three crises in a row—the stock market crash of 1929, the Great Depression, and World War II—and into the nuclear era, it is perhaps to be expected that Americans voiced anxiety about the future often and diversely in all kinds of media. Despite a reputation for safety and tranquility gained during the more obviously turbulent Vietnam War era, the postwar years were themselves full not just of unease, but also upheaval. As they had in previous eras, home economists in the postwar years offered their services as mediators of crisis.

The kind of help they offered now, however, was different from what they had proffered in the past. In part this was because the crisis was different and in part it is because they were.[8]

These differences were of course part of a larger change in thinking about society and in particular the role of education in shaping America's future. As World War II drew to a close, Americans concerned with the future instituted a variety of plans to ensure stability and prosperity both at home and abroad. The Marshall Plan to restore the nations of Europe was part of this project, as was the GI Bill that provided returning soldiers with money for college or for a down payment on a home. The Marshall Plan, which included home economics training for women in war-ravaged countries, was intended to prevent the kind of bitterness and economic chaos that had followed World War I. The GI Bill prevented a flood of workers returning to an economy that, scaling down from wartime production, could not have absorbed them. It offered young men the chance either to improve on their material circumstances immediately or to invest in their own future social mobility through education.

As historian Lizabeth Cohen has noted, because the bill's funds were available only to men, a woman had to be attached to a man in some way to gain any of the benefits of this bounty. Although marriage rates were already on the rise during the war, the bill certainly supported this trend. Simultaneously it bolstered an ideal that had been on the wane for some fifteen years—that men supported women financially. During the Depression, many women had become the sole breadwinners in their families and during the war, with men away, this trend had continued. The GI Bill, then, made it economically advantageous to Americans to reverse this social transformation.

Educators in this period argued that the future could and must be planned for more carefully and completely than the past had been. As educator C. Mervin Palmer anxiously reported in 1944, "Many institutions of higher learning indicate that they do not expect to go back to pre-war objectives in the training of students. The future must be faced and adjustments, both large and small, must be made. . . . A satisfactory adjustment could help prevent another world catastrophe."[9]

Educators suddenly saw their own responsibility as immense: not just the intellectual development of individual students, but the entire stability of society. To this end, administrators in state education departments and in universities began to focus on a kind of education that would fit students to the society into which they would graduate. Vocational education, federally funded since 1917 and given increased funding in the last years of the Depression, became an important part of the plan to secure America against future chaos, economic or political. In 1946, the George-Barden Act more than doubled the funds that had previously been available, signaling support at the highest levels of government for this approach to the future. Vocational education was supposed to supply to industries the kinds of workers they could hire and to provide students with the kinds of skills that would get them hired. Industry could then feel sure of its labor source while young workers could likewise feel sure of their own place in the economic system. They would be not just laborers but men and women with vocations and a safe place in America's financial future. As such they would be productive and, perhaps more importantly, contented. The contented American was one who would support the society he lived in and not go looking for alternatives in the works of Marx or Nietzsche.

As Florence Fallgatter, president of the AHEA, asked in 1951, "Unless the young people of today find satisfaction in their way of life, can we expect them as parents and citizens of tomorrow to care enough to preserve our free American way of life?"[10] Although the first generation of leaders in the movement— women like Ellen Richards, Isabel Bevier, and Martha Van Rensselaer—had argued that their work would serve as a corrective to misdirected society, postwar home economists presented their strengths as conservative, protective of "values," and supportive of traditions. Just what these values and traditions were, however, was the work of those who lived in the postwar moment to determine.

Vocational education programs emphasized stability and preparedness as values. National programs like the GI Bill and the 1949 and 1954 Housing Acts celebrated the newly built single-family home as an American "tradition." And because these homes were new, they had to be built in undeveloped areas, leading to the embrace of suburbs as appropriate places for young families to live. None of these values or traditions—newness, the nuclear family, and suburbanism—necessarily had roots in American culture, but in order for the postwar society to keep generating its own stability, it was vital to portray them as such. Ideally, young couples moving into freshly built suburban homes would understand and embrace the paradox that this was a new but not different America.[11]

Home economists contributed to the perpetuation of these values and traditions particularly through their work in high schools. Two projects, family education and vocational home economics education, emerged as well-funded trends in postwar high schools. A survey of 630 colleges and universities published in 1948 found that 550 of these institutions already offered courses in marriage and or family life.[12] Although each project had begun before the war, both gained new prominence after 1945 and largely came to define the movement in popular culture. As home economists' answer to the crises of the postwar years—demobilization, the Cold War, and the Korean War—these two projects reflected changes in the field as it passed from the status of a movement to an institution.

## Family Education

Education that addressed marriage and family life had been part of home economics curricula since the 1930s, but such courses had tended to approach the topics analytically, from a sociological and/or historical perspective. In the years after World War II, however, these classes became much more practical in orientation, providing training to help students make adjustments, first to the families in which they were already members and then into those that it was assumed they would form later. This reflected a common social anxiety about the fate of marriage and the family in postwar America.

The Depression had caused many families to dissolve for economic reasons, and the war had forced countless couples into long-distance marriages and families. Divorce rates had also been on the rise since the 1920s, when the practice had begun to lose its social stigma and more liberal laws had made it easier for women to gain custody of their children. Some social commentators also feared that the entry of married women in increasing numbers into the paid workforce would weaken or somehow burst family ties.

In the interest of reversing trends that they believed to be harmful to individuals and to society at large, state governments and universities invested in courses at the high school and college levels that they hoped would reinforce marriage and family.

Because home economists emphasized teamwork in marriage, male students were encouraged and in a few cases even required to enroll in these classes. There is no evidence that men accepted this invitation in any great numbers when it was not required, but that their presence was seen as helpful reflects the distinct philosophy of the home economics movement in its early stages, that marriage is ideally an equal partnership. Because the two types of classes—family and marriage education—covered different topics, they will be addressed here separately although they were sometimes combined into one.

As reflected in movies produced for such classes, family education emphasized unity and cooperation. The 1946 film *You and Your Family* demonstrated an early version of interactive media by providing scenes of common
family conflicts, each followed by three possible responses, and then pausing
to ask the audience for the best way to react.[13] In one conflict, a teenage girl is
invited on a date, asks her parents for permission, and is denied because they
think she is too young. One possible response, offered by the filmmakers, is
to sulk, another is to sneak out without permission, but the third, and obviously favored response, is to ask permission to invite not just the boy but the
whole "gang" over to the family home for an evening that all can enjoy. The
message here is clearly not just that sticking to your family's rules is best but
also, more complexly, that sticking with the family physically is best. By 1946,
this family-based formula for courtship was already outdated as cheaper cars
and more movie theaters offered teenagers escape, but the filmmakers sought
to revive it in the name of maturity.[14]

In a second scenario, a family has just finished dinner when "mother" asks
for help clearing up and doing the dishes. In the first response, no one helps. In
the second, only the youngest son offers and takes the opportunity to complain
about the rest of the family. In the third everyone helps, the work gets done
quickly, and they all have a good time doing it. This third, "correct" response
again emphasizes family unity but also introduces another theme common to
family life education, that mother needs help. In no source is it suggested that
anyone else should take over her roles, but family members are repeatedly encouraged to "pitch in" to help her. This message was new to American domestic
discourse and reflected the attitudes of the home economists who taught family
management courses and consulted on scripts as much or more than it indicated any actual changes in thinking about women's roles in the home. In the
postwar era of increased emphasis on home life, rather than interconnections
between home and community, home economists may have worried that the
bulk of domestic labor would once again fall on "mother."

This interesting theme is even more apparent in a movie about family togetherness through interior design that has interesting parallels to contemporary home repair and family-swapping television shows. In the 1952 film
*Sharing Work at Home*, housework for a family of four has made "Mrs. Taylor" physically ill to the point that she can no longer do it.[15] When the movie
opens, she is absent, having been sent to bed by her doctor. The house, pre-
dictably, is in disarray. With inspiration from the teenage daughter of the
family, who gets "some good ideas from [her] home ec. textbook," the family

divide up the household tasks and do them as a team. Although the daughter of the family takes on cooking, ironing, and preparing meals for the invalid, tasks traditionally associated with her gender, the men of the house also take on some "female" work. Mr. Taylor does the laundry and orders the food from the grocer and his son cleans the house "daily" according to their work plan. Indeed, when Mrs. Taylor recovers and her son proudly boasts, "I don't clean house anymore—that's women's work," his father corrects him: each family member should keep doing their part according to time and ability, not according to whether or not it's "a man's job." This is a message that, while not openly transgressive of established roles, quietly opens the door to reconsidering the gendered nature of work. Family life educators here used the attractive theme of family togetherness to nudge the boundaries of expected behavior.

Lest her family go too far, however, Mrs. Taylor reasserts her role as primary housekeeper. When she asks what her place is in the grand new scheme, her family tells her that her job is to "rest" and "relax," terms a housewife of her era seldom heard. Threatened with obsolescence, she consults the home economics textbook that has been her family's guide during her illness. In it she finds the comforting analysis that since a father's job is mostly outside the house at work, and children's main "job" is going to school, most of the housework still falls to the woman of the home. "So let's include mother," she suggests, conflating her work and her person in a way reminiscent of nineteenth-century domestic fiction. With a new era of cooperation before them, the family all pitch in to redecorate their home, leading the narrator to comment, "Of course, this is more than a story of wallpaper and slipcovers. It's a story of improvements in the Taylors themselves." Although Mrs. Taylor remains "mother" in the traditional sense, gender roles in the household have been renovated to allow for more variation and the home has become everybody's work. By allowing their messages about gender and domestic labor to remain mixed in this way, home economists may have helped to ensure popular dismissal of the field.

## Marriage Education

Closely related to family life and family management courses were home economics courses in marriage. Topics covered in such courses included sex education, state and local marriage laws, psychology, and cultural mores related to courtship and marriage. At the college level, marriage courses were most often taught by male sociologists who came to the field through an interest in the sociology of the family as well as through a conviction that education should be made "functional" for students.[16] It was the work of the women in the home economics movement, however, that had provided these men with the opportunity to bring "real life" onto campus. Some college marriage courses were taught within home economics departments, while others were independent, but because marriage education also embraced child development and discussed women's roles in the home it often overlapped with or complemented such courses in home economics departments. At the high-school level marriage education was folded into family management courses, most of which were taught by women.

Student interests and student participation were emphasized in these classes in ways that set them apart from more traditional subjects such as history or mathematics. For example, four courses in Family Relationships and Preparation for Marriage taught in high schools in Des Moines, Iowa, in the 1946 to 1947 school year began with a questionnaire to determine what subject students would like to cover during the year. Among the many topics offered students were the following provocative issues and questions:

> Why people marry—why some people never marry—Who marries
>   whom?
> Engagement: Woman's point of view—Length of engagement—
>   "stepping out" when engaged—Revealing the past.
> Morality makes sense: Does morality make sense? How?
> Disillusionment and Settling Down—Setting up housekeeping
> Common conflicts in marriage; when crisis comes (family breakdowns—
>   dismemberment—demoralization—Infidelity—Death—ways of
>   dealing with family crisis).[17]

From this smorgasbord of human triumph and tragedy, students in teacher Myrtle Mainquist's two classes chose to focus on relationships, dating, and marriage. The forty-seven young women and twelve young men in her two coed classes designed and completed studies on the dating practices of their peers and on recreational opportunities for teenagers in their area.[18]

Educational films and textbooks about marriage firmly advocated taking a rational approach to the emotions. Hoping to reverse war-time trends in which couples married quickly, with romantic attraction their sole guide, these films encouraged long engagements and thoughtful analysis of each partner's strengths and weaknesses. Films such as *It Takes All Kinds* portrayed a range of personality types, encouraging students to think beyond immediate attraction to an individual to consider behavior patterns.[19] The film was based on the popular textbook *Marriage for Moderns* by Henry Bowman, who was chairman of the Department of Marriage and Family Living at Stephens College.[20] Accompanying a panoramic shot of young couples waiting to apply for marriage licenses, *It Takes All Kinds* opens with a male narrator striking a patriotic note: "Freedom of choice," he intones, "a long-fought for and hard-won freedom." By placing the choice of spouse within the emerging Cold War rhetoric of a dichotomy between "freedom" and totalitarianism, the filmmakers apparently hoped to impress their students with the seriousness of the topic. It is possible also to imagine that speaking to a primarily female audience, the statement might bring up reminders of the women's rights movement that had helped to secure a daughter's right to choose her mate without family intervention.

The film's central argument—that how a person responds to crisis tells you most of what you need to know about him or her—is made in a series of vignettes. Although there is no overt judgment of any of the characters as either a good or a bad potential mate, some are distinctly more likable than others. As a character trait, anxiety is presented in opposition to self-confidence, with the former more conducive to social success. In an age in which social commentators, politicians, and artists in all media constantly referred to uncertainty and unease it is not surprising that decisiveness was portrayed as heroic. As the narrator of *Marriage Today*, another educational film, also released in 1950, describes the era: "It's an age of unrest and change, both individual and social. An age of confused personal values and widespread domestic difficulties culminating in a fabulous rate of divorce."[21]

To avoid contributing to the rise of that "fabulous" rate, *Marriage Today* suggests that "moderns," or young adults of the era, were facing their choice of partner and entering their marriages as realists. As a fictional young wife in the same film says of her husband, "He's a real person and he expects me to be one, too." Indeed, each of the self-assured characters in *It Takes All Kinds* expresses his or her confidence by working with circumstances as they were rather than struggling to try to change them. Similarly, the heroine of another film based on *Marriage for Moderns*, the 1950 *Choosing for Happiness* explains to a never-satisfied friend that in a "course in family relations" she had taken in school, she had "learned that it's a good idea to try to change yourself first if there has to be a change. Changing someone else is practically impossible."[22] I do not think it is inappropriate to see a political subtext in these films, especially since marriage and family life educators repeatedly argued that the family was the base unit of society. If marriage failed, society failed. Films that encouraged personal "adjustment" to the small society of a relationship or marriage clearly advocated it for participation in society at large. In an era that had witnessed the destructive power of personality and the potential ugliness of utopias, this perhaps seemed like sound advice. It may also be understood as a poignant attempt to help Americans live with what *Marriage Today*'s writers referred to as the "terrors" of the age, the threat of war, looming economic depression, and nuclear annihilation.[23]

What these films had to say about gender and work, the topics that concern us here, however, was more complex than the seemingly conservative emphasis on self-adjustment would suggest. Subtly but consistently, marriage education films and textbooks portrayed men and women stepping across traditional gender boundaries in order to maintain family stability. Discussing the issue of whether married women should work, sociologist and marriage counselor James Peterson saw no reason for them not to. In his 1956 *Education for Marriage* he argued, "It is something of an anomaly that many girls who are highly trained in college, and make brilliant starts in their profession are expected to give up their work when they marry." Given that "many women have much to contribute" in diverse fields, he found it "difficult to believe that marriage, ipso facto, must eliminate the possibility of making such contributions." Therefore, men would have to take up some of the slack in the household: "The willingness of the husband to participate in family chores must be assumed and realized." The arrangement might cause tension at first, but with careful attention to the "family time budget" all would be fine and in fact better than fine because the intellectually fulfilled woman made an especially good partner and mother.[24]

The 1950 film *Who's Boss?* dealt openly with the tension of living within gender roles.[25] In this film, presented as a drama with narration, Virginia and Mike are married and both work for the same newspaper, she as a photographer, he as a writer. They are constantly fighting with each other as neither lives up to the other's expectations. Mike expects "Ginnie" to do the kind of domestic and emotional work—such as cleaning up after both him and not competing with him socially or professionally—that was traditionally done by women. Ginnie, for her part, expects a partnership and does not want to be responsible for housework anymore than Mike does. As she says, "I've got a brain of my own and I intend to make the most of my life, too." Although she admits that she would like "a home and kids," she is determined "not to be a fool like mother, bending over a washtub all her life while dad went around as free as air."

In his angriest moments Mike looks back enviously on his parent's marriage, in which his dependent mother "looked up to dad." When he calms down, however, he realizes, "I've been hanging onto a lot of ideas I don't really believe in anymore." In reality, he tells Ginnie, "I like a woman who's doing things. . . . You've got a mind of your own and you've got to use it. It's about time I accepted you as you really are." The two begin to make personal changes—Mike helps around the house, both learn to budget, and they talk about sharing their social lives.

Real change, however, does not come until Ginnie gets pregnant. The couple is shown seven years after the birth of their first child living in "a partnership with no boss." Mike is now the breadwinner, but Ginnie still takes occasional photography jobs and Mike helps around the house because his "dignity is a lot more flexible now he's discovered that a wet baby loves whoever changes her, male or female." As the narrator sums it up, "They've long since stopped worrying about who's breadwinner, who's housemaker." Reflecting home economists' ambiguous stance on gender politics, the film critiques traditional roles even as it reinforces them. Harmony comes only when Ginnie gives up working full time, after all. But it also comes, more complexly, from both partners giving up fixed gender ideology. For Ginnie, the independent creative professional who kept her name when she married, this may be a step backward in feminist terms, but for Mike it is a small step forward, which ought to balance out Ginnie's sacrifice to some extent.

Marriage education repeatedly celebrated equal partnership, or what the 1950 film *Are You Ready for Marriage?* called "paired unity." In terms of household labor this did not seem to mean much more than men helping with dishes and the diapers, but it also allowed for women to work outside of the home. In *Marriage Today*, for example, Cathy, who continues to teach after marrying and having a child, is described as "a free, fulfilled human being." Women who do not work for salaries are consistently portrayed as having made a choice to stay home, rather than having been pressured into it either by husbands or society. Making this choice was acknowledged to be difficult, as it was for "Dottie," the young wife in the 1951 film *Marriage Is a Partnership*.[26] "Sometimes," she confesses, "I regretted that decision to quit my job." She missed her paycheck, saying, "staying home was hard. It was an adjustment I had to work out." As for Cathy, the filmmakers subtly let us know that she works for the love of it—her husband is a successful businessman and they do not need her salary to live well.

As these scenarios suggest, marriage educators had a distinct bias toward middle-class values, one that did not go unnoticed in their own time. In a 1953 article in the journal *Marriage and Family Living*, Herman Lantz, professor of sociology at Southern Illinois University, complained, "Implicit in many of our texts is the point of view that democratic families are better and happier than patriarchal families, that the problems families have to face are such important decisions as how shall they work out a budget on only $500 per month (!)." In reality, Lentz pointed out, most families had incomes of half or less than half that amount and "persons can be and are happy in democratic, patriarchal, and matriarchal families." In particular, he criticized marriage education movies for "being so far removed from reality as to give the impression of viewing life on some other planet." Probably referring to Ginnie and Mike of *Who's Boss*, who had had such a conversation, Lantz noted that most couples had to adjust their budgets not by cutting down on "cocktails and taxi-cab fares" but "by cutting down on food, rent, and clothing."[27]

In a responding comment to Lantz's class critique, sociologist Earl Lomon Koos briefly and revealingly noted, "Even the lower middle and lower class students in college today aspire to middle-class patterns—or they would not be in college!" Rather than denying that marriage educators were privileging one class culture over another, Koos argued that this was exactly what students wanted when they enrolled in college. Whether or not it was the business of colleges to perpetuate patriarchal or advocate for democratic families, it does seem possible that students might have hoped to achieve middle class incomes without necessarily abandoning elements of what Lantz in a rejoinder termed "earlier class patterns that are integral parts of their personalities." Marriage educators certainly hoped their work would relegate such patterns to the past. The narrator of *Marriage Today* confidently informs viewers, "In a modern partnership, the rights and privileges, like the duties and responsibilities, are better balanced when they're equal." Any other arrangement was simply outmoded.[28]

## Vocational Education

The most consistent message in marriage and family education textbooks and films was that students must be prepared to face a future that would be significantly different from that faced by any previous generation. Ignoring the vagaries of history, educators posited a consistent past and a ruptured future. Marriage and family education courses were one way to equip youth to face the new world; vocational education was another.

Beginning in 1946, when the previously mentioned George-Barden Act allocated significant sums to vocational education in agriculture, trade, industry, and home economics, vocational home economics began to overshadow the subject's role as part of general education. Because vocational home economics education was so well funded and so identifiably part of the new trend in education, it came to represent the field in popular perceptions of the movement during the postwar period and beyond. Because the majority of people who encountered home economics encountered it in high school, where courses trained young women for their "vocation" as homemakers, this was the image of the field that had the most staying power.

Home economists themselves consistently worked against this perception—that their field was good only for training wives—but they just as frequently supported it through explicit or ambiguous statements. Examples of the internal contradictions of the movement recur in educational films about career choice. A 1940 film, *Finding Your Life's Work*, offered an early perspective on home economics vocational education that seemed to negate much of what the field actually stood for at the time.[29] The Homemaking Department of the generic high school featured in the film was pointed out as a division that "trains girls to be good housewives" and purchasers. Paid employment was mentioned only in connection with sewing, a skill that a girl might use if she chose to enter "the business world." Here was no mention of working in government agencies, institutions, or corporate divisions.

Eleven years later, *The Home Economics Story* offered more options. In this film, made to recruit high school seniors into home economics majors in college, we follow the college careers of four young women who major in home economics.[30] The four choose a variety of majors and the college placement office magically finds jobs for all of them. All except for the one who becomes engaged. Two even leave for jobs in "the big city" on the very day they graduate. Home economics is presented as a friendly topic, one that helps students to make sense of the world around them and of other academic fields. As one character muses, "All the classes seemed to fit together," and "Even the Physics class was what a girl would like—it was about physics in the home." At the same time that the movie portrays women as willing students of the "hard" sciences, it softens, and thus perhaps weakens that image, by suggesting that "girls" can only handle science if it is domesticated. And although three of the four young women were going on to careers in the field, the narrator reminds the viewers, "Each girl has been preparing for two careers. One her chosen specialty, the other is a career in homemaking." Although home economists had largely succeeded at establishing those "chosen specialties," such as textile science and nutrition, as careers, because the majority of Americans did not accept "homemaker" as a career in the same sense, this statement served to undermine the field as professional education. After all, no one celebrated the math graduate for her ability to balance a checkbook or the literature graduate for his ability to tell his children bedtime stories.

*Why Study Home Economics?*, another recruiting film, offered more options but still presented homemaking as the most likely "career" for graduates.[31] One teenage girl, Carol, offers the standard critique of the field—that "home ec. is a waste of time," because there is no point spending time in school with something "you can learn right here at home or pick up after you get married." Her sister, Janice, wants to take home economics, stating, "It's something I'll need to know about—and so will you. If I'm going to be a homemaker the rest of my life, I want to know what I'm doing." To settle their debate, Janice visits a home economics teacher to find out why the field matters. That such films were made perhaps indicates the field's continuing struggle for full acceptance. Supervised by Edna Hill, chair of the Department of Home Economics at the University of Kansas, the film attempts to redeem the field's reputation by taking a turn to the theoretical. Janice will "need to know more than just how to run a house or an apartment. You need to know why." She will learn nutrition and the "psychology of clothing" and techniques of construction, all to adjust meals and clothing to the individual needs of her family.

As scenes of classroom and family life alternate, we learn that Janice's role in her future family will involve much mediation between family members and the outside world, mostly in her role as consumer. The why is not existential but rather material. Although "many boys . . . are enrolled in home economics" because "they, too, need to learn house design, decorator colors, and money management," Janice's role will be more generalized, because her "real success or failure as a homemaker will be determined by [her] ability to develop good family relationships."

Although Janice sees the wisdom of studying home economics if she is going to get married, she still wonders what her training will be worth is if she does not marry. Her teacher does not entertain the possibility that Janice may never marry, but she nonetheless tells her what her options might be if she does not marry right away. Home economics courses in high school will help prepare her for college science and social science classes and if she wants to advance in the field she will have many career opportunities open to her.

This portrait of home economics as vocational training for wife/motherhood that also gave students some potential career options "before" marriage inverted an earlier vision of the field in which skill in housekeeping was the side benefit and professions the main goal. In 1928, Olive Paul Goodrich of the College of the City of Detroit had complained that students were missing the true worth of the field by focusing on its practical applications. Too many students were focusing only on how home economics courses would help them if they married. More might become interested in the field if home economists "could make girls see that home economics may prepare them for a definite profession which has monetary value."[32]

The perception that the field trained young women to be good wives (even if this was what the students themselves preferred) undermined its leaders' attempts to achieve intellectual status. By 1952, a group of high school homemaking teachers who met to discuss the state of their field also discussed ways to get more students to understand the career opportunities open to them. They were equally interested, however, in empowering homemakers as consumers, developing "human and spiritual values" in communities, and, interestingly, in convincing married women with children to help overcome the shortage of home economics teachers by leaving the home to work. Attempting to lure homemakers into the workplace, the group nonetheless spent little time focusing on how to get younger women involved in home economics careers.[33]

According to a 1950 study of 200 young women, the majority—62 percent—felt that high school had not prepared them for real life; what they seemed to want, however, was not professional education but more training for non-career work in the home. One student who dropped out of school shortly after the study was completed expressed her disappointment in poetic form.

> Imagine me with baby
> When it starts to cry,
> Cooing gently in its ear
> R squared equals Pi.
> So taking all these courses
> Is ruining my young life

Who wants to be an Einstein?
I want to be a wife.[34]

As states reported back to the federal government each year on how they
had spent their George-Barden funds, evidence poured in that students in
home economics classes continued to be most interested in the subject as it
related to their own lives. Reports also showed that teachers were happily allowing students to direct their own education toward these interests. Each
year, with the help of their instructors, students chose an "out-of-school" research project to apply what they had been learning in home economics
classes. In the 1947–48 school year, nearly 42,000 Missouri high school students completed such projects in "home and personal living." Projects in
"provision of family meals" attracted the largest number of students, while
the second largest group was drawn to "personal care and improvement." A
slightly smaller group went to work on the family home, making over some
part of it and reporting on their work to their teachers. By 1952, clothing
projects were the most popular type of project, with food projects second
most popular, but food and home projects were still vastly more popular than
topics such as consumer buying, health, and care for the sick.

And yet, the work that vocational home economics students did in and
out of the classroom was frequently as much other-directed as it was self-
selected. In the 1957 to 1958 school year, vocational home economics students
in Massachusetts set to work outfitting their entire school: "Clothing classes
have made choir stoles for the HS Glee Clubs, altered garments for men
faculty members; shortened shower curtains for the school, made draperies
for the principal's office and classrooms, laundered and mended athletic uniforms; and made carpenters' and printers' aprons for the boys."[35] Anecdotes
from the same year reflected students' sense of their work for others as both
important and satisfying. One student wrote, "Prior to mother's death, I was
enrolled in the College Preparatory Curriculum in High School. After mother
died, I decided to change to the Vocational Homemaking program in order
to be able to serve my father and home better." Although her father had re-
married and now did not need her care, the girl was engaged to be married
after graduation and was looking forward confidently to managing her own
home. Students seem to have perceived the field as modern training for traditional roles rather than for careers.

A California boy found himself in similar, although ultimately less tragic,
circumstances when his mother was hospitalized for a month during the

1952–53 school year. He made it his "home project" to fill her shoes. "Being the oldest of two boys," he explained in his report, "the responsibility fell on me. Planning meals, cooking and managing the house were part of my Boys' Foods class, making it much easier." The food class for boys that he mentioned would have been part of a new development in home economics in which increasing numbers of boys entered the field to train for careers in the food industry. Although his focus in home economics would have been on employment rather than homemaking, the student's experience does seem to have offered valuable insight into "women's work."

The student shopped for and cooked the meals that he and his father planned together once a week and managed his younger brother in smaller household tasks. Betraying a touching uncertainty about his skills, he noted, "The family enjoyed the meals, or so they said," and more confidently reported that his mother was pleased with his work when she came home. The boy felt that his experience would be useful to him "when" he married, he wrote, "Before I get married I will probably live by myself so that I will be able to plan and cook my own meals and put myself on a budget." His brief experience as a wife had brought him closer to maturity.[36]

A mother of a student wrote in to thank the home economics teachers of her daughter's school for a similar transformation, commenting, "Susan has changed in many ways during the past year. . . . Her interest in home life has improved such as enjoying and even preparing full meals, serving for the home with pleasure, doing chores willingly, getting satisfaction from a clean and comfortable home, etc." The satisfied mother summed up the changes as "Susan has grown up." On the one hand this comment may suggest a young woman socialized into restrictive gender roles, but on the other hand we may reflect that home economics education, like no other course offered in high schools, actually taught cooperation and consideration of others, both of which are ingredients for maturity.

Vocational education in home economics reached out to the dinner tables and front porches of families throughout the state, empowering teenage girls to make family decisions. Despite the potential for such projects to cause serious family tensions, home economists blithely reported that there was much interest in and appreciation for their work in communities where they taught and that young married women were attending classes especially designed for them in gratifying numbers. In classes for adults, which became increasingly popular through the 1950s, young married women who were not working outside the home attended evening courses on topics like sewing and child development. That vocational home economics funds supported these classes did put home economists in the business of educating women for wifehood, rather than careers in related fields.

A report on vocational home education activities in North Carolina for the 1947 to 1948 school year proudly announced, "The activities in family life education during the school year 1947–1948 have been those requested by the people. No 'arm chair philosopher' dreamed up something that she thought they ought to do." On the one hand this statement rejected the very authority-as-expert that home economists had been struggling almost fifty years to achieve, but on the other it validated the field as something both wanted and needed by the people of the state.

## Future Homemakers of America

Annual reports of the Vocational Home Economics departments of the states reveal that schools were not the only group encouraging girls to think of their futures primarily in domestic terms. The Future Homemakers of America (FHA), which emerged from diverse state and local home economics clubs, became a national organization in 1944. When the first annual meeting was held in 1945, the group already had more than 92,000 members.

The FHA gained hugely in membership and publicity during the early 1950s, counting half a million members by 1958. Because of the baby boom there were simply more teenaged girls available to join such clubs than there had been before. The FHA's popularity probably also stemmed from its association with an image of American womanhood that was reinforced in popular culture. By joining their local FHA, young women could feel safe that they were conforming to traditional gender roles but doing so in a modern way. In an era in which the realities of women's lives were undergoing significant changes, it might well have seemed reassuring to some girls that there was a club in which to learn and practice their roles.

Like the Future Farmers of America, their brother organization, the FHA had an African American counterpart in the New Homemakers of America (NHA). Both groups for girls organized clubs throughout the states but primarily in more rural and suburban areas. The clubs were jointly sponsored by the United States Office of Education and the AHEA and were closely connected to vocational home economics programs in schools. FHA members undertook community-based projects, such as improving the appearance of

schools, babysitting children during Parent Teacher Association (PTA) meetings, organizing events for children and the elderly, running nutrition education programs, and participating in civil defense exercises. Many chapters also
worked with UNESCO, sending supplies to needy school children around
the world and adopting schools in other countries.

The FHA, like other youth organizations of the era, offered girls a chance
to feel important and connected to the world beyond their homes and
schools. The organization's emblem, which appeared on brooches, rings,
thimbles, charms, and patches, depicted a single-family home held aloft in a
giant pair of hands. Beams of light radiated from the house, a modest Cape
Cod-style structure with a small extension, perhaps suggestive of improvements yet to come through the work of FHA members. The image implied
that each member held the future of the home in her hands, an empowering
idea that at the same time had the potential to be limiting as it tied power for
women to a domestic identity.

The FHA creed declared:

> We are the Future Homemakers of America.
> We face the future with warm courage and high hopes.
> For we are the builders of homes—
> Homes for America's future,
> Homes where living will be the expression
> of everything that is good and fair,
> Homes where truth, love, security,
> and faith will be realities, not dreams.
> We are the Future Homemakers of America.
> We face the future with warm courage and high hopes.[37]

Clearly reflective of war-era anxieties over the fate of democracy, the creed
also echoed Ellen Richards's call to "right living" as a social responsibility.

Security and faith would counteract the insecurity of the atomic age and
forestall the spread of "godless" communism. At the same time, a reminder of
the now faded devotion to William Morris's ideals reiterated the concept of
home life as an "expression" of values. Just like much of home economics
writing of the era of World War I and the Depression had encouraged realism
in the face of crisis, the creed also called on young women to have courage
and hopes rather than confidence and expectations.

Although the creed, because it would have been spoken only by girls, may seem to enforce traditional gender roles unquestioningly, however, it is worth noting that the members swear to be home "builders" rather than makers or keepers. Clearly the girls were not pledging their commitment to learn construction trades, but the statement made a subtle argument for a wider range of roles available to young women. An FHA member could interpret any number of home economics career choices as ultimately helping to "build" homes whether or not she actually raised a family. This openness becomes particularly apparent when the FHA creed is compared to an earlier pledge taken by members of a statewide home economics club in Oklahoma. Members of this group, who took the name Future Homemakers of America in 1930, declared,

> I believe that the home is woman's natural environment. I believe that there is as much art in making a barren house into a glistening, comfortable home as there is in painting a picture or in writing a poem.
>
> I believe that there is a dignity and beauty in service; that as a career for women, homemaking offers greater opportunity for leisure, for growth of mind and spirit, for exercise of the body than any other occupation.
>
> I believe that one who has the intelligence to keep her own house in order is wise enough to be a force in any community.
>
> It is my desire to be one of the countless women in the world to make life sweeter and better because I live and do my work well.[38]

The national organization's pledge did not continue the Oklahoma group's elevation of homemaking to the highest moral status and focus on personal fulfillment. Instead, it celebrated home "building" as work of national importance and disconnected the work of the group from gender identity. The NHA creed was more explicit in the connections it made between homes and society, calling on its members to acknowledge, "If there is harmony and love in the home there will be justice in the nation. If there is justice in the nation there will be peace in the world." For African American home economics students, their education could be conceived of as part of a larger movement for social justice and civil rights. Their invocation of "peace in the world" was unusual in a time when popular culture emphasized strength in resisting totalitarianism, and pacifism was looked on as suspiciously accommodationist. But where white home economics students presented their work as conserving American democracy, members of the NHA apparently saw themselves as part of a campaign to expand democracy within the United States. The FHA merged with the NHA in 1965, a change that may have brought issues of race and culture to national membership.[39]

The FHA quickly became a vital part of vocational home economics programs in public schools. Federally sponsored, the organization served as an extension of classroom home economics activities. In Washington state, for example, in the 1946 to 1947 school year, "The major responsibility of an assistant State supervisor was the development of the FHA program."[40] A report from Iowa several years later focused on the need to "interpret" FHA work to school administrators so that they would see the wisdom of continuing collaboration between the schools and the national organization.[41] Teachers reported to the Office of Education on FHA and NHA activities, particularly noting the growth of the groups in their states, and included FHA and NHA bulletins in the material they submitted with their reports.

Because the groups were so closely connected to the schools, girls who belonged to the FHA and NHA had many opportunities to see connections between what they studied and how they and others in their community lived. They also, like members of the Girl Scouts of America, were able to see themselves as part of state and national associations, a potentially empowering experience. One former FHA member recalled that although "being a Future Homemaker held zero status," and she and her friends joined only because they wanted to go on the annual trip to Orlando, Florida, they came to learn that "subtly, subversive acts were taking place where that group of women and girls gathered." Simply being in an all-female group gave the young women an easy sense of authority as they learned to keep meetings in order, make presentations in public, and raise and manage funds. The former FHA member wrote, "Whether or not she did it purposefully . . . [she] was planting seeds of feminist consciousness. She gave us the basic skills of political involvement, packaged in a club ostensibly devoted to the private realm of homemaking. She helped to awaken our voices."[42] Although this FHA member joined in 1976, after the emergence of the second wave of feminism, the features that she found empowering would have been in place since the beginning of the group's existence. In the FHA, young women learned homemaking skills but they also inevitably learned organizational skills and simultaneously developed a notion of the homemaker's role as one that took her out into her community as a citizen.

By associating vocational home economics so closely with the FHA, however, school home economics programs did align themselves more closely with the popular conception of their field as wife training rather than career preparation. In 1970, the organization added the acronym "HERO" to its name to indicate programs in Home Economics Related Occupations but remained identified in popular imagination with training for work in the home. In 1999, the group changed its name to the Family, Career and Community Leaders of America, although some state branches continued to use the FHA/HERO acronym. The latest change can be understood as an attempt to distance the organization further from popular assumptions that its members are primarily or even solely concerned with filling roles that may seem anachronistic today.

## Civilian Defense and Home Economics

Thriving on the sense that they were valued and their field essential to the stability of American society, home economists sought to support the other great educational innovation of the 1950s, civil defense. Remembered now largely as a mass education in panic and delusion, civil defense seemed essential to educators in the postwar era, particularly as the nuclear era began. civil defense education—lessons in how to survive military attack—presented home economists with a quandary. What did they have to offer in the new era of warfare? Conservation, preservation, and substitution had worked wonders for the food supply during World Wars I and II, but what, beyond stocking the shelves of the fallout shelter, could home economists do to help Americans when the atomic bombs started falling?

Mary Hawkins, a staff writer for the *Journal of Home Economics*, summed up the possibilities in an article in 1951. Hawkins solemnly reminded her readers, "We are again living in a period of national emergency," and predicted, "It seems certain that the emergency is going to last a long time and that increasing pressures are to be expected." In response to this crisis, home economists should organize school lunch programs to be ready to provide "emergency feeding" in case of military attack. They should also consult with government agencies on stockpiling food supplies and prepare civilians for possible shortages of food and clothing. As experts in child care, they should be helping to set up day-care centers in areas mobilized for defense and should be advising families on how to provide "emotional protection" for children during those troubled times. Most of all, Hawkins declared, it was the job of home economists to "find out what needs to be done and do it."[43]

At the annual meeting of the AHEA, president Florence Fallgatter echoed Hawkins's call to action and added a more abstract and perhaps more stirring element. Fallgatter admitted, "We must realize that we are up against the grimmest problem we have ever faced, or may ever face," but she declared that in such circumstances home economists should find their prestige enhanced: "It is natural to look to home economists as authorities for the safeguarding of our food and water supplies . . . for preparing homes for least possible destruction in case of attacks, for arranging temporary living facilities in the home shelter, for protection of children." Anticipating the anxious crowds turning to them for help, "home economists of today," the topic of her speech, were asked to search their souls for (presumably affirmative) answers to the following questions: "Do we believe that the real fundamentals of freedom come from one's early family experiences? Are we convinced that home economics can make a unique contribution to freedom through our various approaches to home and family life? . . . And finally, are we willing to work together for a free world in which homes in all countries can nurture peaceful individuals?"[44] Beyond emergency feeding programs, home economists had the fate of the national character in their hands.

And yet, despite the high-flung rhetoric about the family and society, emergency feeding plans became the staple of the home economics response to the threats of the Cold War. Family education programs took on much of the work of reinforcing democracy in the home, but it was much easier and more immediately satisfying to put a feeding program into practice than it was to judge whether family relationships had been made strong enough to withstand nuclear blasts or hordes of invading communists.

State and local agencies as well as less formal organizations put together plans for mass emergency feeding, usually in school cafeterias. If a bomb fell and chaos threatened to follow, citizens could gather in a common shelter for a nutritious meal. In 1956, rather than waiting for the bomb to come to her, dietician Elizabeth Droescher went to the bomb. Droescher was one of sixty people representing the National Advisory Committee on Emergency Feeding (formed in 1953) who traveled to Nevada to witness a nuclear bomb test. Observers were stationed at "Media," a spot seven miles from ground zero. Droescher, like many others of the era who had complex feelings about nuclear power, described the event in glowing terms: "Just before dawn, kneeling and with special goggles in place, the observers saw the sky light up with the mushrooming majesty of the shot, heard the sound, and felt the accompanying tremor followed by the shimmering fallout that seemed to cover the desert."[45]

Then she served breakfast. Her group had come to demonstrate their preparedness for emergency feeding in the case of nuclear attack, so as soon as the bomb had been detonated, "Emergency equipment was set up and all observers were served a breakfast of orange juice, eggs and bacon, Philadelphia scrapple, hard and soft rolls, coffee, and milk." For a second test, the next day, Droescher's group served a hearty lunch of "tomato juice, beef and vegetable stew, roast beef sandwich, baked beans, apple, candy, coffee, and milk." Droescher, pictured in the *Journal of Home Economics* smiling in her heavy fallout suit, remembered the trip as "a most unusual and interesting experience" during which she felt "heartened" that atomic energy could have constructive as well as destructive uses.

From 1950 to 1953, anxieties about another world war seemed to be realized as the Korean War brought global forces into conflict again. A report of work in vocational home economics education in Washington State referred to the war as significantly shaping the kinds of work being done in local schools. "During the fiscal year ended June 30, 1953," the report explained, "home economics education has been challenged to increase its contribution to better home and family living in a tense world situation." Homemaking classes had been focused on new issues, such as "departure of family members for military service; new patterns of living, resulting from changes to defense-related jobs; increased employment of homemakers outside the home; high marriage rates among young people in their late teens and early twenties; increased urbanization; and high prices of consumer goods."[46] In order to stay useful, the home economics teacher had to keep her material current. Unlike math teachers who had the luxury of unchanging material, home economists felt the pressures of social change acutely. And because relocations due to the defense industry and mobilization in the Cold War continued after the war ended, the need for readjustment continued too.

James Peterson's textbook *Education for Marriage* reflected this ongoing change with the inclusion of an entire chapter on "Military Service as a Factor" in marriage. A student who Peterson had interviewed noted, "Though strictly speaking our time should not be called a time of war, still, it is an undeniable fact that since the beginning of World War II we have been in a continual state of emergency. . . . certainly it can be said that for my generation the distinction is slight." Instead of the fabulous world of prosperity and leisure predicted at the end of World War II, many young men and women were now facing long periods of separation and uncertainty. Marriage and family educators and home economists in general tried to sell themselves to the public as experts ready to assist in all the "adjustments" such an era required.[47]

As an editorial comment in the Journal of *Home Economics* phrased it, "the second half of the twentieth century has started off with a question mark . . . yet though the immediate future may seem uncertain, the goal, the objectives of the AHEA should stand out with an even greater clarity." These goals included "ways of improving home and family living and of meeting any changes that affect them." Such work was "always needed." More concretely, another editorial in the same edition pointed out, "A war in Korea raises the price of wool in Australia and of wool coats on Fifth Avenue." In an era of global entanglements, home economics projects like education of the consumer could only become more complex and important.[48]

## Home Economics in Government

As home economists were trying to maintain their authority in relation to the new challenges of the postwar era, reorganization of agencies at the federal level decreased their public visibility. In 1943, the Bureau of Home Economics had been merged with the Division of Protein and Nutrition Research of the Bureau of Agriculture. The resulting combination, the Bureau of Human Nutrition and Home Economics (BHNHE), reflected the success of professional nutritionists in convincing political leaders of the importance of their field. Although the name change did not limit funding for other home economics projects, the distinction that it implied signaled a new way of thinking about the field in which the interconnectedness of its subject matter would be emphasized less than its practical applications. Practical applications included both the complex kinds of research being performed in the bureau's laboratories and the nutrition departments of major universities and the training of high school-aged women in housekeeping skills. The more philosophical and sociological aspects of the field would no longer draw much public interest. Although critics continued to complain that at the college level young women were being taught abstractions rather than table settings, in reality the field was now focused much more on the concrete than on the more theoretical issue of how to value work in the home.

The 1943 change in the bureau reflected a general governmental reorganization of resources in wartime, but it also represented a transformation in the movement itself. By 1943, home economists had achieved many of the goals

that had first inspired the movement. At this point, home economics really
ceased to be a movement as its leaders, though not averse to innovations
within their field, largely ceased pushing for social change. For many professionals in the field, women who had come of age during the second generation of the movement, it must have seemed that the goals of their foremothers
had been achieved. Home economics was an accepted feature of education at
every level throughout the country, and women with home economics degrees were earning good salaries in corporate and government positions. The
uniformed home economists featured in a promotional film, *A Brighter Day
in Your Kitchen*, produced for Beatrice Foods represented this success. Their
professional appearance and the narrator's claim that "these [were] all graduate home economists" was supposed to assure consumers of the high value of
Beatrice products. State and national legislation had also established a range
of protections for consumers, including the 1938 Food, Drug, and Cosmetic
Act, which established standards that one home economist claimed "served as
a landmark in protecting consumers" from substandard goods.[49]

Home economists had opposed the 1938 amendment to the Federal
Trade Commission Act that protected consumers against "unfair or deceptive
acts in commerce," but only on the grounds that they thought that such authority more properly belonged to the Food and Drug Administration. When
the bill became law, however, home economists were appreciative of the work
performed by the commission to protect consumers from unscrupulous advertisers.[50] And, although advertising was not necessarily a fount of truth,
producers of domestic goods seemed to be paying more attention than ever
before to the woman in the home and what she wanted.

Perhaps home economist's most significant and long-lasting victory was
the introduction of the school lunch program that grew through the 1930s,
funded by a variety of agencies until by 1942 each state had a school lunch
program feeding approximately six million school children. In 1946 Congress passed the School Lunch Act, establishing funding for a nationwide
program, and home economics teachers were frequently placed in charge
of these programs in the schools where they taught. The program had been
inspired by the revelation that one-third of the young men recruited to serve
in the armed forces during the war were unfit because of malnutrition. It
seemed that Americans had finally realized that nutrition was a matter of life
or death.

Home economists had also succeeded in getting Americans not only to
accept but also to seek out the advice of experts on matters to do with their

homes. In their roles as domestic experts, however, they were swiftly losing ground, in the popular imagination at least to commercial interests. Partly this had to do with how advertising and marketing worked in the postwar years, but more importantly, home economists never managed to change the way Americans thought about gender and the work performed in their homes.

Although there was not a general uproar among home economists at the reorganization, a skit prepared for the annual meeting of the AHEA in 1948 seems to reflect widespread frustration with the relationship between government-funded home economics and the U.S. Congress. In this skit, which also was part of the celebration of twenty-five years since the Bureau of Home Economics had been created, a fictional "Senator Claghorn, from Down in Dixie, Where Families Are Still Produced," agrees to fund home economics only with absurd stipulations. These include "a cost-of-living study of congressmen and their families that will help us discover why $12,000 per year looks so big in Podunk and so small in Washington," and the hiring of more congressmen's wives as BHNHE researchers.[51]

Most telling of the kinds of criticism home economists were accustomed to, Claghorn was scripted to ask why bulletins were constantly being updated. "Since Mrs. America lives in an obsolete house," Claghorn pointed out, and "is now busily adjusting obsolete clothing to present needs, has obsolete equipment for home canning, why not continue the obsolete canning direction? Why not help Mrs. America to be consistent?" Beneath this mockery of congressional ignorance was the home economist's persistent belief that without their help "Mrs. America" would be left behind in the idealized march of human progress. Claghorn then went on to suggest that freeing up American women from their household chores by modernizing farm homes would result in trauma to the family because women would be moving beyond their proper sphere. Although they were themselves deep in a transition from focus on the house as home to the family, home economists still found reason to mock critics who worried that women's participation as equal members in civil society would destroy the family.

More indicative still of the field's troubled times than political satire were the actual arrangements for the celebration. Despite the group's plan to toast the bureau's growth from a $10,000 "Look," their playful, fashion-related term for their budget, to a "$1,000,000 Look," there was no lavish banquet such as food conservation veterans had enjoyed in 1923. The 1948 celebration was held in the Department of Agriculture cafeteria and attendees paid for their own meals. As a poem prepared for the event explained, the planning committee had limited resources to work with:

It put out a plan with bated breath
But everyone gave it the kiss of death.
In a land that flows with milk and honey
No one in Home Economics had any money.[52]

In 1952 another governmental reorganization began that further lowered the profile of home economists in government. Despite the objections of representatives from the AHEA, there would no longer be a bureau dedicated to their work. Human Nutrition and Home Economics were again divided, but now each became a subunit of the Agricultural Research Service. Meanwhile, school lunch work was removed to the Agricultural Marketing Service, and vocational work in home economics continued to exist as part of an entirely other agency, the Department of Health, Education, and Welfare. Although Hazel Stiebeling, previously the chief of the BHNHE, remarked gamely that she thought the reorganization would improve research in the field, the fact remained that authority over the work of home economists now belonged in the office of Byron Shaw, not the "woman of executive ability" envisioned by the founders of the original office of home economics in 1923.[53]

The shift from female to male leadership was part of a larger trend in the field, described by historian Margaret Rossiter as a loss for the field. Although the arrival of men in top positions in college and university home economics departments reflected increased funding for departments, which Rossiter argues is what attracted men in the first place, it was also part of the devolution of the original unity of home economics. For example, through the 1940s the numbers of men enrolled in institutional management classes in the College of Home Economics at Cornell University increased significantly. Male students were specifically preparing themselves to become hotel and restaurant managers as well as chefs.[54]

Such careers became more and more possible as domestic tourism in the United States increased with the building of roads, the lowered costs of cars and gas, the battering of Europe (making it a less desirable vacation spot), and, with the emerging war economy, more disposable income. Although home economics classes for boys and men were generally designed to train them for careers in hospitality, writers in the popular press could not resist the image of a man in an apron as an easy laugh. An article in the *New York Times* declared "Only Man in Class Is Best Homemaker" when the only male member of a New York University class of home economics majors won a prestigious scholarship.[55] David Hertzson, the winner, was not studying to be a "wife" but rather was an ex-GI who came from a family of hotel owners and cooked for a living. When another man won the same scholarship five years later, the newspaper again reported on what they took to be an amusing anomaly. An article about a home economics "chef class" offered to boys in Floral Park, New York, reaffirmed their masculinity in order to heighten the humor by describing the students as "sixteen stalwart youngsters, including two football players and a center half back on the soccer team." This description was then balanced for comic effect by a demonstration of their studies in which "service, on a lace tablecloth, was impeccable." The punch line of the article was delivered by the president of the senior class, who commented that such a course was valuable because it could "round a person out."[56]

The numbers of men in the home economics department at Cornell and their concentration in one area led to the creation of the now well-regarded College of Hotel Management there in 1954. A few other universities followed this lead, while others, without the resources to create separate colleges, established distinct departments that distinguished between home economics and hotel management. The division can be understood as a success for the field in that home economists had helped to create a career path lucrative enough to be desirable to men, who traditionally had more options than women. In practical terms, however, it significantly reduced the department's staff, students, and potential alumni donors. Indeed, one of the problems with running departments in which the majority of graduates would not pursue a career was that there were not likely to be many wealthy alumni to help support their alma mater.

The creation of the hotel school at Cornell may also have represented a loss for home economists by giving the sense that men did not want to be identified with the field. And, as Rossiter notes, in schools where men were appointed deans of home economics departments, a phenomenon of the 1960s, names of institutions began to change, losing the term "home."

## Home Economics on Television

Just as home economics themes had provided content for early radio shows, domestic matters were the focus of many of the first programs aired on television.

These programs, most of which ran for half-hour segments and focused on cooking, offered a cheap way for networks to experiment with television audiences. Although it now seems inevitable that the medium would attract viewers, early programmers had no such certainty. Although American consumers bought television sets, it was up to broadcasting companies to figure out just what kinds of shows people would watch. This was done largely by trial and error and, in the early days, relying on what had worked on radio. Because women made up the majority of the potential morning viewers and home economics shows had been a reliable element in radio, programmers reasoned that home-focused shows would do well in morning slots. The concepts were generally very simple—a pleasant female personality demonstrated a method of performing some form of domestic work, usually completing a recipe. These shows required no script, a simple set, and only one performer.

Lydia Perera, star of a cooking show in the first years of television, described some of the problems of using the medium to teach cooking. Speed, ambidexterity, and constant patter were requirements of the genre, but just as important was the ability convincingly to suggest "delicious flavor and aroma" because these were qualities that, as Perera dryly noted, "the TV camera [had] not yet learned to convey." A large part of the problem was that because of black and white transmission, "many foods that people find extremely agreeable are indigestible to the TV camera."[57]

Radio cooking shows, of course, had not required real cooking, although in the 1930s Ruth Van Deman of the Bureau of Home Economics advised radio home economists to prepare food for their show's engineers and co-host—the better to fill air time with genuinely appreciative noises. Television finally made the food visible, but ironically less attractive than it had been when its charms were only audible. A segment of the well-regarded *Home* show on NBC in which ground beef was prepared three different ways, for instance, is slightly nauseating shown in shades of glistening gray whereas a radio show that featured salmon croquettes sizzling in lard was surprisingly appetizing.[58]

Home economics-themed television shows, like their radio counterparts, had competition from shows designed solely for entertainment—game shows and dramas, as well as from the variety shows that became popular early in television's history. In some shows, such as *Home*, hosted by the *soignée* Arlene Francis, home economics topics were part of the variety. As television matured, housework and domestic products appeared less in educational segments and more as backdrop for situation comedies or in advertising. Domestic goods producers had long sponsored radio shows and woven endorsements for their products into scripts. On television this strategy took on a new life. Viewers could see for themselves as products were glamorized with lighting and music and the appearance of celebrities. A comparison of segments of two shows, one prepared by professional home economists and the other sponsored by a corporate producer of domestic goods, illustrates some of the ways that television challenged home economists' standards.

*Good Living* was a program produced by the DuMont Network in five distinct segments "designed for you, the modern woman." On Monday viewers could watch *Time to Live* for advice that promised to "save your labor, plan your leisure." On Tuesday, Pat McAlister hosted *Rooms for Improvement*, to help viewers "make [their] house a home." Wednesdays were *All About Baby*, featuring the advice of registered nurse Ruth Crowley. Celeste Carlyle hosted *Individually Yours* on Thursdays. On Fridays beauty hints for "graceful living" were handed out on the grimly titled *Face the Facts*. Few copies of these early homemaking shows remain in existence, but a 1952 episode of *Individually Yours* can give us some idea of what they were like.

*Individually Yours*, as the title suggests, emphasized developing personal style rather than following fashion.[59] Celeste Carlyle, a "nationally known style consultant" answered viewers' questions on design, fashion, and personal appearance. In an episode aired in 1952, Carlyle invited two viewers onto the set. One of them had written to ask how a small woman could best wear prints. She brought along a friend who, once the issue of prints had been resolved (small prints for small women, big prints for big women), asked for advice on how to wear her hair. In interactions with both women, Carlyle advocated homemade solutions; the viewer who asked about prints was complimented for making her own dresses, and her friend was advised to either cut her own hair or get someone in her family to do it. In a later portion of the show, Carlyle advised viewers on how to make homemade dresses look professionally tailored. The show was somewhat didactic, as Carlyle spoke from behind a desk, and, although she created quick sketches in the style of a fashion illustrator, *Individually Yours* was determinedly unglamorous.

In contrast, segments of the *Kate Smith Hour* that featured products of the show's sponsor, Youngstown Kitchens, made the mundane magnificent.[60] Smith, who alternated between singing, introducing other musicians, and interviewing celebrity guests, paused frequently during a 1957 episode of her show to direct viewers into another "room," a model kitchen provided by her show's sponsors. Although made of steel, the Monterey Future Fashion Ensemble kitchen included wood-fronted cabinets "for that warm look." Use of the name "Monterey" would conjure up visions of California and the postwar backyard paradise like the "outdoor fireplaces and patios" invoked by home economist Mildred Swift at the end of World War II. The kitchen was more than a kitchen; it was a sunnier future. Lest such perfection seem unattainable, Smith repeatedly informed her viewers that the kitchen could be purchased in "the same way you buy your wardrobe," piece by piece.

The reference to fashion was an attempt to make women feel personally excited about buying kitchen cabinets while also reassuring them that they would not have to spend a large amount of money all at once. Advertising from this era frequently associated women's fantasy lives with new kitchens, whether to sell new cabinets, appliances, or even new houses.[61] Kate Smith stood like a spokesmodel in the Monterey kitchen, dressed in an evening gown, her arms held slightly open as if welcoming the viewer into a stately home. There was no suggestion that this was or ever would be a place for labor. To further glamorize the Monterey kitchen, Smith announced that brochures about it would come with her own *Celebrity Supper Menu*, a cookbook of recipes for meals that Smith had served to famous guests. American housewives would truly be living like Hollywood stars—all they had to do was buy, piece by piece, the dream kitchen.

The essential difference between these two representations of domesticity—Carlyle's project-centered and Smith's fantasy-fueled—was that one was produced as education, to sell ideas, while the other was created to sell products. While Smith's show had its commercials built in, Carlyle's paused for public service spots encouraging young women to join the Women's Auxiliary Corps of the Army and urging citizens to help control inflation. Both shows used methods pioneered by home economists, Carlyle by encouraging the development of self-sufficiency through domestic skills and Smith by endorsing the idea that a "modern" kitchen was a better kitchen. Because the Smith version of domestic education was profit driven, however, it became the dominant model during the 1950s and up to the present day, although, as we will see later, Martha Stewart complicated this trend. Celeste Carlyle's advice served as a corrective to consumerism, even as an attempt to intervene in capitalism. But because Carlyle's message ran counter to sponsors' desire to sell products, her kind of show became less and less likely to be produced.

More typically, cooking segments appeared in "magazine"-style programs, such as *Home*, where Arlene Francis's assistant not only cooked all of her ground beef recipes using Heinz ketchup but also showed viewers that the recipes were available in a Heinz advertisement in the latest edition of *Life* magazine, thereby giving yet another product placement. Arlene Francis compounded the consumerism by remarking, "H is for Home. And now I find H is really for Heinz." The conflation of domestic space with brand-name domestic goods was complete. Because *Home* issued its own endorsement of each product used on the show, this connection would have had extra power for viewers.

## Consumer Culture

Television's greatest contribution in changing how Americans thought about their homes came through advertising. Because television could bring domestic goods to life in a way that even the best, full-color print advertising could not, it became the most powerful medium for introducing goods to potential consumers. Television advertising recreated a viewer's own active admiration as cameras caressed chrome trim, sliding the viewer's gaze over surfaces in an experience that was almost tactile. The new intimacy of television as a medium that engaged two senses rather than just one allowed for new methods in advertising. Creating what might today be called "synergy," ads blended the marketable personality of a television show's host with a variety of marketed products. More and less naturally, television personalities moved between their own shows and the commercials. Barbara Barkley, a cooking show host in San Francisco, was praised by a writer for her "handling of commercials": Barkley "weaves them into the program, leaving the audience friends of the sponsor and product."[62]

The emphasis on "friendship" between audience and product reflected a new era in advertising and marketing in which corporations attempted to develop customer loyalty. Marketing agents worked to create a sense that the corporation listened to the public and that there was truly a relationship between consumer needs and desires and what companies like General Mills and Westinghouse produced. This connection was the theme of an advertising film created in 1960 by the Corning Glass Works, titled *American Women, Partners in Research*.[63] As historian Regina Lee Blaszczyk has revealed, Corning was a company that had a particular obsession with providing customers products they would use. *Partners in Research* depicted this obsession in an attempt to convince consumers that it was they—the women of America—who really created Corning's products. Presumably if a woman could feel implicated in a product's design, she would feel personally connected to it and responsible for its purchase as the last stage in its production history. In the film, Corning labs were portrayed as constantly in communication with consumers. Although a male presenter commented that the design process "starts with men," he was quick to add, "Good as these designers are, they know that women have ideas of their own. They've learned to seek the help of the American housewife." Following the process of designing a coffee percolator made from material called Pyroceran, originally designed for the nose cones of rockets, the presenter concluded that "Mrs. Research has her final say" about the product at the store.

Although the film was clearly created to sell Corning products, it used tropes created by the home economics movement to do so. Homemaker as researcher, consumer in command of production, home as vanguard of modernity, and domestic life that was not only important, but a matter of national security, all worked as subtle themes in the film. By pointing out that the coffee pot was made of the same material as a rocket's nose cone, Corning flattered its female consumers with images of themselves as living on the cutting edge of technology and interacting with geopolitical forces. By 1960 rockets represented both space travel and the arms race. Home economists' messages that the family and home were the essential protectors of democracy were reinforced through association.

Constant references back to the female consumer created a sense of empowerment for the viewer. Corning engineers might have advanced degrees and high salaries, but they were all at the beck and call of a housewife's preferences. And, although in the ad's final scene, set in a department store, a husband was warned that when she likes a product, "It doesn't do any good to argue logically with your wife," women were consistently portrayed as thoughtful and rational as they participated in focus groups during the many phases of product development.

Homemaker as choice-maker was a recurrent theme of advertising in the 1950s Corporate producers of domestic goods portrayed women as savvy consumers who demanded options. Thus the Youngstown Kitchen came in pieces rather than as one unit so that a consumer could feel that she was creating her own kitchen, not accepting someone else's vision. Whether or not this was actually true—women probably did not mix and match kitchen components, for instance—was beside the point. Marketing and advertising firms wanted women to think that they were seen as independent and rational. An early television show, *The Television Shopper*, with Kathi Norris, was just one of several shows that addressed viewers as shoppers and offered them education in the finer points of new products. What such shows did not do, of course, was criticize products, only presenting those that had passed various tests. *Home* featured a segment in which a male cast member introduced viewers to domestic products, such as vacuum cleaners, that had the *Home* "seal of approval," the program's own version of the *Good Housekeeping* seal. Like the magazine, the television show had adapted the notions of neutrality and expertise to sell products and thereby support sponsors.

The persona that home economists had developed for American women, that of the educated consumer who followed her own common sense over fashion, worked remarkably well in corporate advertising despite the seeming conflict of interest. In *A Word to the Wives*, a 1955 advertising film produced to support building trades, a woman with a brand-new kitchen attempted to help her friend achieve the same.[64] "What about the fifth freedom?" the woman with the new kitchen asked, "Freedom from unnecessary drudgery, freedom to go shopping when the urge hits you or when there's a sale going on." Recast as an issue of rights in an era obsessed with rejection of totalitarianism, consumerism became democracy itself.

Although in reality one would suspect that buying a newly constructed home—for this was how the movie suggested consumers acquire new kitchens—might at least temporarily limit a family's ability to spend on whim, the film's sponsors suggested otherwise. These sponsors (Whirlpool, Caloric, Formica, and Republic Steel Kitchens) implied that with the increased efficiency that would come from a new kitchen, the woman of the house would be saving money and time, both of which she could then expend on shopping sprees. Not made explicit but present nonetheless in this scenario was home economist's oft-repeated argument that in their role as educated consumers women were central to the economic health of the nation. The already modernized woman in the film even referred to an outside source for confirmation of the product's worth, asking, "By the way, did you know that this kitchen won an award from the *Women's Home Companion*?"

As Karal Ann Marling notes in her study of the effect of television on American culture, advertisers learned to offer women each product in a range of colors or with simple variations so that they could enjoy the powerful sensation of having made a choice even if that choice were meaningless in reality. Home economists in schools and colleges had prepared several generations of women to think of themselves as material analysts; advertisers now took advantage of this self-image to sell domestic goods in the kinds of numbers that helped keep the postwar economy booming.[65]

One of these goods was the television itself, which created new problems of interior design as homemakers pondered the correct model to buy for their personal décor and how to integrate the large, attention-absorbing fixture into their homes.[66] The trend immediately following the war in which kitchens were opened up and connected to common living space was soon after complicated by the retreat of the entire family into dens or television rooms where décor was a matter of finding the most comfortable way for a family to watch television together. Televisions as family entertainment fit in well with the postwar emphasis on family unity and self-sufficiency. A woman who reported in a newspaper article in 1948 that she used her television as a babysitter in the morning also noted that the family now seldom required babysitters in the evening because she and her husband were happy to stay home watching programs with their children instead of going out alone or with other adults. The family itself was not enough to keep them home, but the family in front of the television was.[67]

The addition of televisions to ordinary American homes seemed to fit into some home economics ideals of domestic life—that it was entertaining, that it was connected to the world beyond, and that it was a place for togetherness. The consumer culture that television helped foster, however, presented many challenges to home economists. As American housekeepers increasingly got their information about products from the manufacturers of these same goods, home economists fought to stay relevant.

A new culture of consumerism in which, historian Lizabeth Cohen reveals, shopping was presented as a patriotic duty threatened to drown out the gospel of rational domesticity. Home economists had attempted to empower American women to control markets through judicious consumption; now the identity of savvy shopper had been manipulated by advertising firms to sell more products. Advertising complimented women in advance for their excellent choices, presenting them to themselves as levelheaded and not to be tricked. Sometimes, the consumer was shown in league with the corporation against men—husbands or fathers—who were usually portrayed as bombastic but also ill informed and malleable.

A short film advertising Whirlpool washing machines, for example, took the form of a situation comedy in which a group of young women tricked their fathers into buying new washer and dryer sets for their wives, the girls' mothers. Although they would be the beneficiaries of the scheme, the mothers remained remote in the story, leaving all of the action to the younger women. The film, *Mother Takes a Holiday*, encouraged viewers to identify with the girls as modern women, a new generation removed from the old ways of scrubbing and wringing laundry.[68] That the mothers could not get new equipment for themselves, either by using their own money or asking their husbands for it, merely underscored the theme that the older paradigm of long-suffering wifehood was on the way out. One needed to be young to really take advantage not only of new technologies and products but also of new gender norms.

Advertisers used images of women as independent and in control to sell products that were closely tied to cultural mores that actually kept women dependent and distanced them from power. In the short film, a group of girls take their mothers away on a camping trip, leaving their fathers to do the laundry and to discover how much easier it is to do with modern equipment. There is no suggestion that having bought the new equipment, the men will now become regular launderers. Indeed, with their cigars and bumbling, the audience does not want them to. Women will continue to wash, but they will have achieved liberation (handed to mothers by daughters, in a reversal of the suffrage movement) because their work has been made lighter if not less. Except for the essential fact that the whole scenario was designed to push one particular brand of equipment, the story was a home economics classic.

And yet that essential fact remained. Women's very egos were being defined and targeted by corporate producers of domestic goods. By 1961, the trend had become so blatant that the AHEA dedicated an entire session at its annual conference to the topic of consumerism. What should or could home economists—nutritionists, dieticians, child development experts, equipment testers, textile designers—do about it? One thing they could not do, Agnes Reasor Olmstead told her peers, was fight it.

Although it was "a little frightening to sit back and contemplate the all-encompassing field of home economics and to realize the tremendous influence if all home economists exercised their full potential," Olmstead believed that contemporary trends in consumer culture would ultimately direct that influence rather than vice versa. For too long, she suggested, "We [have] been so busy with curriculums, ripping seams, stewing prunes, selling food or equipment, patterns or refrigerators, that we have not fully assumed our responsibilities to the American family."[69]

Where an earlier generation of home economists had tried to arm consumers against fashion, training them to ignore the trivial in favor of the enduring, Olmstead now encouraged her peers to help Americans buy what they wanted when and how they wanted. Quoting a state extension supervisor who argued, "Young people do not wish to wait until they can afford things," Olmstead urged home economists to help such consumers figure out how to function in a credit economy. Rather than lecturing them on the wisdom of thrift and danger of debt, home economists should be recognizing the culture as it was and helping Americans to live successfully by its rules.[70]

Instead of sneering at modern trends such as processed foods, Olmstead called on her colleagues to "face up to the convenience foods." Since 10–20 percent of family food budgets in 1960 were spent on such items, Olmstead argued, "don't fight them. . . . Learn about them . . . buy them . . . use them. Then form an intelligent opinion so that we can help families make wise decisions"(ellipses in original).

The moment to shape the future of consumption had passed. The best role for home economists now was to go along for the ride and offer palatable advice where convenient. "Once in a while," she urged her peers, "let's REALLY think like a consumer, let's be one, let's laugh at home economics," (capitals in original) in the service of making messages more acceptable. The consumer and her tastes must become more central and home economists should continually ask themselves, "In our consumer work or teaching, how mouthwatering do we make a lesson? . . . Do we translate proteins into heavenly hamburger, a mile-high cheese soufflé, or even a popular peanut butter sandwich?"[71]

Almost forty years later, home economist Hazel Reed remembered the postwar period as a time of transition for the field: "As homemakers had more money to spend," she explained, "extension programs became more consumer-oriented. Projects had less emphasis on 'how to' and more about how to buy, what qualities to look for" in factory-made goods.[72]

Other home economists were less eager to abandon the movement's corrective spirit, but they were hardpressed to come up with viable ways to challenge consumerism. Speaking at the 1961 conference, home economist Rose White proposed a campaign of consumer vigilance in a last-ditch effort to control markets. If a store sold multiple brands of one product, the consumer should always buy the brand with more informative labeling. Furthermore, she should not only buy this brand, even if it was more expensive and less appealing, but she should also make sure that the store clerks saw what she was doing.[73]

The strategy seemed sadly outdated in an era of larger and larger chain supermarkets where a clerk would have no connection at all to purchasers for the store or to its owners. Asking consumers to buy something they might not like just because its packaging was more didactic was going to be a very hard sell at any time and particularly in an era when choice and style were emphasized in advertising. As women were encouraged more and more by advertising and popular culture imagery to think of themselves as spenders but not earners, home economists would have to approach their audience differently.

Home economists reacted to the growth of consumer culture in many different ways, but in general the field shifted toward a new emphasis on the consumer as subject of study and analysis. The study of consumer behavior actually aligned home economists with some aspects of the counterculture movement that developed in the mid-1960s. At the same moment, however, home economics was understood by many involved in countercultural lifestyles as a reactionary force in society, the opposite of their own impulses toward nonconformity and independence.

CHAPTER FOUR

# Burn Your Braisers

ON A SEPTEMBER afternoon advertised as "a groovy day on the Boardwalk in the sun with our sisters" a group of women protested the 1968 Miss America Pageant. Among other things, they demanded an end to "The Consumer Con-Game" through which Miss America and other spokesmodels became "a walking commercial" for corporate sponsors. The festive protesters also derided Miss America as an empty role model for girls, mocked her built-in obsolescence, and objected that there had never been an African American winner. One woman expressed the disjuncture between the ideal represented by the pageant and the realities of women's lives by vacuuming the boardwalk while holding cooking pots and a doll, with a child tugging at her hand. The statement that the protesters issued was a manifesto and call to action rather than a carefully constructed position piece, yet it managed to reflect developing social tensions that shaped how home economics would be understood in years to come.[1]

By objecting to Miss America as corporate "shill," the protesters were suggesting deeper connections between gender ideology and consumer culture. Their rejection of popular versions of womanhood propagated in advertising was simultaneously a rejection of consumerism itself. Not buying the corporate image of womanhood meant also not buying the corporate definition of the female self as consumer. In the "freedom trash can" that the protesters provided, they invited participants and onlookers to throw items of "woman-garbage" such as bras, curlers, wigs, and girdles, all products that symbolized attempted conformity to a single ideal of the female. They also planned to discard "representative issues" of several women's magazines. *Cosmopolitan, Ladies'*

Figure 14. A masked protester at the 1968 Miss America pageant in Atlantic City, New Jersey, performs traditional women's roles as political theater. Image copyright by Jo Freeman, www.jofreeman.com.

*Home Journal,* and *Family Circle* were mentioned specifically, and it was implied that others were also welcome. That they lumped together two very different genres of women's magazines indicated that they wanted to reject all proscriptions for womanhood as by nature equally oppressive. Liberation would come only through self-determination unadulterated by messages intended to sell consumer goods. The recipes and childcare tips of *Family Circle* were just as invidious as the beauty and fashion advice doled out in *Cosmopolitan.* The "career gal" reading about how to catch a man was in the same cultural prison as the housewife reading about how to keep hers. Idealized figures like Miss America had been used to sell American women not only products but also a false sense of themselves and their potential.

It would probably have shocked these protesters deeply to know that their basic message was one that home economists had been advocating since the beginning of the twentieth century. And it might have shocked home economists just as much to realize that the Miss America pranksters were on their side. For, after all, the early and persistent message of home economists until the postwar period had been that women must seize control of all forces and elements having to do with domestic space and activities. Whenever possible, for example, a woman should design her kitchen to fit her body, not the other way around. She should make her clothing as a way of achieving independence from image makers, and her clothing should conform not to fashion but to usage and to her own aesthetic. In the marketplace she should be confident of her power as consumer, rejecting substandard goods and rewarding those producers who offered her quality merchandise at reasonable prices. Furthermore, she should know the basics of providing for herself so that she could retain independence from suppliers. In public, as in her home, she should be directed by her own intellect rather than by whim or outside expectations.

As corporate producers had grown savvier during the 1920s and advertising appeared to overwhelm the consumer, home economists sought ways to fight this trend. Simultaneously, they created numerous new career opportunities for women and strove doggedly, though unsuccessfully, to earn respect for the homemaker who toiled alone in her own home, arguing that work should not be devalued because it was traditionally performed by women. During the marriage and baby boom of the 1950s, home economists preached autonomy and partnership within marriage. And as more and more married women joined the waged work force, these students of the domestic sphere focused on what this might mean for family life and looked for ways that women could achieve satisfaction in all areas of their lives. They even pioneered courses that focused on women's changing roles in society and worked within government at its highest levels to provide support for working women and their children.

And yet home economists appeared to second-wave feminists as "the enemy," which was how self-proclaimed radical feminist Robin Morgan addressed them when she spoke before a meeting of home economists in 1971. That encounter will be discussed further below, but it is important to note first that Morgan's antagonism had a history. When members of the AHEA invited Betty Friedan to speak at their annual conference in 1963, they presumably knew that she would not speak in wholehearted praise of their work. In her culture-altering book, *The Feminine Mystique*, which had been published earlier in the year, she rejected outright the idea that housework could be fulfilling and implicitly condemned all projects that offered to help women find satisfaction in traditional housewifery. Although she did not openly engage home economics as an "enemy" of women's liberation, she warned against what she termed "sex-directed education." Despite being offered "for the best of helpful reasons," courses in "life adjustment" would lead, she feared, not only to limited opportunities for women but also to limited imaginations among them. Interestingly, there does not seem to be a record of what Friedan actually said at the 1963 conference. Her archived papers provide no evidence and the *Journal of Home Economics*, which traditionally published abstracts of what guest speakers said at the annual conference, mentioned the speech only in passing. A caption to a photograph of Friedan intriguingly reads, "Betty Friedan, author of the *Feminine Mystique* who spoke at the Pacesetter Luncheon, excited much comment from the audience."[2] It is reasonable to assume that Friedan, ever unafraid of causing offense, applied the same criticisms in person that she presented in her book.

In *The Feminine Mystique*, Friedan blamed marriage education in particular for young women's declining interest in careers outside the home. Although those who taught these courses believed that their curricula would empower young men and women to avoid the traumas associated with lack of sexual knowledge and the difficulties that sometimes follow youthful marriages, Friedan argued that to offer these courses condemned female students to imagining their future only in terms of marriage and motherhood. Because marriage education had spread so far and so fast through high schools and colleges during the 1950s, Friedan claimed, young women now refused to invest any part of themselves in intellectual education, remaining willfully disinterested in college courses while they waited to marry and begin housekeeping.

Home economics courses in fields other than human relationships attracted little of her attention, although at two points she referred to courses in the field as unchallenging. Similarly, a seventeen-year-old feminist profiled in *McCall's* magazine noted, "In lower-class schools, girls are tracked into home economics," while in what she apparently esteemed "higher-class" schools such as her own, "girl artists, like me, are tracked into fashion illustration or advertising, never architecture."[3] In fact, fashion illustration and, potentially, advertising were also fields that college programs in home economics might prepare students for, so although she did not realize it, this particular student was also being indirectly "tracked" into home economics. Her assessment of home economics as not of her world, however, suggests more general assumptions that the field had been fighting since its earliest days. The vocational program in high schools had seemingly made this problem worse. Despite proud rhetoric that defined home economics as the marriage of art and science, the public at large continued to see it as a craft. Home economics was simply handwork, something to occupy the simple. The seventeen-year-old feminist saw home economics as a sterile endeavor, productive of neither fulfillment nor money.

In *The Feminine Mystique* Friedan quoted a young woman who had consciously stepped back from an intense interest in bacteriology to major in home economics. The reason she gave was that she wanted to spend more time in less academically serious pursuits, particularly in socializing with female friends. Although she was less interested in home economics than in bacteriology, she thought that the change of majors would bring more balance to her life. The irony of this story, in the context of the history of home economics, was that bacteriology had been one of the cornerstones of home economics, so the student could presumably continue her work in the field, except that she would now be studying it as an applied science. Friedan, missing this nuance, interpreted the story to mean that the student had given up on rigorous scholarship because she wanted to be more attractive to men. Although academic home economists never even remotely suggested that women who trained in the "hard" sciences were doing wrong or would be unappealing personally, they did often emphasize that their field gave women competencies in two areas—a chosen field and home life—which assumed that while women could choose their career, they would not be able to choose whether or not to do housework.[4]

Friedan briefly alluded to this problematic position when she noted that sex-directed educators, "Instead of challenging the girls' childish, rigid, parochial preconception of a woman's role . . . cater to it by offering them a pot-pourri of liberal-arts courses, suitable only for a wifely veneer, or narrow programs such as 'institutional dietetics' well beneath their abilities and suitable only for a 'stop-gap' job between college and marriage."[5] Again it seems that Friedan was not aware of the degree to which home economics had established real and potentially fulfilling career opportunities for both women and men. Graduates with degrees in institutional dietetics could attain high levels of responsibility and status in the workforce and perform jobs of significant social importance. Nonetheless, home economics educators such as the guidance counselor portrayed in the film *Why Study Home Economics* did attempt to sell their field as one that prepared women not only for careers but simultaneously for their presumed other "career" as wife and mother. Although home economists had hoped to help women make the best of their gender roles both through education and through challenging housework's status, leaders of feminism's "second wave" argued for women's total disconnection from housework. Because the project to professionalize housework had not resulted in its popular perception as a gender-neutral pursuit, these women believed that the only way to free women from the stigma of housework was for them to stop doing it.

## Who Cleans the Freedom House?

For many of the leaders of the women's movement that emerged in the mid-1960s, recognition of gender oppression came in domestic moments. As Casey Hayden and Mary King wrote in one of the first attempts to raise the issue of sexism in radical activist groups, "Within the movement, questions arise in situations ranging from relationships of women organizers to men in the community, to who cleans the freedom house."[6] Female activists in the civil rights movement also found that "they had spent their time . . . making coffee for and cleaning up after the boys." Cleaning the "freedom house" and making coffee for the revolution revealed to these women that gender expectations would not change without pressure, that they would not simply fall away as a generation rejected their parents' standards and ideals.[7]

This awareness famously led some women who were already involved in other political movements such as the civil rights movement, the antiwar movement, and the free speech movement, as well as others who were less political but still members of the counterculture, to join in revealing gender inequalities throughout society. In some of the best-loved statements of the movement, feminist writers pointed to the home as the first line of oppression. Pat Mainardi, for example, in *The Politics of Housework*, listed the many excuses her husband offered for not doing housework, thereby revealing the many ways in which ordinary expectations for women as workers within the home contributed to gender inequality. Her humorous decoding of everyday events would probably have made sense to most female readers in 1970, regardless of their stance on feminism or women's liberation. Both men and women had been socialized to accept a gendered division of labor in the home and Mainardi noted that although the "liberated" man would attempt to reject this socialization he would quickly find that it was to his advantage to maintain it.[8]

Because Mainardi and her husband "both had careers, [and] both had to work a couple of days a week to earn enough to live on," she suggested that they share the housework, and he agreed because, as she noted wryly, "most men are too hip to turn you down flat." Then "an interesting thing happened": he did less and less of the housework while she did more and more. A canny social critic, Mainardi blamed both her husband and herself. Her own fault lay in accepting the mass-marketed vision of womanhood in which "television women [were] in ecstasy over their shiny waxed floors or breaking down over their dirty shirt collars." Absorbing this imagery over the years, Mainardi, like most women of her generation, had accepted the idea that housework was an integral part of her identity. If poorly done it reflected badly on her character. Mainardi did not mention it, but the public schools had contributed to this problem by frequently requiring female students to take home economics, linking the work with their gender.

Mainardi's husband, like all men of the era, had "no such conditioning. [Men] recognize the essential fact of housework right from the very beginning. Which is that it stinks." Free to understand this, Mainardi's husband began offering excuses for not doing his share of the work. First among them was that he did not know how to do household work and that, even when he did know, she was better at it. These arguments relied on the ancient notion that women were naturally rather than culturally associated with housework. This basic belief had been bolstered throughout his and Mainardi's childhoods by the presence of home economics education in public schools. Having seen female schoolmates march off to kitchen classrooms, he could at least suspect that his wife would know more about housework than he.

Home economists had worked tirelessly to combat the idea that housework was essentially female by arguing that in fact most women had no idea how to keep house or raise their families well and that only formal education could prepare them for the job. Simultaneously, however, they had undone their own work by allowing the subject to be taught only to girls in most schools. Although there is no evidence that home economists resisted gender integration in their classrooms and although they seem to have been generally interested in and proud of courses for boys or mixed courses, there is also no evidence of collective efforts to integrate. An image from a booklet about ideal kitchen design produced in 1952 by the Cornell Center for Housing and Environment Studies illustrates this blind spot. In a design described as "Family Centered Living" (reflective of the broader cultural emphasis on family togetherness), a father figure and a male adolescent lounge in the foreground while a mother figure works alone in her kitchen, peeping out between the bars of her modernist jail formed by free-floating shelving that marks off her space from theirs.

Although in hindsight it might appear to have been an important strategy for changing the status of housework to teach schoolboys the same things they taught schoolgirls and to present housework as shared work, it is also difficult to imagine how home economists would have pushed for this. An essential part of their justification for teaching the topic in schools was that no matter what career a girl pursued, the social reality was that she would still have to take care of her home. Because the male housekeeper did not exist in popular imagination except as a figure of fun, it would have been difficult and perhaps dangerous to argue that men would face the same problem when they became independent. The mystery of how men manage without women was sometimes suggested but never fully confronted in courses with titles such as Bachelor Cookery. In large part this remains true in popular culture today, where male celebrity chefs square off in culinary battles rather than offering tips on dinner for one or after-school snacks for the playground set. Unglamorous everyday domestic cookery remains largely women's domain.

As Pat Mainardi reminded her readers, most men before they married "had a rich rewarding bachelor life during which they did not starve or become encrusted with crud or buried under the liner," yet the strengths that pulled them through that assumed-to-be transitional period were, Mainardi argued, strangely never internalized as part of the male identity or resurrected in married life. In this one case, male self-sufficiency was not a source of pride. Mainardi recommended a new regime in the home based in an understanding that most housework is inherently unrewarding and uninteresting. Having mutually acknowledged this to be so, she suggested that both partners would see the justice of sharing the work. She acknowledged an important difficulty that could arise in such an arrangement, which was that men and women would have different standards as to when a chore was complete. Although men might expect a certain level of quality if women were performing the work, they would be willing to settle for lower standards when they themselves were the workers. Women, however, had been socialized to think that housework was complete only when perfection had been achieved.

Mainardi's solution was that women would have to "keep checking up" on the men in their homes to make sure that they were not avoiding any of the work that must be done to keep a home functioning comfortably. This solution would seem less than ideal, as it tied women to the role of "nag" or enforcer of standards and therefore "expert" on housework. Betty Friedan, in contrast, endorsed a new set of standards, encouraging her readers to think of housework as that which should be done as quickly as possible and with the greatest number of shortcuts, particularly in the area of food preparation. In essence, Friedan was asking women to ignore or unlearn what they knew about housekeeping in order to overturn gender-based oppression in their homes. Once liberated from their proscriptive relationships with sex-directed educators and with purveyors of household products, women could use their dishwashers and powdered potatoes "for what they [were] truly worth—to save time that can be used in more creative ways."[9]

Such a position was implicitly anti-home economics in that it rejected domestic labor—even cooking—as inherently worthless. More recently, philosopher Linda Hirshman has urged women to "never know how much milk is left," as a symbol of their equality in the household. Rather than educating men into domestic responsibility, women should abdicate theirs. If neither partner is recognized as "naturally" in touch with such problems, she implies, both will become equally responsible. There may be some milkless days in the transition period, but once the revolution is completed and responsibility becomes shared, shortages will be a thing of the past. Hirshman explicitly rejected "home economics" as gendered knowledge leading to self-imposed oppression: "The home-economics trap involves superior female knowledge and superior female sanitation. The solutions are ignorance and dust. . . . If women never start playing the household-manager role, the house will be dirty, but the realities of the physical world will trump the pull of gender ideology. Either the other adult in the family will take a hand or the children will grow up with robust immune systems."[10]

Although this may prove an unpopular argument in our era of Purell, second-wave feminists and those involved in countercultural lifestyles in the early 1970s struggled to liberate themselves from household standards that seemed unnecessarily high, created, as Friedan argued, to fill the time of women "stuck" in the home. In a poignant description, however, of a mostly lesbian, all-female collective near Moline, Illinois, Vivian Cadden discovered that the problem of housework did not disappear when women lived without men. "The major stumbling block of the collective," she wrote, of the group who lived communally and published a feminist newsletter, "seems to be the allocation of drudgery. Any kind of work that isn't creative, enjoyable, or mind expanding is referred to by a terse four-letter word, and the question of who does such work is a constant drag."[11]

## Hippie Home Economics

The counterculture that emerged in the mid-1960s often actually created more work for women through its rejection of corporate consumer culture. That small segment of society that went "back to the land" in the late 1960s and early 1970s, for example, returned to women's lives many of the household tasks that had been eliminated by the developments of industrial production. Idealistic young women found themselves living in log cabins in Vermont, stuffing woodstoves with heavy armfuls of fuel in order to heat the bathwater or even to make a simple pot of coffee. They took up ancient arts of spinning, dying, weaving, and knitting to save their families from the soulless convenience of department store clothing and became self-trained biochemists with yogurt cultures and yeasty, dark-floured breads.

As Americans participated to greater and lesser degrees in the rejection of consumer culture, they developed increasing interest in nutrition and "health food." "Natural" replaced "modern" in some circles as the word of highest value. The past suddenly became much trendier than the future. Indeed, those newly conscious of and concerned about food sources and contents, while rejecting technological "progress" in some ways, revived the ideas and many of the techniques of the first generation of home economists, whose focus had been on the autonomous consumer. As food historian Warren Belasco winningly remembers of his and his wife's own early experiences rejecting corporate consumer culture in the late 1960s, "We got an old USDA pamphlet on home pickling and bought our first dozen Ball jars. Mastering the pressure cooker, blender, canning kettle, and sourdough starter, we felt free, grounded, and right."[12]

As had been true for generations before, however, the new choices about food, clothing, and domestic space were still largely made by women, although they now had the approval of men who saw them as anti-corporate, sometimes anti-capitalist gestures. Belasco notes, for example, that in the radical Diggers movement of the mid-1960s, which focused its activism on food, it was the "overworked Digger women who did most of the gardening and cooking" that made the group's actions possible.[13]

The movement culture of the 1960s and early 1970s involved much more than taking political action. Because it embraced wholesale rejection of what were considered sterile and inauthentic lifestyles of the parental generation, movement culture, especially among whites, had to come up with new versions of "home" in which to relocate identities. And although the young men and women involved in establishing these alternatives were generally loath to recreate old hierarchies, much remained of traditional family structures in their utopias. Women might birth their children at home and name them Moonbeam, but they were still primary caregivers and, as such, bound to homes in ways that men were not. Living in communal arrangements with shared child-care and group dinners of sprouts and handmade tofu no doubt made many a young man feel like he was finally independent from "the system," but what these men seldom recognized was that they still relied on "wives"—whether legal, common-law, or freely volunteered—to achieve the counterculture.

Ironically, the women whose work supported alternative lifestyles relied on homemaking skills that had been out of fashion since the era of their great-grandmothers. Had home economics not appeared to be the work of the "man" oppressing women into pre-feminist gender roles, more young idealists might have found in it a way out of the pervasive sexism of their domestic arrangements as well as some excellent recipes for whole-wheat bread. First-generation home economists, like the hippies of the late 1960s and 1970s, located value in personal interactions and expressions, elevating the hand-made above the "refined" in sympathy with the ideals of the Arts and Crafts movement. Hippies also, like early home economists, tended to find their idealized "authentic" aesthetic in folk cultures outside of America. Counterculture practitioners in the 1970s turned to peasant cuisines and decorative motifs of south Asia and South America, while founders of the home economics movement had turned to Japanese, English, and German folk histories for inspiration in the domestic sphere. What Warren Belasco notes of the hippies was true also of the home economists, that they celebrated all that was "brown" in direct opposition to all that was "white"—whole wheat bread instead of white bread, molasses instead of sugar, unbleached textiles instead of bright colors.

Although relegation to traditionally female roles within the social movements of the 1960s has been cited often as an important motivation for many women to reflect on gender inequality, radical domesticity could also be empowering as women rediscovered the tremendous sustaining labors of female ancestors. Reclaiming womanhood as a self-made rather than media-created phenomenon frequently led feminists into home economics territory. In rejecting the prepackaged femininity that was used in ubiquity to sell household goods as well as beauty and fashion products, they rejected consumerism itself. As Belasco notes, for example, the feminist newsletter *Great Speckled Bird* "attacked the Pillsbury Bakeoff for now favoring contestants who used convenience foods," because "by downgrading older folk recipes, a male-run corporation was wresting power and skill away from women."[14] Domestic knowledge had dignity and profound value, these activists argued, just as women like Ellen Richards and Martha Van Rensselaer had argued before them. Modern corporations undermined the power that had traditionally inhered in women's culture by creating anxieties and replacements that destabilized older and more reliable ways of knowing. The Boston Women's Health Book Collective's *Our Bodies Ourselves* was after all just a more forthright version of a domestic manual's section on illnesses and also represented women's rights to professional, scientific knowledge about their own (intimate) sphere.

## In Laurel's Kitchen

A fascinating artifact of this overlap between home economics and counterculture lifestyles was the very popular *Laurel's Kitchen*, "a handbook for vegetarian cookery and nutrition," published first by a small alternative press in Berkeley in 1976. After going through five printings in two years, it was picked up in 1978 by Bantam Books, where it remained very popular, being reprinted thirteen times in the next four years. These numbers tell us that its popularity reached well beyond the small population of Americans who lived entirely countercultural lives. The book was in fact composed as an invitation to men and women living more conventional lives to make significant changes not just in what they ate, but also in how they considered consumption. Whether or not the book's readers accepted this invitation, that there was such a high level of interest in what was advertised as alternative domesticity is interesting. The popularity of the book may reflect dissatisfaction with domesticity as represented in the popular media of magazines and television as well as the gradual mainstreaming of previously alternative choices. It also suggests the growing market in lifestyles that is so prevalent today.[15]

*Laurel's Kitchen* was as much a lifestyle guide as it was a cookbook. The reader did not learn to replicate just Laurel's recipes but also, and more importantly, her kitchen and the ethos of that space. Carol Flinders introduced the philosophy of the book in a section titled "Giving the Gift of Life." The phrase referred to the idea that vegetarians save lives by not killing animals for food, but it also reflected the author's promise to her readers that the book itself would give them a new, more satisfying and ethically comfortable life. Recipes and hand-drawn illustrations were provided by Laurel Robertson, whose approach to food, family, and community served as the inspiration for the book. Robertson was described in the authors' notes as being "Pennsylvania Dutch out of southern California," an ethnic identity that connected her both to the American past and to its future because California continued to be associated in the popular imagination with all things new and exciting and particularly, in this era, with youth and alternative lifestyles.

The authors' notes and Flinders's introduction explained that Robertson had learned to cook from her grandmother and mother, establishing her skill as traditional and traditionally gendered in opposition to professional training, whether acquired in an educational or commercial setting. If connection to a famously progress-averse culture were not enough to establish Robertson's credentials as a "natural," Flinders further described her as person of "strong intuitive powers when it came to food."[16]

This characterization of Robertson's knowledge rejected contemporary ideas of women's abilities. Home economists had been arguing for seventy-five years that women did not have innate household wisdom and therefore needed the education that the movement offered. Manufacturers of food products had taken up this argument and bent it to their own needs, presenting the female consumer as one always directed toward "the latest" in ingredients or methodology and simultaneously almost too busy to learn what was new in the frozen-foods aisle. Both home economists and food corporation executives told women that they needed professional help to perform their expected gender roles.

*Laurel's Kitchen* also suggested that a woman needed help, but the help that Robertson, Flinders, and Godfrey advocated was communal and served to complement women's work rather than to direct it. For example, one woman might prepare bread for her neighbors while they supplied her with yogurt or with one of the many bean spreads that were basic to the book's cuisine. Sometimes they would work together in one kitchen, at other times separately, but they remained connected because each made a contribution to the whole.

Indeed, the cooperative nature of the book itself—composed by three authors, each contributing from her own strengths—modeled the process they hoped to see emerging in communities of readers. By advocating a community of women producers, *Laurel's Kitchen* provided a possible antidote to the suburban alienation at the heart of *The Feminine Mystique* and the countless magazine articles it had inspired. Yet the remedy it proposed actually returned women to the gender roles they had outgrown with the emergence of the middle and working classes in the 1830s. During this period in American history a shift in methods of production and in living conditions released middle-class women from most productive labor. Although such productive tasks as bread making and child rearing still took place in their homes, middle-class women were more likely to hire servants to help them than to do it themselves. The vegetarian woman of *Laurel's Kitchen* then returned to the world of the colonial-era goodwife whose productive activities and community involvement defined success in fulfilling her gender identity.

For all its aura of newness, even of the radical, *Laurel's Kitchen* was steeped in the same kind of progressive nostalgia that can be found in the writings of the early home economics movement. The 1982 Bantam paperback edition of the book included a frontispiece featuring the three authors gathered around a simple, old oak table. The room around them is wood paneled and almost austerely simple. The only decorative elements clearly visible are a potted plant and a woven straw bowl of fruit. A simple white coffeepot and mugs on the table suggest fellowship. The room is composed—decorated would be the wrong term—entirely in the Arts and Crafts aesthetic. Both William Morris and Ellen Richards would have been perfectly at home in the room. The women's own mothers, however, who came of age in the era of the dream kitchen, might not have been so comfortable there.

In the frontispiece, Flinders, Godfrey, and Robertson are dressed to match the room, in simple, monochromatic tops and floor-length skirts, their hair piled on their heads in simple buns. Although there is nothing in their choice of clothing that is overtly unfashionable or "retro"—maxi skirts and turtlenecks were common at the time—it is striking how much they are dressed like women of the Progressive Era, the period in which the Arts and Crafts aesthetic was born. Among the many fashion choices available, they have chosen the ones that will link them with the past rather than the present or future.

Interestingly, the authors look not at the photographer but at each other, reinforcing the message that the reader will acquire community through the book, first with Flinders, Godfrey, and Robertson, and then, as she follows their example, with other women in her neighborhood. She too will have faithful female friends with whom to share household tasks, coffee, and—as the three authors appear to be doing—private jokes. The text beneath this image elaborated on the implicit message that *Laurel's Kitchen* offered a recipe for a more satisfying way of life: "Sun splashing on wood and crockery, bright colors and green houseplants, the aroma of baking bread and bubbling soups. . . . Now let Laurel and her friends introduce you to the art of cooking with delicious natural foods. They will help you rediscover the joys of your own kitchen, where wholesome meals artfully prepared and lovingly served amid talk and laughter reunite the home."[17]

Although blurbs such as this are often considered trivial, it is worth taking a look at how the book's publishers attempted to sell their product, since they were so successful in doing so. What would the casual reader respond to in this description that could made her buy the book and take it home? Offered first was an aesthetic of the natural—natural light and live houseplants—and an ethic of taking time; both breads and soups can take hours to make. The publishers promised their readers access to a way of life that was the opposite of most mass-marketed domesticity. It did not take place in a hurry, did not depend on metal gadgets, and was not performed in a coolly futuristic environment or for an audience. The world of Laurel's kitchen was presented as new but not new, a rediscovery of ancient truths, a reunion with traditional values. The three women's modesty in looking at each other rather than at the camera subtly reinforced this message.

These truths and values were unstated but implicit: working for her family truly was fulfilling for a woman and her work was essential to the health of the family as an institution. In an era when feminism and the women's liberation movement ardently rejected the conflation of woman with home, *Laurel's Kitchen* reinscribed this connection as itself liberationist. Like the first generation of home economists, however, Robertson, Flinders, and Godfrey defined liberation not in terms of gender but as freedom from the dictates of the market. As we shall see shortly when we look closely at Carol Flinders's introduction to the book, gender difference did not necessarily result in gender inequality in Laurel's world.

Having picked up on the marketable aspects of feminism, mass producers of domestic goods had, by 1976, when *Laurel's Kitchen* was first published, begun to sell women a vision of themselves as too liberated to bother with old-fashioned domesticity but still responsible for their home and family's well-being. These busy creatures were offered all kinds of convenience products to make their domestic life easier so that they could pursue whatever fabulous feminist future they desired. Most of the money, of course, was to be made in exploiting the contradiction—liberated yet still responsible—that had the potential to bring on identity crises in American women. Typically, if marketing and advertising professionals can trap a market in continuous self-doubt, they have secured themselves generations of steady income. Carol Flinders, Laurel Robertson, and Bronwen Godfrey hoped to free women from this trap by encouraging them to embrace domesticity as itself liberating.

Flinders's two-part introduction to *Laurel's Kitchen*, "Giving the Gift of Life," first told the story of her own conversion to vegetarian living and then explored the issue of women's roles within the countercultural lifestyle that she and her husband had chosen for their family. Her conversion narrative featured Laurel Robertson as a catalyst and guide who helped Flinders move in a direction that she had preexisting interest in. Briefly, Flinders and her husband lived in Berkeley, had two children, and practiced meditation under the tutelage of a yogi. Through that practice they became interested in vegetarianism but remained unsure of how to make this shift successfully. Flinders's friendship with Robertson, who she described as a person without artifice and in possession of what might be termed "natural wisdom," assisted the family in making this change. For Flinders, Robertson became both friend and guru. Neither Robertson nor Flinders worked outside the home, although both were active in radical causes in Berkeley in the early 1970s. Their cookbook/lifestyle guide advocated spending lots of time in the kitchen and slowing down processes that had been speeded up during the 1950s. Laurel's kitchen served as a space where she and her friends could actively resist the mass media representation of women's lives as harried and anxious.

The complicated gender politics of this vision burst through the surface of Flinders's introduction in several places. Flinders seemed to make a feminist argument against mass-media representations of women when she argued that her transition to a vegetarian diet was partly inspired when she realized that "something was terribly wrong with our whole culture's attitude toward food." This wrongness had a lot to do with how women were targeted by mass media. "Leaf through a women's magazine," she invited her reader, "or a standard cookbook," and one would see that "A whole language has been worked up to convince us that a well-prepared blintz is just this side of Nirvana."[18] Flinders continued in her comparison of past with present, locating a kind of golden age not very long before her own lifetime, in the late nineteenth century. "In Fannie Farmer's day," she claimed, "You went out to the kitchen and baked a chocolate cake. Big deal. Now you're invited to 'Have the Chocolate Experience.'"[19] She implied that marketers of domestic goods were trying to sell women a vision of domestic life that was more fulfilling than it really was. One might think that she hoped to liberate women from their traditional connection to food and nurture, yet not much further on in the same section she presented an alternative vision that serves to tighten these bonds: "For a wife and mother to carry out her work in the spirit of karma yoga, she needs to try quite literally to see the Lord in the people she loves, clothes, feeds."[20] Admitting that this ideal would be hard to achieve, Flinders added that she nonetheless found it "breathtakingly attractive." Through vegetarian eating, meditation, and participation in radical politics, Flinders merged the above-mentioned colonial era ideal of the goodwife with the antebellum-era ideal of woman as spiritual guardian for her family.

The theme of attraction was elaborated in a voyeuristic scene in which Flinders watched Robertson prepare lunch for her husband, Ed. Flinders recognized this as an intimate act of love for Robertson, who took the greatest care to provide Ed with sufficient nutrients, vitamins, and variety, never neglecting palatability. Flinders admitted to feeling uncomfortable; Robertson's care seemed like a challenge to her own assumption of closeness with her husband, Tim. After watching Robertson, she tells her readers, she became more careful and loving in her lunch preparations, although taking care to be subtle about it, "lest [Tim] lose face with some of our more 'liberated' friends." The implication here is that those who considered themselves anti-sexist would mock Tim for allowing his wife the seemingly subordinate position of loving lunch-maker. The "liberated" woman either would not make her husband's lunch, or would do so resentfully. Flinders herself seemed unsure whether she was or wasn't liberated, defensive of her friend's practices, but still sensitive to how feminists might see her own behavior.

As she explained in the second part of her introduction, "The Keeper of the Keys," her involvement with Robertson led Flinders to ask difficult questions of herself. Having come to the conclusion that "we women ourselves are a valuable and often misused resource," an idea that again echoes early home economists' justification for their movement, she then had to ask a question that she recognized was a "troubled and troubling question—in some circles, even, an explosive one: How is my time best spent?" Flinders recognized that "to 'retrench' and return to less mechanized and commercialized methods of homemaking may mean [one] won't have time for a job" or hobbies, yet the option intrigued her. Even if she conceded that it was a necessary sacrifice, she wondered, "Could I carry it off without feeling, and expressing resentment?"

For Flinders the answer was affirmative, indeed even affirming. The key, as home economists had once argued, was to pay more rather than less attention to the work you were doing in the home. Labor-saving devices and products not only created more work in the end, they degraded the idea of work. If it was something to be done, as Friedan argued, in the least amount of time and with the least effort, then there was no joy in it. But if one paid attention, Flinders claimed, it became meaningful. As if channeling Ellen Richards herself, Flinders asked, "Why compartmentalize our lives so that art is a thing apart? There is an artistic way to carry out even the simplest task, and there is great fulfillment to be had from finding out that way and perfecting it."[21]

Although the gadgetry that Flinders rejected had not yet been created when home economists first gathered in Lake Placid, New York, in 1899 and although they had great hopes that technological advances could ease domestic labor, they had been the first to make Flinders's argument that drudgery was as much a matter of attitude as it was of actual labor. Like these early home economists, Flinders located the "most effective front for social change" in the home, and like them she did not reject women's roles outside the home, but unlike the early or later home economists, she did find an explicit connection between women and home. Using history as her justification, she argued, "Judging by our experience, women are the people who can best accomplish these changes, by bringing warmth, self-sufficiency, and interdependence to our homes and communities."[22] Flinders argued that because of innate or at least culturally nurtured qualities, women were best able to perform the meaningful work of housekeeping. Home economists had argued instead that because women had traditionally done this work, it made sense for them to be educated in it. Simultaneously, they argued that the work should be understood on a larger scale—nutrition rather than just family meals, child psychology rather than just minding baby, and so on. Both Flinders and home economists called for a revision of domesticity in the interests of a healthier society, but where Flinders relied on the "natural" or organic process, home economists offered rationality and expertise.

Flinders's final statement prefigured the "Mommy Wars" of the early twenty-first century in which the issue of a middle-class woman's proper goals and behaviors became fodder for heated debate and much publishing. She recommended, "Any woman about to take a job should think carefully about the pressures compelling her choice and decide which are legitimate and which questionable. She should consider what her home and family and neighborhood stand to lose—and," Flinders added with a tweak on feminism, "she should never underestimate her own worth."[23]

In a doubly ironic twist, when the book's authors wanted advice on nutrition to support their claims for the healthfulness of a vegetarian lifestyle they turned to a male home economist. Bronwen Godfrey wrote the last third of the book, "Nutrition for a Meatless Diet," in consultation with George M. Briggs, professor of nutritional science at the University of California at Berkeley. This section included explanations of basic nutrition as well as food tables that could help readers to balance their own diets. It is worth noting that by the time this book was written, nutrition had so far escaped the stigma of domesticity that Godfrey's adviser was male. A generation earlier, Eleanor Roosevelt had turned to Flora Rose of Cornell for similar data. Godfrey, a trained nurse, turned to home economics when she consulted Briggs to reassure her audience that the vegetarian path was not one of starvation but rather a more healthful way to live and endorsed by at least one traditionally defined expert.

The section begins with an illustration by Robertson that reflected the trio's distinct approach to food habits as lifestyle. In the image, a young woman is holding a clipboard and making notations. Before her is a scientific scale, several beakers full of grains, and a few heavy books, one of which is propped open. Despite the trappings of professionalism, however, the space is clearly domestic and not a laboratory. There is an overstuffed armchair, a vase of flowers, and a bookcase in the background. A door is open to the kitchen, suggesting that her research will never stray far from that practical space. In one sense she is the home economist's dream girl because she is treating her home scientifically, but she also potentially represents the de-professionalization of domestic knowledge because she works outside the world of professional home economics. Godfrey's introductory words reflect the foundational principles of nutrition and echo earlier statements by Ellen Richards. Calling on readers to "reeducate our tastes and rethink many of our old eating habits," she argued, "Food should have value. . . . It is not enough for food to look and taste good; it should be nourishing, too." Admitting that this was a difficult focus to maintain "amidst the barrage of advertising and the clamor of old habits," she nonetheless advocated it as the route to "wellbeing."[24]

The concept of self-reeducation of one's attitudes was a common theme in writing during this period, just as "adjustment" had been a theme in the

1950s. With the Cold War still raging, the bitter aftertaste of the Vietnam War in the air, and much unrest at home, Americans still grappled with the question of whether to remake society or themselves and retained a persistent sense of social dissonance.

*Laurel's Kitchen*, with its scientifically endorsed pseudo-traditionalism, offered readers a solution to their confusion: a contemplative cuisine resulted in an ethically sound life. Godfrey provided food value charts that could serve as a map to this idealized future while Flinders offered a justifying philosophy of separate-spheres feminism and Robertson contributed recipes to fill a woman's day with virtuous production. For the authors of *Laurel's Kitchen*, consumerism, not gender inequality, was the major problem of modern society. The solution lay, therefore, in celebrating the value of women's unpaid traditional work in the home.

## The Rewards of Housework

While Flinders, Godfrey, and Robertson found implicit value in housework, other contemporary social critics wondered whether demanding wages for women's work in the home could solve the problem of gender inequality. This idea had emerged earlier in the first wave of the feminist movement, simultaneous to the development of home economics as a discipline. When asked her opinion of this idea, Martha Van Rensselaer, dean of the College of Home Economics at Cornell, had answered that housewives earned a "psychic reward" for their work.[25] To quantify it in terms of capitalist production would be impossible and was unnecessary. The housekeeper worked out of love for the end-goal, the ideal home. Van Rensselaer did not suggest that the work was innately female or that it had, indeed, anything to do with gender, but, given that women did perform the great majority of housework, her statement might be understood as a restatement of separate-spheres ideology in which the male sphere was all that was outside the home and was governed by the rules of the market while the complementary female sphere was interior and based in emotional and moral values. The idea of psychic reward also would seem to undermine Van Rensselaer's being involved in creating "domestic" careers outside of the home for women, including herself.

When the question of why women were not paid for housework reemerged in the late 1960s, the disconnection between how people relate to work in their own home and the capitalist system in which labor is sold became problematic again. Men and women who considered themselves Marxists and who hoped to reorder society in a more equitable fashion could not agree on how housework fit into their understanding of economic life. Were housewives creating value through their labor as maintainers of working men? Were they somehow productive because they sent forth new workers into the economy by giving birth to and raising their own children? Were women the original proletariat, oppressed by the men who themselves claimed oppression at the hands of bosses? Many questions were posed but few new scenarios suggested.[26]

In 1975, the Women's Work Study Group, a collective of socialist feminist scholars, sought to understand how housework functions in a capitalist economy. Although they struggled to apply terms to work that sometimes seemed the opposite of productive waged labor, the group concluded that "housework is valuable and important." The oft-repeated woman's apology "I'm just a housewife," they argued, reflected women's awareness that their labor was undervalued. "In America today," they argued, "there is a tendency to demean the work women do in the home" resulting in "an undervaluation of her contributions to people's welfare and to the maintenance of the capitalist system."[27] The housewife proved a complex issue for feminists; they did not want to be her, but to reject her life as meaningless was to alienate the majority of their potential audience and comrades. First-wave feminists found themselves in the uncomfortable position of convincing the majority of women that, personal feelings of satisfaction and trust in their own judgment aside, they were being oppressed. The Women's Work Study Group recommended a course of political organizing that addressed needs of women with waged work and housewives simultaneously.

While some pondered where the housewife's wages might come from (her husband? the state?) and whether they would be standardized and women's work subject to inspection by professionals, others thought the question was best avoided altogether because payment for housework could potentially legitimate "keeping" women in the home. The work was not the problem, these feminists argued. The problem, as ever, was who had the power. The idea of psychic reward drifted in and out of this debate, too, as women wondered how it would feel to be paid to look after one's own children as if the relationship were strictly business and not one with emotional elements. But then again, should a person be willing to work for free just because she loved the work?

Conversations that home economists had had in a previous generation about the interconnectedness of labor and life and art and science might have been useful here, but were in a sense culturally inaccessible to this generation. Betty Friedan's impassioned and impractical call for all women to discover and pursue what would really fulfill them as human beings perhaps only added a layer of confusion to the lives of women who did not have the economic resources to finance soul-searching. As Judith Viorst, a regular columnist in *Redbook*, pointed out as she voiced concerns about feminism, "It's true that some women are, in the dreariest meaning of the phrase 'just a housewife.' But some of them are 'just a lawyer,' too."[28] In the end, it may have been the emotional component of motherhood that caused this debate to stagnate. The "Mommy Wars" of today indicate that although how one keeps one's house is no longer an issue for public debate, who cares for one's children remains a violently divisive issue. The question of whether it is "right" to pay someone else to look after your children is hotly debated in books, articles, and parenting web logs by those who have the means to do so while the question of whether it would be ethical to accept wages to look after them yourself remains obscured. Because the common sense of our era retains something of the separate spheres ideology in which love is set in opposition to money, it is difficult to even imagine the transaction between employer husband and employee wife as anything but alienating and perhaps even degrading.

## Home Economists' Response to Feminism

Because they generally considered themselves progressive and concerned with raising the social status of women, home economists were shocked to discover that second-wave feminists did not see them as allies. When Robin Morgan addressed the American Home Economics Association as "the enemy" in 1971, the association was so disturbed that, as with Betty Friedan's remarks, it did not immediately publish her statement in its report of the annual conference, noting only that it had "touched off spirited discussion."[29] It took two years for the *Journal of Home Economics* to publish her attack, but when they did so, they embedded "What Robin Morgan Said" in a transcribed discussion among leaders in the field that gave deep consideration to her criticism and delved into the difficult issues of home economics in the age of women's liberation. Having assumed their own feminism, home economics leaders now looked for ways to connect to a new generation of women who seemed simultaneously to be reintroducing ideas pioneered by the movement and to be rejecting everything it stood for.

In Morgan's address to the AHEA she called on her audience to "quit [their] jobs," because their work supported all of the institutions—marriage, the nuclear family, and the consumer society—that "the radical women's movement [was] out to destroy." Where home economists saw themselves as mediators of these institutions, Morgan saw them as apologists. She claimed that the home economics courses that the average American schoolgirl had to pass through usually left her "a limp, jibbering mass of jelly waiting for marriage." Marriage itself she rejected as economic exploitation. If her audience still insisted on keeping their jobs, she urged them at least to work for change. Her first two, slightly contradictory, recommendations were that home economics no longer be required and then, that if it were required, that male students also be forced take it. Echoing Pat Mainardi's "The Politics of Housework," she suggested, "If men are trained in [household] jobs, they can't use the cop-out of saying, 'If I washed a dish, I'd break it.'"[30]

Many of Morgan's assumptions about home economists and her attacks on the field suggested that she did not know very much about it. For example, she upbraided the assembled home economists for failing to pay attention to environmental issues while in reality a concurrent session of the conference was addressing just this issue and the movement had itself been founded alongside the study of ecology. Similarly, identifying the field as "conservative and hypocritical," she called on home economists to "tell the truth about [the] housewife's role and about the way she is regarded and about the despair she faces in her life," glibly ignoring that the field had been organized around this very focus and that she herself had been invited to speak as part of a three-speaker panel on the status of women. The simple act of inviting Morgan (and Friedan before her) signaled an interest in changing ideas about gender and society.[31]

Despite the ferocity and occasional thoughtlessness of Morgan's attack, however, home economists in leadership positions took her words to heart. Forming a Women's Role Committee, the AHEA published proceedings of a conversation that members of this committee participated in during their formation. As Doris Hanson, executive director of the AHEA, explained, "one of the reasons for launching this committee was that when we tried to respond to Robin Morgan to tell her what we do and what we actually stand for, we didn't have it together ourselves."[32] They did not have data that they could present to convince Morgan and others that, they "weren't the problem." Marjorie East, president of the AHEA and head of the department of home economics education at Pennsylvania State University, argued, "[Morgan's attack] was good for the Association because she really did stir us up and made us take a second look at what we are doing." The attack gave home economists a rare moment to return to thinking about themselves as activists in a movement, which, while comfortably ensconced as a national institution, could still operate as a vehicle for social and cultural reform.[33]

East had been confused by Morgan's claim that home economics forced one version of womanhood on girls because in her experience, she said, "We've been teaching dual roles for years."[34] East thought that the problem might be that high school teachers were not successfully sharing this message with their students. Her colleague, Susan Weis, professor of home economics education at Penn State, thought that the problem of portrayal might come from home economists at all levels. Directing attention to a central paradox of the movement from its earliest days, she suggested, "We teach one lifestyle and we ourselves practice another lifestyle." While the *Journal* had published the occasional article about cooking classes for working women, the "normal" home assumed throughout the field was the married heterosexual household with two or more children.[35]

Hanson countered that in fact the "working model" that home economics teachers provided students, that of the "successful working woman who at the same time maintains a home," might be one of the reasons there was "no dearth of girls coming into home economics" courses.[36] A reader, Bernadine Peterson, responded to this discussion in a letter to the editor of the *Journal*'s next edition by asking, "Why do we continue to refer to woman's 'dual role'?" Arguing "that homemaking is sex-assumed in our society," Peterson, a home economics education professor at the University of Wisconsin, urged other home economists to give up the assumption that women were naturally inclined to domesticity. Women, like men, should feel free to define themselves with a single role—professional.[37]

So in fact Morgan had misunderstood the field when she called on home economists to "begin to deal with [their] oppression as women." Some felt that their professional training in the field allowed them to transcend sexism, while others, like Hanson, argued that home economists, because they were professional yet also domestic, had achieved the perfect balance in womanhood. The implications of Hanson's suggestion reflected a continued conflation of women with domesticity that bubbled to the surface throughout the conversation and that drew Peterson's criticism.

Weis, for example, repeated a traditional complaint of the field when she suggested, "The home economics profession has suffered because it was representing women's interests and needs." For Weis, however, the rise of feminism and the women's liberation movement seemed to offer a way out of this trap. Noting that they were "now entering a decade for women," she encouraged her peers to think about "both men and women and their various lifestyles." Arguing that many home economists were "not comfortable with the thought of teaching boys," she nonetheless, or perhaps consequently, argued, "It is timely to consider the ways home economics can benefit boys and men and to build educational programs accurately aimed at the needs and interests of both boys and girls." Progressive as this statement seemed, Susan Weis of the Women's Roles Committee still appeared to be uncomfortable with the idea that boys would simply join girls in home economics classes and that both gender groups would have the same "interests and need," in the home.[38]

An article in the October 1972 issue of the *Journal of Home Economics* had addressed "alternative" lifestyles, and East commented on it favorably, specifically drawing attention to "the willingness of both male and female to interchange roles," which made her hopeful for broader changes in society.[39] The question of how to teach this willingness brought up the crucial fact that although there were significant numbers of men teaching in home economics departments in colleges and universities, there were almost none at the secondary level. Because most of primary and secondary teaching profession was female and this was where the largest number of students would encounter home economics, and because domesticity was culturally coded as female, the topic continued to be identified with women. The cultural element was crucial to this process; although women frequently taught math and history, for example, neither subject became feminized.

The Women's Roles Committee recognized that their own secondary school textbooks perpetuated gender role stereotyping and that the basic lessons of courses at these levels focused on the practical rather than the analytical. A shift away from replicating women's work in the classroom and toward a sociological approach, they reasoned, might attract more men to secondary school education in home economics. One participant suggested that courses include a thorough analysis of the results of gender role stereotyping and others discussed the "masculine mystique" as a phenomenon that stood in the way of men's crossing gender boundaries.[40]

Virginia Trotter, vice chancellor of academic affairs at the University of Nebraska, suggested a "women's study program" that "might evolve out of the home economics curriculum" and that would debunk popular myths about women in the workforce, such as that female managers were more likely to leave a position than male managers. Susan Weis imagined this as an interdisciplinary program, "cooperatively developed with departments such as sociology and political science."[41]

Although none of the women mentioned it, just two years earlier, the University of Wisconsin Stout State University had offered a women's studies course in the home economics department. Listed in the course catalog as Topics in Family Life, the course was actually titled The Social Roles of Women in America. The two women who taught the course described a curriculum that treated social roles "analytically rather than descriptively" and moved "beyond analysis to feminist criticism."[42] There was a small but apparently growing interest in including women's studies in home economics. For Doris Hanson, this made sense historically as "the cause of women's rights has been fought on most universities by the Dean of Home Economics."[43] She might also, and perhaps more relevantly, have recalled that home economics departments in the 1920s had offered courses on women's roles from the perspective of economic history, anthropology, and economics.

Marjorie East, however, advised her colleagues that to infuse home economics programs with women's studies would just "reinforce the myth that we are concerned only about women and not about people." For East, it was crucial to "get to the boys in high school," in order to start changing gender expectations. The conversation ended on a hopeful note as members of the committee reminded themselves that younger colleagues in their profession were "really with it" and "more conscious of" changing gender roles. Ultimately, the group took responsibility for failing to convey the deeper messages of the movement to teachers at the primary and secondary levels and committed themselves to continuing discussion and improving communications about gender issues.

## The End of Home Economics

As much as the members of the Women's Role Committee seemed both to be surprised by Morgan's attack and to take it to heart, the truth was that home economics was already undergoing important changes by the time she made her critique. Transformations were particularly visible in higher education, where many departments and colleges of home economics were actually renaming themselves in order to present a new face to the public. In a 1954 letter to the *Journal of Home Economics*, Catherine Landreth, professor of child psychology at the University of Chicago, noted, "In a recent publication

Dr. Agnes Fay Morgan points out that the name 'home economics' does not describe the purpose and activities of members of our association on university campuses." Landreth agreed with Morgan, who had been a pioneer in the movement, establishing the home economics program at Berkeley, and offered a critique of alternatives that had been offered. Rejecting as "pretentious" the term "human ecology," which would later prove a popular choice, she settled on "home and family studies" as a name that would "indicate not only [their] area of interest and method of approach but also the multiple character of [their] undertaking." Rather than attempting to mask the multidisciplinary nature of the field, Landreth's suggestion foregrounded it.[44]

The name of the field had been an issue of debate from the movement's early days, but as Landreth's letter implies, this debate was finally producing actual change. The same year that Landreth asked, "Is There a Better Name for Home Economics?" the home economics department at Teachers College, Columbia, ceased to exist when it merged with the department of Marriage and Family Life to form the new Department of Home and Family Life. Teachers College had been one of the first institutions to invest in home economics education and some of the field's founding mothers and fathers had been Teachers College faculty, so the name change here might reasonably be seen as a bellwether. And indeed, name changes spread slowly but steadily through the field, signaling an end at least semantically to home economics.

Asking, "What's in a Name?" Patricia Durey Murphy, a doctoral candidate in home economics education at the University of Minnesota, provided a brief history of the debate over what to call the field. Looking back from 1967, Murphy noted that although attendees at the Lake Placid conference had chosen the name "home economics" in 1902, "through the years the question of the name of the field has continued to be discussed."[45] Although historian Margaret Rossiter argues that the name changes that began in the 1950s were part of the male incursion into home economics and a subsequent decline in female authority within the field, Murphy's article argued that the majority of home economists, most of whom were women, rejected the name themselves.[46] Intriguingly, she suggested that this was because home economics was stigmatized as women's work. "Apparently from all the controversy," Murphy reasoned, "This name just doesn't satisfy the needs of many for identity. Both Francena Miller and Mary Beth Minden speak of the unwillingness of professionals in the field to identify themselves as home economists. This may be due partly to the predominance of women in the field and/or to the nuances associated with it."[47]

Francena Miller was dean of home economics at the University of Connecticut and also served as executive director of the American Association of University Women, the nation's most powerful professional organization for academic women. Mary Beth Minden worked for the U.S. Department of Agriculture and was active in the AHEA. Both were influential figures and their acknowledgment that there was major dissatisfaction among home economists was itself important. It indicated that women with long-term commitments to the field and whose own self-definition was linked to it were open to fundamental change in the field.

Murphy's suggestion that women did not want to be associated with home economics because home economics was associated with women might well have reflected the growing influence of feminism and persistent gender inequality in the work world. Some young home economists might want to distance themselves from the field because of feminist vilification of it, whether or not they considered this perspective justified. Although individually they knew that they were not cooking and/or sewing for a living, their professional lives would certainly become more comfortable if this was not the predominant assumption connected to the term "home economics."

The study of women's roles in society, too, a pursuit that home economists had early helped to introduce to the academic and corporate world, now revealed the ghettoization of women in particular professions and encouraged younger women to define themselves according to professions rather than gender. The common culture of the generation entering college in the 1960s, too, which privileged personal self-determination over conformity, probably contributed to rejection of a name that seemed to tie practitioners to just one identity, that of housewife.

If this was the case, then the entrance of men into home economics, particularly at the top levels of academic administration, could have been experienced as a gain by female home economists, even while it might have disturbed the established culture of their field. In cases where men took over jobs previously held by women this was part of a generational as well as a gender shift as the first generation of home economists—women like Agnes Fay Morgan at Berkeley—retired after long careers in the field. Because men had traditionally enjoyed seemingly infinite opportunities in the professions and in business, their entrance into home economics ultimately can be seen as a sign of the field's success. There were now sufficient resources and potential for social status and cultural authority to attract men. The growing numbers of men in the field did not necessarily eclipse the truth that women had been responsible for the work of establishing the many subfields of home economics as viable professions.

It made sense for men who entered the field to push for name changes in order to secure social status for themselves. This should not be surprising, as home economists of the first generation had worried continually about whether their name adequately expressed their seriousness of purpose, expertise, and mission. In a sense, they too had worried whether it was not too "female," as the culture defined that term. These same women had still never been able to shake off the assumption, bolstered by vocational home economics classes in high schools, that their entire discipline was devoted to teaching cooking and sewing to future housewives. When men entered home economics as nutritionists or dieticians, child psychologists, or sociologists of marriage and the family, they would have wanted to bring with them the cultural gravitas that merely being male entitled them to. And simultaneously they would not have brought with them the naturalized connection to the domestic that women carried. A man who trained as a food scientist was not assumed to be simultaneously training for an "inevitable" role as cook for his family.

Because the original mission of home economics—to elevate homemaking to a profession—had failed, male home economists needed to dissociate themselves from the title in order to maintain status. And because gender inequality did really exist in power relations, female home economists were less able to accomplish this transformation by themselves at the time, despite the real interest in doing so that Miller and Minden cited. Simply put, they could have renamed their field "astrophysics" and the fact that they were women would have mattered more than the name that they chose. So although Rossiter is undoubtedly correct to point out the simple mathematics of power—men at helms of home economics programs resulted in exactly that many fewer women in these positions and the consequent loss of role models for younger women—the gender integration of the field did not drive women out and may in fact have served to raise the social status of the various divisions of home economics over time. Although numbers of women in former home economics departments did decline, they did so because of increased opportunities for women in all the other fields of academia and business.

Further complicating the narrative of transformation, not all departmental name changes were initiated by men. As Patricia Murphy noted, there were "family sociologists, family economists, family food scientists, human nutritionists, consumer economists, dieticians and others" who did not identify as home economists. Many prominent departments remained under female

women in those departments proposed name changes in order
. in the focus or methodology of the field that they themselves

ion in one area had led to emotional disconnection from the
general field. Although this can happen in any academically defined area of expertise, home economics presented a special case because subfields like nutrition and textile science were connected through a terrain—the home—that
experts in either field might never deal with directly. The faculty members of
foreign language departments presumably do not all speak each other's lan-
guages, yet they do share a common material—language itself. The same might
be said to be true of physicists, that although they practice in widely divergent
ways, they share a common methodology. The case of home economics was
not unique, however, and similar problems vex more recently created fields
such as business and communications. Because home economics had been
pieced together from other existing fields as well as new areas of focus, ties between departments did not have the strength of shared material or approach.
In the end, the connections could sometimes just seem like coincidences.

Renaming can be seen as an attempt to reconnect the pieces and to make a
new claim for legitimacy, so it will be worthwhile to consider briefly the implications of the field's new names. Despite the lack of a unified position on what
the field should be called, there does seem to have been a widespread consensus that a new name would mean both more precision and more power. The
two most common choices were "family and consumer sciences" and "human
ecology," each name reflecting a different approach to the field's public relations problems.

Family and consumer sciences emphasized the home economist's role as
mediator between individual and society as well as establishing the field as
contemporary in its deep involvement with consumer culture. The name also
implied variety within the field, suggesting that one might encounter family
scientists and consumer scientists but not necessarily a family *and* consumer
scientist. The name indicated that practitioners in the field would be analytical and experimental, scholars rather than housewives. Home economics,
while it had indicated an academic field of inquiry, also remained tied to a
single space—the domestic environment, whereas families and consumers
operated in a variety of spheres. At least rhetorically, this name change extended the field beyond the four walls of home.

"Human ecology" as a name similarly stretched the boundaries of the
field's material. No longer focused on just the home, nor even just the family,

now (former) home economists could be considered experts on the human condition in all its variety. Landreth argued that home economics could not live up to this name "without subsuming the entire content of the biological and social sciences." Nonetheless, several prominent departments, Cornell University notable among them, chose this title in the late 1960s.

The term "human ecology" was actually appropriated from an already existing but little-noticed subfield of sociology that emerged in the 1920s. Human ecology was the study of human interaction with our natural and constructed environments. The name "human ecology" appealed to some home economists because it was noticeably free of gender associations and also, like family and consumer sciences, suggested the study of phenomena rather than the practical application of skills to tasks. The generality of the name allowed for the retention of all of the core subjects of home economics while the field at large could be repositioned as more concerned with the larger themes of human existence than with the day-to-day.

Less popular than "family and community sciences" or "human ecology," names with some variation on the theme of "human development" were also common as home economics departments joined the renaming trend. "Life sciences" and "human services" were two others. All of the new names shared a flavor of objectivity as home economists made a final attempt to establish their authority over home life as originating outside that institution.

When the New Mexico State University Board of Regents changed the name of the home economics department there in 1997, the head of the department, Mary Ellen McKay, explained, "We think the name, family and consumer sciences, is really more representative of what we teach. . . . In the past when people heard about home economics, they thought our focus was entirely on the family. Today, we also focus on the consumer, so the name change is appropriate."⁴⁹ For decades, then, home economists in this and other schools had been laboring under false identities. Similarly, when Washington State University's College of Agriculture and Home Economics changed its name in 2003 to the College of Agriculture, Human, and Natural Sciences, Dean James Cook said, "the name change was necessary to update the college's image. Home economics has been a discipline at WSU for 100 years. But the nature of the field has changed dramatically and the term home economics no longer describes well the field of study." Noting that his institution was one of the very last to change its name, Cook looked optimistically to the future of this renamed field: "The name change reflects the fact that home economics has grown into the field known today as human sciences, now one of the fastest-growing areas in teaching, research and outreach in the United States."[50]

Despite the potential vagueness of terms like "human sciences" or "human ecology" for the general public, the fact remains that home economists like McKay and Cook have successfully liberated their field from automatic associations with women's lives and, by extension, with the trivial. Because of the failure of home economics to raise the status of "women's work," they have been forced to find another route to legitimacy and we cannot fault them if, like many an academic before them, they take refuge in the obscure. While home economics departments, then, have ceased to exist on American campuses, nutritionists have revised the "food pyramid," textile scientists have given us Lycra, and child development experts thrive in the era of standardized testing and medicalized childhood. And furthermore, as anyone who has turned on a television or glanced at a magazine rack in the past ten years knows, the American hunger to "work on" the domestic in all its variety is seemingly insatiable.

# Flip This Housewife

IN A SERIES of television commercials for Reynolds Wrap aluminum foil that began appearing in 2000, a pair of lab-coated women appeared onscreen and identified themselves as Pat and Betty, home economists. A Web site, the Reynolds Kitchen, features Pat and Betty and their extended tips on how to use the company's products around the house. Despite what one might think, given television advertising's habit of using actors to play experts, Pat and Betty really are home economists. Both have degrees in the field as well as many years' experience working in test kitchens and, in Pat's case, for state agencies.

I was very surprised to see the two women on my television set and wondered what their sudden appearance might mean, for Pat and Betty are obsolete signifiers. There was a time from the 1930s to the 1950s when the home economist was a cultural figure. Certainly, she was not as widely recognized as the Fuller Brush man, but she had a post on the staff of major women's magazines, she taught courses in public high schools, and she served on government advisory boards. Now, however, the home economist has passed into the mists of collective memory. Pat and Betty made me think about what impact home economics has had on popular culture. How has it survived outside of the Family and Consumer Science Programs, the Colleges of Human Ecology? What difference has it made to our culture?

Americans still expect and accept advice from professionals who are home economists, but they think of them as nutritionists, interior designers, family psychologists, and textile chemists. By the time the American Home Economics Association changed its name to the American Association of Family and

Consumer Sciences in 1994, most home economics departments had long since changed their names to rid themselves of the word "home."

Most people associate home economics with a high school class they may have been required to take in which they were offered obscure wisdom about casseroles or rolled hems. Because home economics as a unified topic has lingered longest in secondary schools, this is the image that remains. As Rima D. Apple, professor of human ecology and women's studies at the University of Wisconsin, writes, "Rather than training girls in critical thinking and urging women to reach outside the domestic sphere, twentieth century home economics in the public schools taught a narrow spectrum of domestic tasks."[1] Indeed, when I began this project, almost every one I mentioned it to immediately associated it with an unpleasant or confusing high school experience. Because of Title IX of the Educational Amendment Acts of 1972, which ended gender segregation in public school courses, some of the people who regaled me with bad memories of home economics are male. Since Title IX took effect, schools with home economics classes have opened them to boys while girls have also attended "shop" classes. In theory, this ought to have helped to realize some of the goals of home economists, disconnecting housework from gender stereotypes, but in practice, this does not seem to have been the result. This is largely because high school home economics never did include the kind of social analysis or abstract thinking that college programs did, foregoing theory for skills. So although a friend remembers making English muffin pizzas in her home economics class in Kentucky, she does not remember any related discussion about working parents who might rely on children to make their own after-school snacks. Without some kind of context for these skills, students seem not to respond with much enthusiasm.

Adults, however, have been known to get agitated. In 1975, a Baptist minister in New Milford, Connecticut, led a protest against a public school there where boys were assigned to home economics classes and girls to woodworking and metalworking classes. Reverend Lynn Mays argued, "By having a young boy cook or sew, wearing an apron, we're pushing a boy into homosexuality." His protest drew mainly negative responses, including one from a former marine, who asked if Mays "assumed that every veteran is a queer because he once stood mess hall duty or sewed on a new pair of chevrons after promotion."[2] Despite Mays's fears and feminists's, hopes, however, a 1980 study showed that putting girls in "shop" and boys in home economics was not yet breaking down gender stereotypes among youth.[3]

Even under its many new names, home economics still struggles to define itself against negative expectations. Virginia B. Vincenti, a professor of family and consumer sciences at the University of Wyoming, describes her field as "in an almost continual state of rethinking itself."[4] In 1984, when Marjorie Brown, a professor of home economics at the University of Massachusetts, was asked to help prepare a report on the field, she criticized home economists for what she saw as a relationship too friendly with manufacturers and "challenged the profession to ask itself constantly, 'Whose interests do we really serve?'"[5] The conflict that the first generation experienced between the project to establish themselves as expert academics and their mission to improve the lives of ordinary women continues to trouble their heirs. Vincenti herself calls for change, arguing, "Until our culture becomes less gender-biased, we will continue to have many societal problems that result from the marginalization of women, their ideas and values."[6] In other words, by sidelining women and "women's work," our culture shortchanges itself.

Pat and Betty, the Reynolds Wrap home economists, do not appear on our television sets to tell us about the ongoing identity crisis and commitment to social change in the field of home economics. They do not represent a sudden cultural yearning for the wisdom of Ellen Richards. They come to sell us tinfoil. Pat and Betty are a revival of the ideal home economists of an earlier era, but with an odd twist because that ideal has been out of circulation for so long. Rather than making the two women seem like agents of the modern, their lab coats and advanced degrees actually give them a retro charm. They put the kitsch in kitchen and this is probably where their value as advertising characters lies.

Another aspect of the Pat and Betty ads that struck me as noteworthy was that they are shown teaching a man how to cook. In fact, more and more adds for domestic goods are directed at men. Although this would seem to be a good thing, it is actually a sign of a movement away from valuing the work done in homes. Ads directed to men feature products that require absolutely no assembly or cleanup. Pat and Betty, for example instruct a young man on the wonders of cooking with aluminum foil—you just wrap the food in it, bake it, and then toss out the foil. And in the heretofore uncharted territory of male laundering, a detergent company offers men little pouches of detergent to toss into the wash. Presumably, measuring washing powder is one of those mysterious things, like breastfeeding, that only women can do. Similarly, Nestle offers men and boys "Hot Pockets," a calzone-like item that is kept in the freezer and heated in the microwave. It is advertised as a meal in one, not even requiring utensils, those fussy feminine implements.

Men, of course, are not the only people being offered simplified domesticity. Advertising domestic products to men is possible only because of a continuing trend to convince both women and men that housework of all kinds is "too much" and that no one has time for it. The January 2007 edition of the homemaking magazine *Real Simple*, for example, features a clock on its cover and the promise that nothing described in the magazine will take more than fifteen minutes to do. A nervous breakdown can even be averted by reading a brief article titled "In 15 minutes you can . . . snap out of a funk."[7] The February issue of *Better Homes and Gardens* for the same year includes a feature on how to get the most out of your "organizer-binder." The appointment books of three very busy "real" women are showcased, and tips such as color-coding types of appointments are revealed.[8]

The trend, both in domestic products and in domestic ideology, is obsessively to break down our days and activities into bite-sized segments that can be managed with to-do lists and containers of various sizes, colors, and textures. Soups that one drinks straight from the can are advertised (by Campbell's) as the perfect solution for women who are too busy to stop for lunch. And because these same women are probably also too busy for breakfast, several companies offer them sippable yogurts while Kellogg's provides cereal bars with a frosting-like layer of milk built in. No bowls, no spoons.

The message remains that housework is women's work and advertising continues to insist that a woman's social status depends on her ability to keep her house smelling like apple pie or ocean breezes rather than dogs, cigars, and sweat—the male world. But advertisers have picked up on the idea that women think of themselves as busier than ever, or at least that this idea can be used to sell more products. Whether women today are actually busier than their mothers were is hardly the point. What matters is that we live in a culture that values busyness for its own sake. Those who are not constantly on the run between activities (preferably a variety of money-making and physical improvement) are suspect. *Martha Stewart Living* magazine even urged readers to begin 2007 by painting walls of their homes with chalkboard paint so that to-do and to-buy lists could become part of the décor.[9] Feeding into and off of this culture, advertisers assure consumers that they are sympathetic to the plight of the modern woman, almost always coded as a mom. She wants to do the best for her kids but she just doesn't have time.

Simple processes like roasting a chicken or making a cake are presented as Herculean labors. The subtext can be described as consumerist-feminist: "Who has time to be Betty Crocker anymore? We have active lives to live." In reality, manufacturers do not want people to make their own pot roasts or use baking soda as a scouring powder because they want to sell dinners and cleansers. What is happening in advertising, then, is not that men are being treated like women, not that it is becoming acceptable for men to engage in domestic work, but that women are being treated more like men—people who have no time for domestic tasks.

There is still an important difference in the portrayal of gender roles in advertising around domestic goods. A detergent is not sold to men and women in the same way. The little pouches of detergent marketed to men might at first seem to suggest that men are simply too stupid to do their own laundry. The real message, of course, is that men are a sort of gender aristocracy who have much more important things to do than clutter their minds with domestic knowledge. A man does not need to know how much soap to put in the washing machine because there are women, and now major manufacturers, to figure it out for him. Although women are being appealed to now as impossibly busy people, the responsibility for domestic work is still upon them. This is part of their busyness. When men do the laundry it is not because they are super dads but because they need clean clothes and are not married. When men microwave foods like Hot Pockets it is to feed themselves, not provide a "home-cooked" meal for their family. Even in the instances where a man is shown preparing dinner for his family, his way is made easier by prepared foods. In an ad for Hamburger Helper, when a wife jokes that her husband's "cooking" (adding pre-packaged ingredients to meat) is something she could get used to, he reacts with a frightened look. The message is that male involvement in domestic work is only ad hoc, not a question of identity. The nutritious breakfast, the white shirt collar, the "mountain-fresh" bathroom are still all markers of a woman's success at achieving her gender. It is now also a marker of her gender that she feels oppressed by all that is expected of her—housework and personal fulfillment cannot coexist easily.

This internal tension is at the root of the "Mommy Wars," which although tangential to contemporary home economics are nonetheless worth noting here. The Mommy Wars are the result of ideals in conflict as a generation of middle-class, educated women raised in a largely pro-feminist culture bore children and discovered that it is difficult to be successful in the professional and domestic worlds simultaneously. Some adamantly defend their choice to leave the waged world of work and devote their time to raising their children. Others just as firmly defend their choice to work professionally and balance this with a combination of paid child care and personal intervention. Both sides tend to pay lip service to the concept of respecting other's choices while not very subtly suggesting that their own decisions are best for everyone. The debates themselves are strictly bound by factors of class. Most American women, after all, are not able to "choose" to stay home. Just what qualifies as "staying home" is also unclear as some "stay-at-homes" earn money or at least spend time writing about their lifestyle for a public audience.

The debates are also curiously bound by blindness to an even larger context, that of the meaning of labor and its relation to our happiness. The debate is always phrased in terms of the failures and successes of feminism and for this reason, men are generally left out of the equation. While combatants in the Mommy Wars wrangle over whether a woman is more valuable to her children as a constant presence or as a wage-earning role model who experiences satisfaction from her work, no one asks the same of men. It is assumed that their highest value to their families is in their paychecks. Some "stay-at-home dads" are beginning to challenge this assumption, but they are still rare enough to be remarkable. And it is notable that middle-class women who work outside their homes still feel compelled to justify their choices by arguing that child care and housekeeping can still be kept to a high standard.

Curiously, women can now escape temporarily from the stress-laden torments of household responsibilities into the worlds of Home and Garden Television (HGTV) or a domestic arts and crafts project detailed in one of the many housekeeping magazines or companion web sites. The occupational therapy approach to domesticity of course began with Martha Stewart, who established a business empire by teaching women (her assumed audience) to concentrate on the decorative aspects of life. Stewart's name and aesthetic are more pervasive in discussions of modern domesticity and in the market for domestic goods than any other person's today, although her rivals have multiplied significantly since she began her career. Stewart's wide appeal comes from her promises to give her audience the ability to live beyond their means through the power of do-it-yourself cuisine and decoration. In the process, she firmly separates science from the home. First-generation home economists might have admired Stewart for making such a good living through marketing domestic expertise, but they would probably have bewailed her disinterest in science and labor.

The domestic projects Stewart models on her television show and in her magazine focus on making things pretty rather than efficient. Stewart never appears in uniform and there is no sense that she is experimenting with anything. Her projects are not learning experiences. She offers her audience a way to climb the class ladder, if only aesthetically. Each object a woman makes under Stewart's remote tutelage gives her home "class." She knows this because Stewart herself is classy. Calm, blond, irreproachably (though falsely) Yankee, Stewart cultivates an air of old money. Her crafts are not about showing off how much money one has. Instead, they are about an imagined and constructed quality known as "graciousness." Graciousness is the opposite of the frenzied female lifestyle that advertisements portray. The gracious lady always has time to make her own soup and to sit and eat it out of a lovely china bowl. She probably wove the place mats herself. Many of Stewart's projects have a homey quality, but this is there to make them seem "traditional" rather than folksy. The craft activities are designed to make it possible for middle-class women to acquire many of the decorative touches that wealthier women inherit or buy.

Stewart shares with the first generation of home economists the goal of making a profession out of domesticity, with one very important exception: Stewart's goals are limited to her own career. She has made a fortune out of presenting herself as the single most reliable expert on gracious domesticity, rather than presenting ways in which other women (and men?) can use domestic arts to advance their own careers. Her message is not that any home can be professionalized, but that it can be prettified. Indeed, the prettiness she encourages is subtly offered as an escape from the professional. Nothing she makes is necessary. All of her projects require us to disconnect from our workaday lives in order to calmly apply decoupage to plain glass bud vases. Her lessons in arrangement serve the purpose of a kind of collective occupational therapy. This is done in the interest of achieving graciousness in our homes to contrast with the assumed busyness of our non-craft oriented lives.

Stewart's persona as businesswoman never intrudes into her domestic classroom. She doesn't talk about board meetings, market shares, or insider trading but gives the impression that she is always just puttering about the house, efficiently creating beauty with every step. For her primarily female audience, she represents yet another set of impossible goals. Her steely calm never cracks as she challenges her audience to be never frazzled and always dexterous.

To her credit, Stewart attempts to convince her audience that there is pleasure in domestic work, that just being at home and enjoying domestic life can be "a good thing." She is able to make so much money doing this, however, precisely because of all the other market forces telling women that they do not have time for homemaking and telling men that it is not any of their business. Attention to domestic aesthetics and to food made "from scratch" becomes a hobby, something like fly tying or model building, rather than a vital part of everyday life. We follow Martha's instructions to make braided rugs out of old towels or hand-blown Easter eggs in order to "reconnect" with some romanticized version of womanhood when women's lives were themselves decorative, rather than actually productive or participatory.

Cheryl Mendelson, author of *Home Comforts*, the best-selling housekeeping encyclopedia published in 1999, similarly encourages readers to find pleasure in domesticity, although her approach is less decorative and more microscopic.[10] Mendelson's work echoes the tone of early home economists who sought to arm the housekeeper with the most contemporary wisdom about their homes. Her approach, particularly when she talks about household germs, is scientific, if perhaps also a little alarmist. For Mendelson there is far too much dust in the world and far too little ironing. Like the first generation of home economists, too, Mendelson writes of the home in the context of the world around it. She gives legal advice and suggests effective ways to organize a home office, acknowledging that a housekeeper may have other roles, too.

Unlike professional home economists, however, and like Stewart, Mendelson makes it plain that her expertise is based in personal experience rather than professional training and research. She has borrowed much of her material from sources created by home economics professionals, but her own voice is that of a skilled amateur. Since *Home Comforts* was published, many have dwelt on what the popularity of Mendelson's book can tell us about women's culture in America at the beginning of the twenty-first century. Ultimately, however, because Mendelson sells neither products nor a personality, as Stewart does, her work has had little impact on the culture at large.

Cultural critic Katha Pollitt attacked the book on several fronts, lumping it with Martha Stewart's work in decorative domesticity, despite Mendelson's own rejection of what she describes as "playing house instead of making house."[11] Pollitt argues that Mendelson's devotion to the work of the home is both a symptom of severe class division in America and antifeminist in its spirit. Because only an upper-middle-class woman would actually have the time and economic support to take up Mendelson's call, the book reflects our culture's failure to recognize the difficult circumstances of most women's lives that do not allow time or space for hanging out the laundry and later ironing the sheets. To revere domesticity also, she argues, is to ignore the realities of women's lives and simultaneously to limit women's opportunities for self-fulfillment.[12]

Caitlin Flanagan, of Mommy Wars fame, declared Mendelson's book "this generation's most important book on" housekeeping, although admitting that, because of her own lassitude, she would probably not follow much of the advice therein.[13] Flanagan praised the book for its attempt to restore dignity to housework, seeing in this a critique of second-wave feminism's attempt to reject domesticity—and the stay-at-home mom. Indeed, Mendelson gently suggests such a criticism when she writes that when "Feminist historians" argue that technological advances in domestic life in the 1950s merely freed housewives for "superfluous" tasks, "they devalue the goals of that era's housewives." She writes, "I am not convinced that they are being fair."[14] Now, she suspects, a generation of young women await her book, women who were taught by their mothers to reject housekeeping, but who in reality "have confided to me, sadly, that they sometimes felt as though they were being driven from things feminine and domestic by mothers," and now, although "supercompetent" in their professional lives, "feel inept and lack confidence when they find themselves wanting to make a home of their own." Although Mendelson admits that "you can be male and be domestic," it is important to note that by being "kept from" domestic knowledge, these sad young women were being severed from their femininity.[15]

The popularity of Mendelson's book may indeed come partly from the author's attempt to reclaim housework for women who do not like to think of themselves as housewives. Proudly informing her readers that she has practiced law and has taught philosophy at the college level, Mendelson wants to reassure her audience that she is not "just a housewife." Her self-identification is complicated by her attempt to rehabilitate housewifery while avoiding talking about gender roles. This is an awkwardness that ironically probably helped to sell her book.

Women who have forged their adult identities through waged work but now find themselves concentrating on domestic life would seem to be her ideal audience. Home Comforts can make such women feel professional about home life, but the book does not actually do the work that home economists originally attempted, the work of changing the social status of housekeeping. In a statement seemingly designed to reassure women who feel uncomfortable about having made a choice to focus on home, Mendelson unconsciously echoes an earlier writer on the tensions between feminism and domesticity. As mentioned earlier, Judith Viorst, writing in *Redbook* in 1974, noted that while it was true that some women were miserably "just housewives," others were miserably "just lawyers," too. Mendelson goes one step further, asserting, "I can assure you that it is actually lawyers who are most familiar with the experience of unintelligent drudgery."[16]

The problem revealed by Mendelson's justification is that different kinds of work have always been valued differently by society and that this differential, frequently based in ideas about gender, has been internalized by most people by the time they reach early adulthood. Although a lawyer might experience more actual drudgery than the housewife, he or she is usually compensated handsomely with money and social status for such work and at a rate that is today (pretty much) gender neutral. The homemaker, meanwhile, must rely on her own sense of her importance to her family for her reward. It is exactly because domestic work in one's own home is unpaid and low-status that Martha Stewart and the many domestic shows and magazines have been able to succeed. For those who do this work, Stewart and others offer validation. Homemaking is newsworthy, the housewife a valued commodity.

Stewart's empire has spawned much imitation, but it has also caused a subtle kind of backlash that defines contemporary domestic expertise in American culture. This backlash is evident in a variety of domestic "personalities," including Rachael Ray and Paula Deen and in the new "quick-fix" gospel of homemaking magazines, television shows, and web sites. Perhaps the perfect example of this genre is *Semi-homemade*, a show on the Food Network that features perky, slender Sandra Lee assembling treats from prepackaged ingredients. An especially entertaining example has her mauling a store-bought apple pie to use its innards as filling for two layers of frozen puff pastry in the construction of a napoleon. Of course she tops it off with some liquor-spiked Reddi-wip.

Looking at contemporary domestic advice media, it seems that Martha's perfectionism finally exhausted some of her audience. While they may still buy her magazine, watch her show, and enjoy thinking about one day possibly starting one of her projects, they have made room for other domestic divas in their hearts. These divas, some of whom are men, are slapdash, even slovenly. Watching Paula Deen prepare fried chicken on a recent episode of *Paula's Home Cooking*, I was distracted from the action by a fat old dog lying in a corner of her kitchen. When I determined that the dog was actually alive, my attention drifted around her knick-knack-filled kitchen as I wondered where she would roll out a pie crust or put down a bag of groceries. And all the while, Deen was frying pieces of chicken and slathering them in honey pecan sauce, diffidently reminding us that it was not *her* recipe, but one borrowed from a friend.[17] Deen's charm for her fans, presumably, is in her "realness," her unpolished humanity and good cheer, her un-Marthaness. She is like a modern incarnation of Aunt Jenny, the radio character who made everything with Spry shortening and told stories sent in by her listeners. Deen's authority, like that of Aunt Jenny before her, resides in her experience, not her expertise. Now even the amateur expert, like Martha, has become too oppressive, and consumers look for someone friendlike and abundantly mortal.

Similarly, Rachael Ray is "real," a bundle of energy who just tosses things together, licks her fingers, invents words as she goes along, and is often convulsed in giggles. It is clear that there is much that she does not know and that her lack of knowledge does not bother her. She is the archetypal good-time gal, and her kitchen reflects it. Although the kitchen itself is spacious and equipped with top-of-the-line appliances, its backdrop—a cityscape seen through a window set in a brick wall—undermines all this. We are supposed to imagine that Ray lives in an apartment in a somewhat rough part of a northeastern city. The aesthetic is a direct challenge to Stewart's refined country-home milieu. Ray's appliances do not match, and all are brightly colored, suggesting "working class" and "1950s" simultaneously. The viewer is supposed to understand that Ray offers neither the finest nor the latest techniques. Rachael Ray is in no way better than you, and for that reason you should trust her.

Where Paula Deen and Rachael Ray democratize the kitchen by insisting on their own amateurism, many popular television shows do similar work in the world of interior design. *While You Were Out* and *Trading Spaces* give ordinary people the opportunity to redecorate other people's homes in an odd kind of competitive and possibly vindictive act. Who will finish first? Who will be most aesthetically outrageous? Skill is not much of an issue in such shows, even as the teams are coached by professional decorators. Glue guns, heavy-duty staplers, and slipcovers do much of the work. For all the representations of luxury and personal expression that are part of *Extreme Makeover: Home Edition*, with its manic yet soulful host, Ty Pennington, that the houses are built and decorated in two weeks suggests a kind of ephemerality to the domestic that might be unsettling. For producers of domestic products, however, this representation of the home as a quickly demolished, instantly remodeled "gift" (the family does not pay for its new house) is surely welcome.[18]

Although the mania for decorating shows began with a focus on renovation, allowing for constant product and vendor endorsement, the home itself quickly became a commodity and the number of shows about selling private homes seems to be increasing. In these shows, viewers learn, for example, which are the key changes to make to their homes to maximize resale prices and how to attract buyers. Where home economists celebrated the home as a permanent expression of a family's character, shows like *Flip This House* and *Curb Appeal* present it solely as a commodity. Home is an asset not a refuge. Herbert Hoover once called the home the basic unit of society; in these shows it has become a unit of currency. In this new way of thinking about the home, the housewife becomes marketing agent as well as consumer. Managing the home is still her profession, but on *Flip This House* that management is depersonalized and domesticity is finally fully immersed in the cash economy. Investing has become more important than nesting.

The personal aesthetic, an elusive entity that early home economists sought to develop down the particular paths of naturalistic minimalism, is now also for sale. If a homeowner lacks a strong design sense, she or he need only consult the HGTV web site, where a quiz divides the hapless into sixteen categories, each category a genre in commercial furniture production. I, for example, am traditional, transitional, and (Ellen Richards would be glad to know) Arts and Crafts.[19] And if I feel unrepresented by these styles, I am welcome to consider how my horoscope should direct my aesthetic with the program *What's Your Sign? Design*.

Aside from this turn to the astrological, much of the advice presented on home shows, magazines, and web sites is standard home economics wisdom. A brief video posted on the HGTV web site, "Go with the Kitchen Flow," even notes, "In the 1950s, Cornell University developed the triangle as a way of conceptualizing" the relationship between a kitchen's three main appliances, the sink, refrigerator, and stove.[20] Another such instructional slide show, "Five Steps to the Perfect Sanctuary," explains that "to build a working space you need to first break it down. And that all boils down to function." Prepackaged aesthetics are all very well, but rooms still have to work for their inhabitants physically, as well as emotionally.[21]

The "common-sense," as opposed to the commodified, approach to domestic life, is most evident in the growing field of child-care advice as entertainment. Television has been slower to introduce shows on this topic than on any other angle of domestic life and this is notably something that both Martha Stewart and Cheryl Mendelson avoid. I suspect that this is because child rearing is both as personal and infinitely more important than drape selection or appetizer choice. People feel more strongly defensive of their choices in this area than in any others. After all, a poorly raised child cannot just be "flipped."

A series of shows on Discovery Health Channel treads the dangerous terrain of childrearing carefully, attempting to provide a generalized mood of supportiveness, rather than prescription. *Yummy Mummy*, a Discovery Health Channel show, advertises itself as "for mothers of the MTV generation," suggesting that there is a whole cohort of women who reject the traditional image of mothers as willingly sacrificing their individuality for the sake of their children. Child-care issues are interspersed with beauty "news" and strategies for finding "some priceless personal time for yourself." More boldly, Jo Frost, a notably sensible English woman, enters real homes and makes real changes. She is not, however, a child psychologist or family therapist; she is "Supernanny." One hundred years of home economics research and education are all subverted by Mary Poppins.

Professionals do turn up in housekeeping magazines, where their brief articles routinely either reassure the anxious or alarm the complacent. Even in magazines, however, the child psychologist does not enjoy total authority. Just as often as experts are consulted, "real" women (and sometimes men) offer lessons from their own experience that are presented as just as valid as theories developed through research and analysis. Americans, it seems, want lots of advice, but they do not want to have to evaluate any of it. As choices are increasingly presented exclusively in terms of products, evaluation becomes selection based on available options rather than critical thinking.

Analysis was at the heart of the home economics project, and the elusiveness of this quality in our culture is probably both cause and result of the movement's failure to transform us. Recently, an emerging popular interest in environmentalism has directed new attention to how we use resources in our homes, and this may be positive change towards the best kind of thinking that home economists encouraged.

By thinking about resources and achieving a basic level of self-sufficiency as to our daily lives, we maintain a measure of independence from forces of the consumer economy. Simply put, if you can sew a button on your shirt, you do not have to rely on a dry cleaner to do it for you (or a department store to sell you a whole new shirt). If you can make your own soup, you do not contribute to the mass homogenization of tastes, and you take some control over your own diet. Much of domestic work may even provide opportunities for self-expression. That said, I am a terrible housekeeper and would rather never dust again in my life. Yet I do it because I know that despite my loathing it is perfectly easy to do and something that I can do on my own without even the latest implements. A piece of an old t-shirt does the trick.

The culture that home economics was created in response to has changed, but this culture has not yet become more amenable to the movement's message. Domestic work is still unvalued except, in the case of Martha Stewart, as a hobby, or as entertainment on television shows such as *Mission: Organization*, where messy closets are presented as major crises. Ordinary women are encouraged to think of housework as an albatross. Ordinary men are not encouraged to think about it at all. Women's connection to food, home, and children is generally portrayed as both natural and a burden, one that can be lightened (with new, improved products), but not one that can really be shared with men. *Real Simple* includes in its list of "kitchen shortcuts" an encouragement to "enlist help, even if it's just for one task," because "kids and spouses make terrific herb washers, lemon squeezers, ingredients adders, and stirrers."[22] Family members can help, but the ultimate responsibility for the kitchen devolves on just one adult and, reflected in columns, photography, and advertising alike, that adult is female.

There has been some movement, beginning in the very late twentieth century, toward increasing male involvement in child rearing and this may lead to an increased connection to the domestic as, presumably, women's close relation to children is how they got stuck in the household to begin with. Men appear on cooking shows, although traditionally they do so as professional chefs, while women, like Rachael Ray, are often "just" cooks. In addition, the increasing cultural acceptance of homosexuality has somewhat loosened or broadened definitions of masculinity. The hit television series *Queer Eye for the Straight Guy* introduced the American viewing public to men who cooked, decorated, and dressed stylishly. However, because they were gay, stereotyped as "feminine," their attention to domestic detail never challenged traditional ideas of masculinity. Indeed, their makeover project proved his heterosexuality through his ignorance of all things designed.

When home economists set out to change the world, they did so within the confines of their culture. They attempted to make both women and men believe that domestic work has intrinsic worth and that knowing the best methods connects a person more powerfully to the world around her. They failed in this goal partly because advertising professionals saw that money could be made by exploiting the notion of housework as drudgery and partly because they themselves were not ready to shift half the burden of domestic work onto men. The first generation wanted to raise the status of domestic work and domestic workers so they made a modern, professional, analytical science out of all that related to home life. They stopped short, however, of calling for an end to the pervasive conflation of women with the domestic. They made domestic work "fit" for men to do—serious and scientific—but were only able to achieve this transformation outside of the home, in corporate labs and academic departments. Although by the 1950s increasing numbers of men were drawn to home economics work in fields such as nutrition, child psychology, textile science, and institutional management, most men still do not connect their self-worth to domesticity in the way that many women more or less comfortably do.

The culture in which the first generation lived and worked could not conceive of domestic work as something to be shared and enjoyed equally by both men and women. The work was so deeply gender coded that even the people who revolutionized it in every other way could not think of insisting that it was gender neutral. Home economists of the first generation did not emphasize the sociopolitical aspects of their thinking. They believed that housework was something that had to be learned in order to be done well. Its secrets were not lodged in a woman at birth nor could she just pick it up effectively at her mother's knee. They even went so far as to offer home economics classes to boys and men, but they did not take the next step of pushing for domestic work equality.

In part they did not see the need for this step because so many of them did  not live with men and so did not experience this inequality first hand. They balanced professional and domestic lives but when they encountered sexism it was much more likely to be in the context of the professional world than at home. Another factor in determining the limits of the politicization of the home economics movement was that the idea of married women in the paid workforce was still new and the numbers of women with families who worked still relatively low. The idea that women would pursue professions just as many men did was also new. As we know, this idea still causes cultural confusion, mostly because the work world was designed for male heads of families who relinquished all child-rearing and housekeeping responsibilities to women in an age-old pattern of gender partnership. As historian Alice Kessler Harris argues in *In Pursuit of Equity*, gender ideology has very often obscured conceptual possibilities as well as limited opportunities day-to-day.[23] Of course, it is pure speculation to suggest that had the conceptual restrictions of their times been removed, home economists of the first half of the century would have argued loudly and persuasively for change in gender ideology. It is impossible to imagine precisely because it did not happen.

I think that there can no longer be any doubt that leaders of the first generation of the home economics movement intended their work to expand professional and social opportunities for women. Although, as Sarah Stage commented in 1997, "Historians have for the most part dismissed the home economics movement as a force for expanding women's options," this oversight has been significantly repaired by the collection of essays that Stage herself edited with Virginia Vincenti.[24] In addition, the expansion of the field of cultural history has begun to allow us to understand more and more of human experience as actually "political," in ways that we did not recognize before.

A movement need not be either radical or conservative, nor even successful to deserve attention. Historians who interest themselves in chronicling shades of gray suggest that it is perfectly possible to be both liberationist and restrictive at once. My own sense of the home economics movement is that many of its leaders experienced the movement as liberationist in their own lives. By creating it they created themselves, establishing positions that were at once outside and also compatible with traditional gender roles. Because they did not have the category of gender to work with in the same way that we have today they were able to express the liberationist potential of the home economics education only in limited ways. They could and did envision women making new roles for themselves in the professional world and believed, too, that they could change the valuation of women's work in the unpaid domestic sector. Because they focused all their efforts on changing the lives of women, rather than on attacking gender categories, however, their work was limited in its success as a vehicle for critique of society.

# NOTES

INTRODUCTION

1. Abigail Tucker, "Beyond Homemaking," *The Post-Star* (Glens Falls, N.Y.), March 11, 2003.

2. Survey, conducted by the National Restaurant Association, quoted in "U.S. Restaurant Chains Find There Is Not Too Much," *New York Times*, July 28, 2006.

3. One of the most controversial contributors to what have come to be known as the "Mommy Wars" is Caitlin Flanagan, author of *To Hell with All That: Loving and Loathing Our Inner Housewife* (New York: Little Brown, 2006), whose columns in the *Atlantic* have dealt with issues such as what working mothers sacrifice in terms of family ties and fair pay for nannies.

4. Alice B. Neale, "Furnishing; or Two Ways of Commencing Life," *Godey's Lady's Book*, November 1850.

5. Catharine Beecher and Harriet Beecher Stowe, *The American Woman's Home* (New York: J. B. Ford and Company, 1869), p. 19. Much has been written about Catharine Beecher. The best place to begin is still with Kathryn Kish Sklar's biography, *Catharine Beecher: A Study in American Domesticity* (New York: W. W. Norton and Company, 1976).

6. Beecher and Stowe, *The American Woman's Home*, p. 17.

7. M. O. J., "Aunt Martha's Prevention," *Arthur's Home Magazine* (April 1870): 230.

8. Ellen Richards, *The Rumford Kitchen Leaflets* (Boston: Rockwell and Churchill Press, 1899), p. 12. Ellen Richards, *Report to the Massachusetts Board of World's Fair Managers*, December 27, 1893. Permanent online exhibit, MIT Institute Archives and Special Collections, http://libraries.mit.edu/archives/exhibits/esr/; Ellen Richards, *The Rumford Kitchen Leaflets*, p. 16. Although there was also a model kitchen in the Women's Pavilion, Richards and Abel's kitchen was part of the Sanitation and Hygiene "department" housed in the Anthropologic building. The kitchen in the Women's Pavilion, part of Illinois's contribution to the fair, demonstrated many methods of cooking corn, whereas the Rumford Kitchen had a wider focus. Placement with sanitation and hygiene and with anthropology rather than with women's achievements most likely seemed appropriate to home economists who, while not disavowing traditional gender roles, attempted to transcend them.

9. Rumford, who fled America as a loyalist during the Revolution, lived in Europe and was made Count of the Holy Roman Emperor in 1791 for work he had done as an assistant to the Elector of Bavaria. He was one of the great innovators of his day with a broad range of interests typical of intellectuals of the era.

10. Lake Placid Conference on Home Economics Proceedings, 1899, p. 3

11. Ibid., pp. 6–7.

12. See Dolores Hayden, *Grand Domestic Revolution* (Cambridge, Mass.: MIT Press, 1981), for a fascinating discussion of early feminist thinking about domestic space.

13. *Second Annual Conference on Home Economics* (Lake Placid, N.Y., 1900), quote on p. 13.

14. *Fourth Lake Placid Conference on Home Economics* (Lake Placid, N.Y., 1903), p. 11.

15. See Steven Diner, *A City and Its Universities* (Chapel Hill: University of North Carolina Press, 1980), for a discussion of the connection between the development of the modern research university and progressive projects and politics. See also his discussion of women's professions in the Progressive Era in *A Very Different Age* (New York: Hill and Wang, 1998), p. 178.

16. Letter from Sarah Louise Arnold to Martha Van Rennselaer, December 31, 1917, 23/2/749 Series II, Box 14, Folder 38, New York State College of Home Economics Records (NYSCHE Records).

17. "The New Reform Is Better Food," *Fort Wayne Morning Journal-Gazette*, June 23, 1901, p. 16.

18. "Learning Home Arts," *New York Times*, October 31, 1909, p. SM11.

19. "Making Good Wives Is School's Work," *Chicago Daily Tribune*, September 27, 1903, p. 52.

20. Martha Beasley Bruere, "Why Girls Should Not Be Taught to Do Housework," *Independent*, March 20, 1916, pp. 416–17.

21. *Fourth Annual Lake Placid Conference on Home Economics* (Lake Placid, N.Y., 1902), p. 22.

22. Ibid., p. 23.

23. "Living by Chart," *Chicago Tribune*, May 3, 1903, p. 20. The fact that the writer identifies these ideas as belonging to "alumnae," that is college-educated women, from Boston suggests that he or she may have harbored hostilities toward the kinds of women who lived in "Boston marriages," the domestic partnerships of educated women that flourished particularly in this northeastern area, where so many women's colleges could be found. It is too much to suggest that the writer was homophobic, since the term "lesbian" was never used to define these relationships, but it is certainly implied here that women who lived with other women did not understand "real" life.

24. (Mary Hinman Abel?), "The Home Economics Movement in the United States," *Journal of Home Economics* (October 1911): 330, 329.

25. M. Carey Thomas, *Women's College and University Education* (New York: Educational Review, 1908), p. 77. For a discussion of Thomas's reaction to home economics, see Sarah Stage, "Home Economics: What's in a Name?" in Sarah Stage and Virginia B. Vincenti, eds., *Rethinking Home Economics: Women and the History of a Profession,* and Helen

Lefkowitz Horowitz (Ithaca, N.Y.: Cornell University Press, 1997), *The Power and Passion of M. Carey Thomas* (New York: Alfred A. Knopf, 1994).

26. From the Eighth Lake Placid Conference Proceedings, quoted in Anne M. Fields and Tschera Harkness Connel, "Classification and the Definition of a Discipline: The Dewey Decimal Classification and Home Economics," *Libraries and Culture* 39, no. 3 (Summer 2004): 253. In a traditional Anglo-American folk song, "Billy Boy," a mother questions her son about his sweetheart's domestic abilities.

27. Undated note card in "Public Addresses on Home Economics," Box 1, RG12 130, Bureau of Home Economics papers, National Archives and Records Administration (NARA).

28. Undated interview with Flora Rose, c. 1953, conducted by Mary Philips, Box 32, Folder 14, NYSCHE Records.

CHAPTER ONE

1. Lita Bane, *The Story of Isabel Bevier* (Peoria, Ill.: Chas. A. Bennett Co., Inc., 1955), p. 37.

2. Ibid., 40–41.

3. Mary Philips, interview with Flora Rose, c. 1953, Box 32, Folder 14, New York State College of Home Economics Records, Cornell University Division of Rare and Manuscript Library, Ithaca, N.Y. (NYSCHE Records).

4. Caroline Percival, *Martha Van Rensselaer* (Ithaca, N.Y.: Alumni Association of the New York State College of Home Economics at Cornell University, 1957), p. 6. Nancy Tomes also refers to this anecdote in *The Gospel of Germs* (Cambridge, Mass.: Harvard University Press, 1998), p. 141, noting, "Home economists sought to teach not only the rules for disease prevention but also the scientific rationale for why their observance was so important."

5. Sanitary Science Club of the Association of Collegiate Alumnae, *Home Sanitation: A Manual for Housekeepers* (Boston: Ticknor, 1887), p. 8.

6. Bane, *The Story of Isabel Bevier,* p. 36.

7. "Bevier Anecdotes, 1929" (Recollections collected in 1932), Box 2, Bevier Papers, University of Illinois Archives, Urbana-Champaign (UIUC Archives).

8. Tomes, *Gospel of Germs,* p. 138.

9. Ellen Richards, *The Chemistry of Cooking and Cleaning* (Boston: Estes & Lauriat, 1882), p. 4.

10. Whitman H. Jordan *Principles of Human Nutrition: A Practical Study in Dietetics* (New York: Macmillan Co., 1912), p. 123.

11. Quoted in Benjamin Andrews, *Education for the Home,* Bulletin of the Bureau of Education of the United States (Washington, D.C.: Government Printing Office), part III, p. 35.

12. Mary T. Dowd and Jean Jameson, *Food: Its Composition and Preparation* (New York: John Wiley & Sons, 1918), p. 23.

13. Ellen Richards et al., *The Rumford Kitchen Leaflets* (Boston: Rockwell and Churchill Press, 1899), p. 16.

14. "Government Experts Develop Recipes and New Cooking Methods That Recognize the Importance of Flavor in Nutrition," *New York Times*, April 3, 1927, p. 22.

15. See Laura Shapiro, *Perfection Salad* (New York: Farrar, Strauss, and Giroux, 1986), for a critique of the food aesthetic common to home economics professionals at the turn of the century. Although Shapiro finds the cooking school teachers and domestic science manual writers of the turn of the century actively resistant to finding pleasure in food, I argue that the recipes they created offer ample evidence that they truly liked to eat. Indeed, my research in this area of home economics has always left me ravenous. Rather than condemning the food choices of the past, as it has been easy for writers to do, it is more useful to regard food aesthetics of the past in much the same way we think of cuisines of other cultures, as different in specific and revelatory ways rather than simply good or bad. Time or historical era, an often neglected element of culture in general, determines what people eat.

16. Simmons College Bulletin, 1911; Cornell University Bulletin, 1936–37; Benjamin Ide Wheeler, memo to finance committee April 3, 1913, Domestic Science Committee Papers, Ser. 1 CO5 60:86, University of California at Berkeley University Archives (UCB Archives).

17. Bane, *The Story of Isabel Bevier*, p. 34.

18. 1920–21 Annual Report, Department of Home Economics, Box 37, Folder 1, NYSCHE Records.

19. Quoted in Shapiro, *Perfection Salad*, p. 138

20. Caroline Hunt, *Life of Ellen H. Richards* (Boston:Whitcomb & Barrows, 1912), p. 215.

21. Charles Langworthy, "Maria Parloa," *Journal of Home Economics* 1, no. 4 (October 1909): 378.

22. Undated interview with Flora Rose, c. 1953, conducted by Mary Philips, Box 32, Folder 14, NYSCHE Records.

23. Mabel Thacher Wellman, *Food Study: A Textbook in Home Economics for High Schools* (Boston: Little, Brown, and Co., 1917).

24. Nancy Berlage, "The Establishment of an Applied Social Science: Home Economists, Science, and Reform at Cornell University, 1870–1930," in Helen Silverberg, ed., *Gender and American Social Science: The Formative Years* (Princeton, N.J.: Princeton University Press, 1998). Berlage uses the story as an example of male faculty members not taking female home economists seriously.

25. Emma Conley, *Nutrition and Diet* (New York: American Book Company, 1913), p. 155.

26. "Hour by Hour, 5 U.S. Experts Eat Lamb," *Chicago Daily Tribune*, June 5, 1931, p. 21.

27. "Government Experts Develop Recipes and New Cooking Methods that Recognize the Importance of Flavor in Nutrition," *New York Times*, April 3, 1927, p. 22. Cornell Bulletin for Homemakers, February, 1939–41, p. 23. It should be noted that white beans have traditionally been used to make pies in the south but that this practice has not become widespread. Soy bran muffin recipe from "Soybean's Virtues Told Housewives," *Los Angeles Times*, October 6, 1943, p. A7. Marian Manners, home economics columnist for

the *Los Angeles Times*, cautioned readers not to try to use soy products as replacements in old recipes but rather to follow the advice of the professionals on best uses for them.

28. "Nutrition Investigation," newspaper clipping n.d., Box 1, Folder "1897," Bevier Papers, UIUC Archives.

29. John Leeds, *The Household Budget* (Germantown, Philadelphia: J. B. Leeds, 1918), p. 11. Leeds received his Ph.D. from Columbia University in political science and was chair of the social science department at Temple University, teaching sociology and economics as well as household economics.

30. Bertha Terrill, quoted in Benjamin Andrews, *Education for the Home* (Washington, D.C.: Government Printing Office, 1914–15), p. 55.

31. Helen Kinne, *Shelter and Clothing* (New York: Macmillan Company, 1914), p. 4.

32. Susan Ware, *Partner and I* (New Haven, Conn.: Yale University Press, 1987), pp. 38–39.

33. Simmons College Bulletin, 1917–18, Box 3, Folder 2, Simmons College Department of Nutrition Records, Simmons College Archives, Boston, Mass. (Simmons College Archives).

34. Edna D. Day, "Home Economics at the University of Missouri," *Journal of Home Economics* 1 (June 1909): 232.

35. Caroline Hunt, "Woman's Public Work for the Home an Ethical Substitute for Cooperative Housekeeping," *Journal of Home Economics* 1 (June 1909): 220.

36. Anna B. Cooley and Helen Kinne, *Shelter and Clothing* (New York: Macmillan Company, 1913), p. 97. Cooley and Kinne encouraged readers to make their own underwear by claiming that "there is an indefinable charm about handmade lingerie" and that factory-made underwear is often produced in such "insanitary" conditions that it must be washed before use (pp. 200–202).

37. Helen Goodrich Buttrick, *Principles of Clothing Selection* (New York: Macmillan Company, 1924), p. 4.

38. Mary Schenck Woolman and Ellen Beers McGowan, *Textiles; A Handbook for the Student and the Consumer* (New York: Macmillan Company, 1919).

39. Cooley and Kinne, *Shelter and Clothing*, p. 1.

40. Helen Kinne, *The Home and the Family* (New York: Macmillan, 1917), p. 55.

41. As a specific example of this transition, we can look to wallpaper. Jan Jennings, "Controlling Passion: The Turn-of-the-Century Wallpaper Dilemma." *Winterthur Portfolio* 31, no. 4 (Winter 1996): 243–64, reveals the way in which during the first two decades of the twentieth century wallpaper became an issue of morality for home economists because it represented a woman's ability to control her environment. Home economists urged women to educate themselves in color theory and design principles so as not to be manipulated by salesmen. They also argued that wallpaper harbored vermin. Above all, however, they urged the simplification of pattern or removal of wallpaper because it represented an aesthetic that they considered unhealthy. Jennings notes that Helen Brinkerd Young, a Cornell-educated architect who became head of the college's Department of Domestic Art, wrote that wallpaper had a direct impact on the character of a home and its inhabitants. Busy patterns that hinted at three dimensions and anything in the color red Brinkerd

thought tended to encourage uncontrolled passions. In the place of pulsating florals or martial motifs, home economists like Young suggested simple earth tones. The purposes of the home—sanctuary and workplace, rather than temple—should be uppermost in the minds of decorators.

42. Roosevelt's decision to renovate the working parts of the White House rather than the display areas undoubtedly reflected national conditions at the time that her husband took office as much as it also reflected her own personality. While the Great Depression denied many Americans the means to get by, spending tax money on redecorating would have seemed the height of callousness. Redesigning the kitchen to make work better for the employed would have seemed a more practical and hopeful gesture.

43. Beecher encouraged women to wear "stiff jackets" rather than corsets because of the damage that corsets did to internal organs, causing severe problems in digestion and breathing. She also proposed domestic architecture that made it easier for women to move between their kitchens and other parts of their homes in order to make their labor more efficient.

44. Kate Heintz Watson, *Textiles and Clothing* (Chicago: American School of Economics, 1907), p. 203.

45. In the field of domestic architecture, streamlining was also idealized. As Dolores Hayden writes in Grand Domestic Revolution (Cambridge, Mass.: MIT Press, 1981), by 1900, a small but vocal group of people had already introduced the notion that woman's relationship to the domestic could be altered for the better. Hayden's "domestic feminists" were people like Charlotte Perkins Gilman and Edward Bellamy who wrote about ideal future worlds in which women's gender identity was disconnected from domestic work. Domestic feminists imagined, designed, and occasionally even built homes (usually apartment blocks) in which there was no kitchen. If you removed the prison from the home, Gilman and others argued, there was no way to keep women locked up.

Homes designed by Hayden's domestic feminists were semi-communal endeavors. Buildings included common kitchens and laundries staffed by paid workers. Many provided cleaning services and some had day-care centers as well. As Hayden points out, most of the visionaries who wrote about such homes of the future assumed that these paid employees would be female but did not address the problem created, or perpetuated, by this assumption. Women's work would still be done by women, just not by middle-class women. Rather than finding a way to pay women for the work they did in their own homes, domestic feminists more often suggested paying other women to do it for middle-class women, leaving open the question of who would cook, clean, and care for the children of the working class.

46. Swann Harding, "How to Fritter Away Your Money," *Scientific American* (August 1933): 53–55.

47. Illinois also opened a practice apartment, both to make room for more household management students and to address the particular issues of living in an apartment.

48. "Learning Home Arts," *New York Times*, October 31, 1909, p. SM11.

49. "Flower Pot Is Work of Coeds," *Los Angeles Times*, September 7, 1921, p. 16. The students named their house the Flower Pot and ran a tea room in the space as well as using it to practice household management.

50. There was also much affection for the children in the entire college community. Their pictures were featured in student newspapers and faculty doted on them. In a letter to Amy Daniels, who worked at the Child Welfare Research Station at the University of Iowa, Flora Rose wrote of Cornell's practice baby, "We have had much pleasure this spring and summer in feeding our practice house baby. . . . He is now six months old and weighs eighteen pounds. That sounds very heavy, but he is not a fat baby. His flesh is firm and pink, and his eyes a brilliant blue. For a common, or garden baby, we all think him quite remarkable." (Rose to Daniels, February 23, 1921, Box 11, Folder 32, NYSCHE Records.) In a letter of May 12, 1928, Van Rensselaer told Stanley that there were two practice-house infants available, one who must go to a Catholic home, and one who might go to a Protestant home. On May Stanley answered that Willebrandt "will be very glad to have you send me a statement about the protestant boy," but that she might not be able to decide anything quickly. Box 8, Folder of letters from Van Rensselaer and Rose to Stanley, Office of Home Economics Papers, National Archives and Records Administration, College Park, Md. (NARA).

51. Newspaper clipping, no title, n.d., Box 19, Folder 45, NYSCHE Records; Katherine Glover, "Apprenticing for Motherhood," *Today's Housewife* (July 1924); "Baby Loses Thirty Mothers," *Los Angeles Times*, June 6, 1931, p. 4.

52. Morris Bishop and J. H. Mason, "The Practice Baby," *Saturday Evening Post*, May 5, 1928, p. 34.

53. "A Few of the Model Mamas," "The Reply," *Home Economics Reminder: A Quarterly Publication by the New York State College of Home Economics at Cornell University* (September 1928), Box 32, Folder 12, NYSCHE Records.

54. Helen Mougey Jordan and Ruth Lindquist, *A Study of Institutional Policies and Recommendations Regarding Children in Home Management Houses*, c. 1931, p. 8, Box 19, Folder 43, NYSCHE Records.

55. Press release, May 21, 1937, Box 2, Agricultural, Consumer, and Environmental Sciences Dean's Office Papers, UIUC Archives.

56. The fact that so many academic home economists lived in long term loving partnerships with other women is very interesting. I discuss this facet of the movement in depth in my article "Model Mamas: The Domestic Partnership of Home Economics Pioneers Flora Rose and Martha Van Rensselaer," *Journal of the History of Sexuality* 15, no. 1 (January 2006): 65–88.

57. New York State College of Agriculture, *New York State College of Agriculture Bulletin, 1908–1909*, NYSCHE Records.

58. New York State College of Agriculture, *New York State College of Agriculture Bulletin, 1907–1908*, NYSCHE Records. In the 1903–4 academic year Van Rensselaer had offered a course in Woman's Work and Domestic Science, in which she discussed the history of women's work in the home and how modern developments might change and improve this labor. The course addressed "social conditions, past and present" of American women as well as sanitation, decoration, clothing, and food science. New York State College of Agriculture, *New York State College of Agriculture Bulletin, 1903–1904; New York State College of Agriculture Bulletin 1904–1905*, NYSCHE Records.

59. Andrews, *Education for the Home*, pp. 22–26.

60. Annual Report of the Department of Home Economics, New York State College of Agriculture, 1918–19, Box 37, Folder 13, NYSCHE Records. Also see the biography of Hazard on Cornell's excellent history of home economics web site, http://rmc.library.cornell.edu/homeEc/bios/blanchehazard.html.

61. Merasi Nerad, *The Academic Kitchen* (Albany: State University of New York Press, 1999), p. 36.

62. May Haggenbotham, *Handbook for Domestic Science and Household Arts for Use in Elementary Schools* (New York: Macmillan Company, 1900), p. 7.

63. Sarah Comstock, "Intelligent Homemaking," *Collier's* March 25, 1911, p. 18.

64. Mabel Barbara Trilling et al., *Home Economics in American Schools* (Chicago: University of Chicago Press, 1920), p. 1. Trilling, who was a professor of home economics at Carnegie Institute of Technology, wrote several home economics textbooks with coauthor Florence Williams Nichols. The other authors of *Home Economics in American Schools* included Clara Blanche Knapp, the first female professor at Middlebury College, and Bertha Miller Rugg, wife of Harold Ordway Rugg, a well-known progressive educator who was also credited with having helped to organize the book.

65. Ibid., p. 5.

66. Lucy Langdon Williams Wilson, *Handbook for Domestic Science and Household Arts for use in Elementary Schools* (New York: Macmillan & Co., Ltd., 1911), p. 147.

67. Lewis Terman, "A School Where Girls Are Taught Home-Making," *Craftsman* (April 1911): 65.

68. Ella Hollenbeck, "Home Tinkering for Girls and Home Economics for Boys," *Journal of Home Economics* 22 (August 1930): 659.

69. Maude Wilson Dunn, "Family Adjustments: A Course for Senior High School Boys," *Journal of Home Economics* 23 (January 1931): 9.

70. Letter from Margaret Wilkinson (Mrs. Henry Martyn) Bindt to President Sproul, January 12, 1932, UCB Archives.

71. Beulah I. Coon, "A Survey of Studies Related to the College Curriculum in Home Economics," *Journal of Home Economics* 29 (February 1937): 78.

72. Agnes Fay Morgan, "Undergraduate and Graduate Preparation for Home Economics Research," *Journal of Home Economics* 31 (December 1939): 685.

73. Elizabeth Kelly Lahines, "Uplift from the Kitchen," *Collier's*, May 23, 1914, pp. 22–23.

74. Irene Westbrook, "Us Brides of a Year," *Household Magazine* 29 (May 1929): 30.

75. Benjamin Andrews, Series 8/11/20, Box 2, Folder "Bevier Anecdotes," 1929 UIUC Archives.

76. Lita Bane, address delivered to the American Home Economics Association, June 23, 1932, Atlanta, Ga., Agricultural, Consumer & Environmental Sciences Dean's Office Papers, Series 8/11/5, Box 2, UIUC Archives.

77. Ibid.

78. Clara Brown, "Appraisal of Trends in Home Economics Education," *Journal of Home Economics* 29, no. 9 (November 1937): 604.

79. Frances Zuill, "New Frontiers in Home Economics Education," *Journal of Home Economics* 25 (August/September 1933): 555.

80. Effie Raitt, "Annual Message of the President of the American Home Economics Association," *Journal of Home Economics* 27 (October 1935): 481–85.

81. Agnes Samuelson, "An Administrator Looks at Home Economics," *Journal of Home Economics* 28 (October 1936): 522.

CHAPTER TWO

1. Paul V. Bettoes, *The Bureau of Home Economics: Its History, Activities and Organization* (Washington, D.C.: Brookings Institution, 1930), p. 41. The office was opened in the United States Department of Agriculture's States Relations Service, which was created in 1915 to support agricultural education.

2. Toward the time when the Office became the Bureau of Home Economics (1923), members of the staff began to realize "the importance of economic data in the consideration of home economics problems," shifting focus from the home as center of production to the home as center of consumption. The bureau was established with a mandate to "investigate the relative utility and economy of agricultural products for food, clothing and other uses in the home and with special suggestions of plans and methods for the more effective utilization of such products for these purposes, and to disseminate useful information on this subject." In a sense, then, the bureau was established to consider American agriculture from the demand side, while other offices within the USDA considered problems of supply. Bettoes, *Bureau of Home Economics*, p. 42.

3. Elizabeth Israels Perry, *Belle Moskowitz* (New York: Oxford University Press, 1987), p. xiii.

4. "Women Must be Trained," *New York Times*, June 10, 1917, p. 8.

5. The Collegiate Section of the U.S. Food Administration, *Food and the War: A Textbook for College Classes* (Boston: Houghton Mifflin Company, 1918).

6. "Schools Aiding War Charities," *New York Times*, September 30, 1917, p. E2.

7. "Girl Food Savers," *New York Times*, May 19, 1918, p. 61.

8. "Domesticated Men," *Los Angeles Times*, copied from the *Baltimore Star*, January 27, 1918, p. III 18.

9. "All-Potato Dinner," *New York Times*, May 12, 1918, p. 80.

10. "Schools Aiding War Charities," *New York Times*, September 30, 1917, p. E2.

11. As Barry Karl observes, "[progressives] looked to the war to make their point for them, to prove to public opinion . . . that their prescriptions must be followed. . . . Nothing could be further off the mark. All down the line . . . progressives simply turned out to be wrong." Barry Karl, *The Uneasy State: The United States from 1915 to 1945* (Chicago: University of Chicago Press, 1983), p. 47.

12. Herbert Hoover, *The Memoirs of Herbert Hoover: Years of Adventure* (New York: Macmillan, 1951), p. 250.

13. James Ford, *Annotated Bibliography of Consumers' Cooperation: The Survey* 39, p. 57, February 9, 1918, quoted in The Collegiate Section of the U.S. Food Administration, *Food and the War*.

14. Program for reunion of National Food Administration workers, 1923, Box 1, Folder 16, Sarah Louise Arnold Papers, Series I, Simmons College Archives, Boston, Mass. (Simmons College Archives).

15. Box I, Folder 16, Sarah Louise Arnold Papers, Series II, Simmons College Archives.

16. The Smith-Lever Act, coauthored by Senator Hoke Smith of Georgia and Representative A. F. Lever of South Carolina, created the Cooperative Extension Service and stipulated that home economics education should be provided for farm women. The act was followed in 1917 by the Smith-Hughes Act, which provided funds for state vocational education in agriculture and home economics. Rima D. Apple argues that this legislation was a mixed blessing: "Though the act spread home economics education into school systems across the country . . . the act's implementation undermined some of the basic principles espoused by home economics reformers, particularly scientific research as a basis for the continued development of the profession." Rima D. Apple, "Liberal Arts or Vocational Training?" *Rethinking Home Economics: Women and the History of a Profession* (Ithaca, N.Y.: Cornell University Press, 1997), p. 86.

At Cornell, students of one clothing course "donated all things made or remade to Belgian relief or Red Cross" as part of their semester's work. Their professors wanted them to have personal experience of the potential importance of domestic work. Annual Report of the School of Home Economics, New York State College of Agriculture at Cornell University, Ithaca, N.Y., 1917–18, Box 37, Folder 12, New York State College of Home Economics Records, Cornell University Division of Rare and Manuscript Collections, Ithaca, N.Y. (NYSCHE Records).

17. "Women's Institutes in North Carolina" (editorial), *Journal of Home Economics* 1 (April 1909): 163. The North Carolina car actually made between three and ten stops a day, while the University of Illinois car made visits of up to five days in communities along its route. Brochure, University of Illinois Home Economics Extension Service 1917–18, Box 2, Folder 1917, Bevier Papers, University of Illinois Archives, Urbana-Champaign, Ill. (UIUC Archives).

18. Flora Rose to Miss M. B. Benson, U.S. Food Administration, June 8, 1918, Box 11, Folder 24, NYSCHE Records. During the 1930s and 1940s, Cornell also sponsored the Wattmobile, a van that had been customized to bring exhibitions on and demonstrations of electrification to rural areas. ("What Was Home Economics?" online exhibition, http://rmc.library.cornell.edu/homeEc/5formats/wattmobile.html.)

19. Flora Rose to Miss M. B. Benson, June 8, 1918, NYSCHE Records.

20. "Food Reserve Train Starts," *New York Times*, May 22, 1917, p. 7.

21. Mary Williams, "Teaching Domestic Science to Different Nationalities," *Journal of Home Economics* 2 (June 1910): 272.

22. Simmons College Household Economics Department, Annual Report of the Household Economics Department, Box 1, Folder 7, Simmons College Archives.

23. Report of President's Committee on Home Economics Principles and Recommendations, May 23, 1945, UCB Archives.

24. "Graduate Students in Home Economics" (editorial), *Journal of Home Economics* 25 (March 1933): 223.

25. Marjorie M. Heseltine, "Commercial Education Material Used by Home Economists," *Journal of Home Economics* 21 (June 1929): 419.

26. Ibid.

27. Carolyn M. Goldstein sites another corporate home economist, Mary Philips of the North American Dye Corporation, who saw "the home economist's presence as a 'wedge' in the corporation.'" Goldstein quotes Philips arguing that the home economist in business "would be 'a powerful force for betterment and uplift,' and, she implied, would temper the hold that corporations had on American domestic life." Carolyn M. Goldstein, "Part of the Package," in Stage and Vincenti, *Rethinking Home Economics*, pp. 279–80.

28. Helen Crouch Douglas, "Broadcasting Home Economics Talk," *Journal of Home Economics* 27 (November 1935): 568.

29. Ibid., p. 563.

30. Helen Powell Smith, "Reaching Out with Radio," *Journal of Home Economics* 40, no. 8 (October 1948): 455.

31. Ibid., p. 456.

32. Ibid.

33. Helen Stacy, "Home Economists on the Air," *Journal of Home Economics* 29, no.7 (September, 1937): 461–62

34. Theodore Dreiser to Isabel Bevier, September 10, 1908, and September 17, 1908, Box 1, Human and Community Development Department Correspondence, UIUC Archives.

35. In 1925, Van Rensselaer and Flora Rose collaborated on the article "When George and Mary Wish to Marry," for *The Delineator* in which they gave advice to newlyweds about how to run their first home. They concentrated much attention on finances, arguing that money troubles caused gender strife. The article is remarkable for the fact that it was written by two women who had never been married, but who shared a home with each other. Rose and Van Rensselaer earned the same salary. Rose refused to earn more, although her higher degrees entitled her to. The two women, then, had the kind of economic equality within their household that none of their readers was likely to have.

36. See Susan J. Matt, *Keeping Up with the Joneses* (Philadelphia: University of Pennsylvania Press, 2003), for an engaging exploration of how home economists who worked with extension agencies served as apostles for the emerging consumer culture, creating desires among rural women that would lead them directly to corporate producers of domestic goods, all in the pursuit of becoming modern.

37. "Teaching a State to Cook," *Collier's*, January 21, 1911, p. 21. The farm wife portrayed in this story became prettier through home economics not because it taught her beauty tricks but because her work with the program gave her pride, which improved her appearance.

38. Anna Gilbert, "Journal of an Extensionized Farm Woman," *Journal of Home Economics* 13, no. 7 (July 1921): 303.

39. Ibid.

40. See Marilyn Irvin Holt, *Linoleum, Better Babies, and the Modern Farm Woman* (Albuquerque: University of New Mexico Press, 1995) and Kathleen R. Babbitt, "Legitimizing Nutrition Education," in Stage and Vincenti, *Rethinking Home Economics*, for discussions of

relations between home economics extension agents and their intended audience. Holt discusses sources of possible tension between extension agents and rural women in Kansas, finding that home economists adjusted their expectations and approaches to suit the experiences of rural women. She writes, "Certainly the experts and home economics professionals attempted to transmit a defined viewpoint to farm women, but whether they succeeded is an open question" (p. 42). Babbitt, writing about the popularization of nutrition education, notes, "If extension home economists had hoped to attain a certain status as experts in nutrition through their work as rural home demonstration agents, they were sorely disappointed" (p. 151). Particularly during World War I, farmers and their wives distrusted interference by people they associated with the government. Babbitt quotes a New York farm woman who complained, "We do not need to have new (and some of them are entirely absurd and impracticable) recipes handed out to us by people who never baked a loaf of bread in their lives" (p. 148).

41. A. R. Mann, "The Relation of the Extension Specialist to the Resident Staff in Home Economics," *Journal of Home Economics* 14, no. 4 (April 1922): 165.

42. William Leach, *Land of Desire* (New York: Vintage Books, 1994), p. xiii.

43. Resolution of the Western District Federation of Home Bureaus, Box 32, Folder 9, NYSCHE Records.

44. See Regina Lee Blaszczyk, *Imagining Consumers* (Baltimore: Johns Hopkins University Press, 2000), for a discussion of ways in which mass producers of domestic goods have turned to consumers for direction, rather than simply manufacturing desire, as some cultural critics would have it. Blaszczyk offers fascinating evidence of how the Corning Glass Works used a noted home economist to channel the needs of consumers in their successful attempt to create marketable baking dishes.

45. The Ideal Manufacturing Company to Isabel Bevier, January 11, 1909, Box 1, Human and Community Development Department Correspondence, UIUC Archives.

46. Isabel Bevier to American Vacuum Cleaner Company, January 2, 1909, Box 1 Folder 1909, Bevier Papers, UIUC Archives. Some home economics departments offered courses in Household Equipment, which were dependent on manufacturers for samples. See Amy Sue Bix, "Gendered Technical Training and Consumerism in Home Economics," *Technology and Culture* 43 (October 2002).

47. Bevier to American Vacuum Cleaner Company January 2, 1909.

48. John Killian to Robert Underhill, August 30, 1935, Folder 1932, UCB Archives.

49. Engraved card, n.d., Box 33, Folder 42, NYSCHE Records. Despite her early endorsement of the fireless cooker, Van Rensselaer seems to have changed her policy toward manufacturers. In 1920, when Sarah Splint offered to send a representative from Knox gelatin to Cornell for demonstrations, Van Rensselaer politely refused. She explained that the dean of the college did not think it right for a state institution to have such relations with private companies. And, she added, "Miss Rose and I have discovered that we should be careful and are glad to conform to this ruling. The Dean is exceedingly generous about these things and gives his judgment as impartially as possible." Sarah Splint to Martha Van Rensselaer, September 1, 1920; Van Rensselaer to Splint September 19, 1920, Box 33, Folder 42. NYSCHE Records.

50. Janice William Rutherford, *Selling Mrs. Consumer* (Athens: University of Georgia Press, 2003), pp. 146, 147. Rutherford's biography of Frederick provides a brief discussion of home economics as part of the context in which Frederick emerged as a national figure, but primarily portrays Frederick as a self-created expert.

51. Dan Gerber, "The Home Economist in a Business Firm," *Journal of Home Economics* 26, no. 1 (January 1934): 21.

52. Gerber, "The Home Economist in a Business Firm," p. 22.

53. Katherine Parkin, "Campbell's Soup and Traditional Gender Roles," in Sherrie A. Inness, ed., *Kitchen Culture in America* (Philadelphia: University of Pennsylvania Press, 2001), p. 58.

54. 1919 Advertisement for Campbell's Soup, quoted in Katherine Parkin, "Campbell's Soup and Traditional Gender Roles," in Sherrie A. Inness, ed. *Kitchen Culture in America* (Philadelphia: University of Pennsylvania Press, 2001), p. 63.

55. "Thrift Week and the Employment Crisis" (editorial), *Journal of Home Economics* 23, no. 1 (January 1931): 57.

56. Ibid.

57. Van Rensselaer to Hewitt, June 15, 1920, Box 14, Folder 1, NYSCHE Records.

58. Ibid.

59. Stanley to Van Rensselaer, November 23, 1928, Box 11, Folder 28, NYSCHE Records.

60. Pamphlet prepared for the Department of Applied Education General Federation of Women's Clubs by the Savings Division of the Treasury Department; Office of Home Economics and of Extension Work, States Relations Service, Department of Agriculture and the Home Economic Education Service Federal Board for Vocational Education, Box 1, Folder "Misc Mim Material, 1917–1923," Office of Home Economics Papers. See Lisa Jacobson, *Raising Consumers* (New York: University of Columbia Press, 2004), especially Chapter 2, "Reforming the Child Spender," for a discussion of thrift programs in public education. Jacobson finds that although public schools in the 1910s had been assisted by banks in educating students toward thrift, after World War I financial education in schools shifted toward an emphasis on the student as consumer and spender.

61. Department of Applied Education General Federation of Women's Clubs, pamphlet.

62. "White House Gets Milkorno," *Literary Digest*, May 6, 1923, 25.

63. Newspaper clipping, no title, n.d., Box 19, Folder 15, NYSCHE Records.

64. "CWA and ERA Activities in the City," *Fitchburg Sentinel*, June 2, 1934, p. 4. Recipe published in *Hammond Times*, November 15, 1935, p. 20.

65. Mrs. Franklin D. Roosevelt, *It's Up to the Women* (New York: Frederick A. Stokes Company, 1933), pp. 262–63.

66. "Roosevelts Are Eating 'Low Cost Menus' to Publicize Plan and Aid Housewives," unidentified newspaper clipping, with handwritten "Washington, D.C.," March 21, 1933, Box 19, Folder 18, NYSCHE Records. Although the low-cost meal described may not sound especially delicious, it may have actually been an improvement on typical White House fare, which was notoriously unpleasant. See "ER's Revenge: Henrietta Nesbitt Housekeeper," in Blanche Wiesen Cook, *Eleanor Roosevelt*, vol. 2 (New York: Penguin Books, 1999), and Doris

Kearns Goodwin, *No Ordinary Time* (New York: Simon and Schuster, 1995), for discussion of Roosevelt-era White House cuisine. Apparently, the Roosevelt's housekeeper, Henrietta Nesbit, had been hired by Eleanor Roosevelt because she was an acquaintance who needed a job, not because she was a good cook.

67. Lucy H. Gillett, "Using Home Economics to Make the Most of What We Have," *Journal of Home Economics* 25, no. 3 (March 1933): 208–12.

68. Breckenridge was the first woman to receive a Ph.D. from the University of Chicago. She got her degree in political science and helped to establish the school of social work at Chicago.

69. Sophonisba Breckenridge, "Home Economics and the Quest for Economic Security," *Journal of Home Economics* 27, no. 8 (October 1935): 490.

70. "Housework Class Opens," *Los Angeles Times*, June 7, 1936, p. A2.

71. Annette Herr, "Readjustments in Home Demonstration Programs to Meet the Present Economic Situation," *Journal of Home Economics* 25, no. 4 (April 1933): 290.

72. Mary Sweeney, "Responsibility of Home Economics Teachers in Their Communities in the Present Economic Crisis," *Journal of Home Economics* 24, no. 8 (October 1932): 880. Sweeney was principal of the Merril Palmer School in Detroit, a home economics high school.

73. Frances Swain, "Opportunities and Responsibilities of Home Economics in the Present Situation," *Journal of Home Economics* 25, no. 11 (November 1933): 747.

74. I. Thomas Hopkins, "Prospects for Progress in Home Economics Education," *Journal of Home Economics* 23, no. 2 (February 1931): 123.

75. Ibid.

76. "Citizenship First, Scholarship Second," *New York Times*, May 25, 1919, p. 37.

77. "German Developments in Household Management" (editorial), *Journal of Home Economics* 23, no. 3 (March 1931): 262.

78. Anna M. Cooley, "Fifth International Congress of Home Economics," *Journal of Home Economics* 26, no. 12 (December 1934): 622.

79. See Daniel Rodgers, *Atlantic Crossings* (Cambridge, Mass.: Belknap Press, 1998), for a discussion of the international connections between reform movements from the Progressive era to the New Deal.

80. Song quoted in Bonnie S. Anderson and Judith P. Zinsser, *A History of Their Own: Women in Europe from Prehistory to the Present* (New York: Harper Perennial, 1989), 2:213.

81. Marian Manners, "Frozen Fruitcake Goes to War," *Los Angeles Times*, March 18, 1945, p. e9.

82. Ruth Van Deman, "Plain Writing—Easy Reading," article prepared for *American Cookery Magazine*, dated February 8, 1944, Record Group 310, Box 5, Bureau of Home Economics papers, National Archives and Records Administration, College Park, Md. (NARA).

83. Amy Bentley, *Eating for Victory* (Urbana: University of Illinois Press, 1998). Bentley's excellent book addresses issues of gender and race in America's reliance on women to conserve resources during the war.

84. "Dear Mom," Duke University, Digital Scriptorium ad access site, http://scriptorium.lib.duke.edu/dynaweb/adaccess/war/conservation/@Generic__BookTextView/499.

85. Ivol Spafford, "Adjusting Home Economics to Wartime Needs," *School Review* (January 1943): 33–38.

86. Letter to students from Marie Belle Fowler, June 11, 1941, Box 23, Folder 35, NYSCHE Records.

87. Statement of Belief, June 11, 1941, Box 23, Folder 35, NYSCHE Records.

88. Alvin Hansen "After the War—Full Employment" (Washington, D.C.: Government Printing Office, 1942), quoted in *Journal of Home Economics* 34, no. 4 (April 1942): 230. Hansen (1887–1975) was the Harvard professor of political economics who adapted and introduced Keynsian economics to the American situation.

89. "Course Especially for Prospective Brides Offered on University Campus," *Nevada State Journal*, September 26, 1943, 6.

90. Ibid.


CHAPTER THREE


1. Khrushchev visited the United States for thirteen days in September 1959. During his visit he stayed overnight at the farm of Iowan Roswell Gast, who had invited the premier and his wife when they heard he would be touring Iowa. During a tour of the agricultural department at Iowa State he made an unscheduled stop in the home economics department.

2. "Premier Wished Coeds Luck in Husband Hunt," *New York Times*, September 24, 1959, p. 21.

3. "Co-eds in the Kitchen," *Newsweek*, October 5, 1959, p. 79.

4. Ibid.

5. Ibid.

6. Aileen Snoddy, "Marriage Steals Cream of Home Economics Crop," *Warren* (Pa.) *Times-Mirror*, April 6, 1959, p. 3. Dorothy S. Lawson, who was interviewed for the article, worked at the New York State Bureau of Home Economics Education.

7. "Home Ec. Teachers Scarce," *Indiana* (Pa.) *Evening Gazette*, July 24, 1950, p. 16.

8. Among the works that have explored American anxiety in the postwar period, Larry May, ed., *Recasting America* (Chicago: University of Chicago Press, 1989), provides the most multifaceted approach because it is a collection of essays by writers in diverse fields. Like Warren Susman and Jackson Lears, who both contributed pieces to the collection, I am here most interested in perceptions of crisis and yearning for consensus rather than in the actualities of the postwar period because the ways in which home economists portrayed themselves in relation to these perceptions did shape the field in years following this period. Also see Elaine Tyler-May, *Homeward Bound: American Families in the Cold War Era* (New York: Basic Books, 1988), for the essential exploration of gender and culture in the Cold War period. Tyler-May's work reveals ways in which agents of consumer culture attempted to manage women, who were widely perceived as unstable elements in society.

9. C. Mervin Palmer, "Are Colleges Preparing Students for the Postwar Period?" *Journal of Higher Education* (April 1944): 230.

10. Florence Fallgatter, *Journal of Home Economics* 43, no. 7 (September 1951): 502.

11. The Housing Act of 1949 provided federal support for urban redevelopment and slum-clearing programs with an emphasis on new construction and provision of support for development of communities on open land. The 1954 Act added funds to help rehabilitate existing housing and neighborhoods as well as building new ones.

12. Howard Becker, *Family, Marriage, and Parenthood* (Washington, D.C.: Heath, 1948), p. 798.

13. *You and Your Family,* Blake (BK) Inc., 1946.

14. For more on the history of courtship in America, see Beth L. Bailey, *From Front Porch to Back Seat* (Baltimore: Johns Hopkins University Press, 1989).

15. *Sharing Work at Home,* Coronet Instructional Films, Glenview, Ill., 1949.

16. For a brief history of the marriage education movement, see Beth Bailey, "Scientific Truth . . . and Love," *Journal of Social History* 20, no. 4 (Summer 1987): 711–32. Bailey discusses the movement in terms of the rise of the expert in American culture rather than as a response to postwar social anxiety about gender roles and family functions.

17. 1947 Descriptive Report of Vocational Education: Home Economics, Iowa, Box 9 RG12 150-54-26, National Archives and Records Administration, College Park, Md. (NARA).

18. 1947 Descriptive Report of Vocational Education: Home Economics, Iowa, Box 9 RG12 150-54-26, NARA.

19. *It Takes All Kinds,* Affiliated Film Producers, New York, N.Y., 1960.

20. Henry A. Bowman, *Marriage for Moderns* (New York: McGraw Hill Book Company, Inc., 1960).

21. *Marriage Today,* Affiliated Film Producers, New York, N.Y., 1950.

22. *Choosing for Happiness,* Affiliated Film Producers, New York, N.Y., 1950.

23. Although there was no economic depression in the postwar period, Americans remained frightened by the prospect of another Great Depression into the 1950s.

24. James A. Peterson, *Education for Marriage* (New York: Charles Scribner's Sons, 1956), pp. 346–47.

25. *Who's Boss?,* Affiliated Film Producers, New York, N.Y., 1950.

26. *Marriage Is a Partnership,* Coronet Instructional Films, Glenview, Ill., 1951.

27. Herman Lantz, "Problem Areas in Marriage Education," *Marriage and Family Living* (May 1953): 116–17. Lantz was well known as a sociologist of the family, pioneering in the development of this field.

28. Earl Lomon Koos, "Comment," *Marriage and Family Living* (May 1953): 18; Herman Lantz, "Rejoinder," *Marriage and Family Living* (May 1953): 19.

29. *Finding Your Life's Work,* Holmes (Burton) Films, Inc., Chicago, Ill., 1940.

30. *The Home Economics Story,* Iowa State Teachers' College, Ames, Iowa, 1951.

31. *Why Study Home Economics?* Centron Corporation, Lawrence, Kans., 1955.

32. Olive Paul Goodrich, "Gainful Occupations Open to Girls Having Home Economics Training," report prepared for U.S. Bureau of Education, Record Group 12–130, Box 1, Folder "Department of Supervisors and Teachers of Home Economics," Bureau of Education Papers, NARA.

33. Oneita Pierce, "Training Conference Uses Family Life Project Materials," *Journal of Home Economics* 45, no. 1 (January 1953): 40.

34. Charles G. Spiegler, "Are Our Girls Getting Boys' Education?" *New York Times*, May 14, 1950, p. 197

35. Descriptive Report of Vocational Education, Massachusetts, 1957–58, Box 13, p. 28, NARA.

36. Descriptive Report of Vocational Education, Massachusetts, 1952–53, Box 13, p. 18, NARA.

37. The FFA creed appeared in the organization's publication, *Teen Times*. It was revised slightly in 1999 to reflect the organization's change of name and mission, when the FHA became the Family, Career and Community Leaders of America. The FCCLA creed can be found on the Web site www.fccla.org. The creed of the Future Farmers of America, in contrast to that of the FHA, had six wordy paragraphs, beginning with the romantic statement "I believe in the future of agriculture, with a faith born not of words but of deeds— achievements won by the present and past generations of agriculturists; in the promise of better days through better ways, even as the better things we now enjoy have come to us from the struggles of former years."

38. "Girl Students in Rally," *Weekly Kansas City Star*, March 24, 1930, p. 7.

39. North Carolina Home Economics Vocational Education Annual Report, 1947–48, (n.p.), Box 21, NARA.

40. Washington State Home Economics Vocational Education Report, 1946–47, p. 29, Box 27, NARA.

41. Iowa State Home Economics Vocational Education Report, 1953–53, p. 16, Box 9, NARA.

42. Dori Grinenko Baker, "Future Homemakers and Feminist Awakenings: Autoethnography as a Method in Theological Education and Research," *Religious Education* (Summer 2001).

43. Mary Hawkins, "Home Economists Plan for Defense," *Journal of Home Economics* 43, no. 5 (May 1951): 339–41.

44. Florence Fallgatter, "Our Responsibility for Freedom: As Home Economists of Today," *Journal of Home Economics* 43, no. 7 (September 1951): 504

45. Elizabeth C. Droescher, "Operation Cue, Las Vegas, Nevada, April 1955," *Journal of Home Economics* 47, no. 8 (October 1955): 625.

46. Washington State Home Economics Vocational Education Report, 1952–53, p. 47, Box 27, NARA.

47. James A. Peterson, *Education for Marriage* (New York: Charles Scribner's Sons, 1956), pp. 175–76.

48. "Comment," *Journal of Home Economics* 43, no. 2 (February 1951): 117.

49. Ardenia Chapman, "Can AHEA Become an Effective Force for Standards?" *Journal of Home Economics* 43, no. 3 (March 1951): 171.

50. Once the bill was approved, articles in the *Journal of Home Economics* ceased to criticize it, and an October 1949 article on the work of the Federal Trade Commission by

Betty Bock, an economic analyst within the agency, presented a favorable view of the commission's work to home economists at large.

51. Skit script, Agricultural Research Services Papers, Box 2, Folder "25th Anniversary of BHNHE," NARA.

52. United States Department of Agriculture Newsletter, July 19, 1948, Agricultural Research Services Papers, Box 2, Folder "25th Anniversary of BHNHE," NARA.

53. Press statement, "Bureau of Human Nutrition and Home Economics Celebrates Its 25th Birthday," Agricultural Research Services papers, Box 2, Folder "25th Anniversary of BHNHE," NARA.

54. Margaret Rossiter, "The Men Move In: Home Economics in Higher Education, 1950–1970," in Sarah Stage and Virginia B. Vincenti, eds., Rethinking Home Economics (Ithaca, N.Y.: Cornell University Press, 1997), pp. 96–117.

55. "Only Man in Class Is Best Homemaker," New York Times, November 18, 1950, p. 9.

56. "L.I. High School Boys Excel as Chefs; Cook Dinner as Culmination of Course," New York Times, May 25, 1958, p. 57.

57. Lydia Perera, "Cooking on Video," New York Times, February 10, 1952, p. 111.

58. Ruth Van Deman, "Newer Educational Devices Available to the Home Economist," Journal of Home Economics 31, no. 8 (October 1939): 538. Both the Home show episode aired in 1954 and the Aunt Jenny's Real Life Stories episode aired in 1939 are archived at the Museum of Television and Radio in New York City.

59. Good Living: Individually Yours, episode aired by WNDQ in 1952, archived at the Museum of Television and Radio, New York City.

60. The Kate Smith Hour, episode aired in 1957, archived at the Museum of Television and Radio, New York City.

61. See Laura Scott Holliday, "Kitchen Technologies: Promises and Alibis," Camera Obscura 47, 16, no. 2 (2001). A particularly blatant attempt to sell a new kitchen as a woman's self-fulfillment can be found in the 1957 industrial film Practical Dreamer, produced for U.S. Steel by the Handy Jam Organization. The film can be viewed online at http://www.archive.org/index.php.

62. Kathleen Donahue, "Stove Lights Way to Success on TV for Girl," Chicago Daily Tribune, August 13, 1950, p. SW10. Despite the title, Barkley was a married woman with several years' experience as a home economics teacher before she became a television show host.

63. American Women, Partners in Research, Holland-Wegman Productions, 1960.

64. Word to the Wives, Telamerica, Inc., c. 1955.

65. Karal Ann Marling, As Seen on TV (Cambridge, Mass.: Harvard University Press, 1994). See especially the chapter "Nixon in Moscow: Appliances, Affluence, and Americanism."

66. Lynn Spigel, Make Room for TV (Chicago: University of Chicago Press, 1992). Spigel examines the appearance of television sets in advertising in women's magazines to reveal the medium's integration into American culture through its physical integration into the American home.

67. "Tele Replaces Sitters, Young Mother Finds," Chicago Daily Tribune, September 19, 1948, p. F8. Elaine Tyler May, in Homeward Bound, argues that the open kitchen plan

that became popular after World War II initially seemed like an empowering trend for women, since it made their work in kitchens visibly part of the family's life, but that it eventually resulted in added anxiety for women as higher standards of aesthetics, cleanliness, and order had to be maintained when the kitchen emerged from behind closed doors. Betty Friedan, in *The Feminine Mystique* (New York: Norton, 1963), also argued that the open plan made more work for women and limited their autonomy by limiting their privacy.

68. *Mother Takes a Holiday*, Handy Jam Organization, Detroit, Mich., 1952.

69. Agnes Reasor Olmstead, "The Home Economist's Responsibility to the Family in the Consumer Age," *Journal of Home Economics* 53, no. 7 (September 1961): 57.

70. Ibid., p. 540.

71. Ibid., p. 542.

72. Hazel Reed, "Reminiscences," in Stage and Vincenti, *Rethinking Home Economics*, p. 183.

73. Rose White, "Standards for the Consumer," *Journal of Home Economics* 53, no. 7 (September 1961): 532.

## CHAPTER FOUR

1. "No More Miss America," Chicago Women's Liberation Union Herstory Web site, www.cwluherstory.org, accessed September 2007.

2. *Journal of Home Economics* 55, no. 7 (September 1963): 503.

3. "Five Passionate Feminists [symposium]" *McCall's* 97, no. 10, p. 113.

4. Betty Friedan, *The Feminine Mystique* (New York: Laurel Books, 1983), pp. 155–56.

5. Ibid., p. 166.

6. Casey Hayden and Mary King, "A Kind of Memo," Chicago Women's Liberation Union Herstory Web site, www.cwluherstory.org, accessed September 2007.

7. Virginia Cadden "Women's Lib? I've Seen It on TV," *Redbook* (February 1972): 94.

8. Pat Mainardi, *The Politics of Housework* (New York: Redstockings, 1970).

9. Friedan, *The Feminine Mystique*, p. 342.

10. Linda Hirshman, "Homeward Bound," *American Prospect Online*, November 21, 2005. Available at www.prospect.org/web/page.ww?section=root&name=ViewWeb&articleId=10659, accessed September 2007.

11. Cadden, "Women's Lib?," p. 94.

12. Warren Belasco, *Appetite for Change: How the Counterculture Took on the Food Industry* (New York: Pantheon Books, 1989), p. 7.

13. Ibid., pp. 19, 34. The Diggers provided free meals in the Haight-Ashberry section of San Francisco as a way of drawing attention to the inequality of world food distribution and the dangers of corporate food production. They were active for a brief period between 1966 and 1968.

14. Belasco, *Appetite for Change*, p. 36. ˙

15. Laurel Robertson, Carol Flinders, and Bronwen Godfrey, *Laurel's Kitchen* (New York: Bantam Books, 1978).

16. Ibid., p. 17.

17. Ibid., frontispiece.

18. Ibid., p. 9. Flinders's details are particularly reflective of her time and culture. That blintzes, a typically Jewish delicacy, had entered the mainstream cuisine indicates larger cultural transformations.

19. Ibid.

20. Ibid., p. 33.

21. Ibid., p. 47

22. Ibid., p. 50.

23. Ibid.

24. Ibid., p. 341.

25. Martha Van Rensselaer to Carrie Chapman Catt, June 23, 1928, Box 33, Folder 25, New York State College of Home Economics Records, Cornell University Division of Rare and Manuscript Collections, Ithaca, N.Y. (NYSCHE Records).

26. See Eva Kaluzynska, "Wiping the Floor with Theory: A Survey of Writings on Housework," *Feminist Review*, no. 6 (1980): 27–54, for a comprehensive, yet lighthearted review of writings that tackle the topic of wages for housework.

27. The Women's Work Study Group, "Loom, Broom, and Womb: Producers, Maintainers, and Reproducers," *Frontiers* (Fall 1975): 8.

28. Judith Viorst, "What Worries Me About Women's Lib," *Redbook* (May 1974): 52.

29. "Today's Frontiers, Tomorrow's Realities—AHEA's 62nd Annual Meeting," *Journal of Home Economics* 63, no. 6 (September 1971): 408.

30. "What Robin Morgan Said at Denver," *Journal of Home Economics* 65, no. 1 (January 1973): 13.

31. Ibid.

32. "The Women's Roles Committee Speaks Out," *Journal of Home Economics* 65, no. 1 (January 1973): 10.

33. Ibid.

34. Ibid.

35. Ibid., p. 11.

36. Ibid.

37. Bernadine H. Peterson, Letter to the Editor, *Journal of Home Economics* 65, no. 4 (April 1973): 2.

38. "The Women's Roles Committee Speaks Out," p. 12.

39. "Alternate Lifestyles, an Individual's Choice," *Journal of Home Economics* 64, no. 7 (October 1972): 4–8. The article was a collection of statements written by people living in five different "alternative" lifestyles. These included an unmarried couple, a single mother who had made a transracial adoption, and a small commune.

40. "The Women's Roles Committee Speaks Out," p. 14.

41. Ibid.

42. Sheila Tobias, "For College Students: A Study of Women, Their Roles and Stereotypes," *Journal of Home Economics* 64, no. 4 (April 1972): 17.

43. "The Women's Roles Committee Speaks Out," p. 14.

44. Letter to the Editor, *Journal of Home Economics* 46, no. 5 (May 1954): 294.

45. Patricia Durey Murphy, "What's in a Name?" *Journal of Home Economics* 59, no. 9 (November 1967): 702.

46. Margaret Rossiter, "The Men Move In: Home Economics in Higher Education, 1950–1970," in Sarah Stage and Virginia B. Vincenti, eds., *Rethinking Home Economics: Women and the History of a Profession* (Ithaca, N.Y.: Cornell University Press, 1997), pp. 96–117.

47. Murphy, "What's in a Name?" p. 705.

48. Ibid., p. 706.

49. Statement posted on New Mexico State University web site, November 1997, http://cahe.nmsu.edu/news/1997/063097_FCS_department.html, accessed September 2007.

50. Press release posted on Washington State University web site, November 2003, http://cahenews.wsu.edu/RELEASES/2003/03055.htm, accessed September 2007.

## EPILOGUE

1. Rima D. Apple, "Liberal Arts or Vocational Training?" in Sarah Stage and Virginia B. Vincenti, eds., *Rethinking Home Economics: Women and the History of a Profession* (Ithaca, N.Y.: Cornell University Press, 1997), p. 94

2. B. Rice, "Coming of Age in Sodom and New Milford," *Psychology Today* (September 1975): 64–6.

3. V. Adams, "Popgun Classroom Feminism," *Psychology Today* (March 1980): 24.

4. Virginia B. Vincenti, "Home Economics Moves into the Twenty-first Century," in Stage and Vincenti, eds., *Rethinking Home Economics*, p. 301.

5. Ibid., p. 304.

6. Ibid., p. 319.

7. *Real Simple* (January 2007): cover and 67.

8. Jeff Bredenberg, "Calendar Girls," *Better Homes and Gardens* (February 2007): 130–34.

9. Kimberly Fusaro, "Get Organized with Chalkboard Paint," *Martha Stewart Living* (January 2007): 131.

10. Cheryl Mendelson, *Home Comforts* (New York: Scribner, 1999).

11. Ibid., p. 7.

12. Katha Polit, "Home Discomforts," *The Nation*, January 24, 2000.

13. Caitlin Flanagan, "Leaving It to the Professionals," *The Atlantic* (March 2002): 110–16.

14. Mendelson, *Home Comforts*, p. 13.

15. Ibid., p. 9

16. Ibid., p. 10.

17. *Paula's Home Cooking*, episode: "Picnic in the Park," aired August 17, 2006, on the Food Network.

18. In a sly commentary on the genre, particularly *Extreme Makeover: Home Edition*, the writers of *The Simpsons* gathered neighbors to rebuild Ned Flanders's ruined house only to see it fall to pieces because of their cheerfully shoddy workmanship

19. "What's Your Style Quiz," HGTV web site, www.hgtv.com/hgtv/pac_ctnt_988/text/0,,HGTV_22056_33320,00.html, accessed September 2007.

20. "Go with the Kitchen Flow," HGTV web site, http://design.hgtv.com/kitchen/video_detail.aspx?id=184, accessed September 2007.

21. Mark McCauley, "F is for Function," in "Five Steps to the Perfect Sanctuary," www.hgtv.com/hgtv/pac_ctnt_988/text/0,,HGTV_22056_49459,00.html, accessed January 2007.

22. "Kitchen Shortcuts," *Real Simple* (February 2007): 152.

23. Alice Kessler Harris, *In Pursuit of Equity: Women, Men, and the Quest for Economic Citizenship in 20<sup>th</sup> Century America* (Oxford: Oxford University Press, 2001).

24. Sarah Stage "Introduction," in Sarah Stage and Vincenti B. Vincenti, eds., *Rethinking Home Economics*, p. 1.

# INDEX

Page numbers in italics indicate images.

between audience and product, 134–35;
home economists' response to, 138–40;
homemaker as choice-maker, 135–38; shopping as patriotic duty, 137; television advertising, 134; television's integration into
home decor and family life, 137, 206n.67
contemporary domestic advice media,
182–86; absence of analysis/evaluation,
185–86; and amateurism, 182–83; child-care
advice television shows, 184–85; home selling television shows, 3, 184; interior design
television shows, 183–84, 210n.18; magazines, 176, 182, 185; the "quick-fix" gospel
of, 182
convenience foods, 3, 139, 175–76, 177
Cook, James, 171, 172
Cooley, Anna, 37, 39, 94–95
Cooperative Extension Service, 198n.16. See
also extension programs
cooperative living, 44–45, 47–48, 95, 151,
153–54. See also practice houses
Cornell Center for Housing and Environment Studies, 148
Cornell Research Foundation, 88
Cornell University, College of Hotel Management, 130
Cornell University, Department of Home
Economics: clothing design students, 38;
courses on the study of women, 49–50,
195n.58; culturally sensitive home economics, 28; "demonstration cars," 69, 70,
198n.18; departmental name change, 171;
Depression-era Milkorno foodstuff, 88–89;
early food science and nutrition courses,
28; male students and institutional management courses (1950s), 129, 130;
post-World War I radio shows, 73; practice-house babies, 44, 45, 45–46, 195n.50;
"Statement of Belief," 98; story of the cabbage-eating legislator, 29–30; World War I-
era extension services, 69, 70, 198n.16,
198n.18; World War II-era educators and
curriculum, 97–98
Cornell University, New York State College
of Agriculture, 80
Corning Glass Works, 134–35, 200n.44
Cosmopolitan magazine, 141–43
counterculture: gender oppression in, 146–47;
hippie home economics and "back to the
land" movement, 150–60; and ideals of
first-generation home economists, 150,

151–52; interest in nutrition and "health
food," 150–51; and Laurel's Kitchen, 152–60;
and marketing of traditional gendered domesticity, 155–56; and self-reeducation of
one's attitudes, 159–60; and women's increased household tasks, 150–51. See also
feminism, second-wave; home economics
in the 1960s and 1970s
Craftsman magazine, 54
Crisco, 2, 84
Crowley, Ruth, 132
Curb Appeal (television program), 184

Daniels, Amy, 24, 195n.50
Day, Edna, 35
Deen, Paula, 182–83
The Delineator (magazine), 77, 78, 199n.35
"demonstration cars," 69, 70, 198nn.17–18
Dennen, Jeanne W., 66–67
Department of Health, Education, and
Welfare, 129
Depression. See home economics in the
Depression (1930s)
design courses and early home economics education, 36–42; aesthetic philosophy,
36–37, 39–41, 43, 193n.41; Arts and Crafts
movement, 39–41, 79, 151; clothing design
and construction, 36–39; collective title of
Household or Domestic Arts, 36; and
courses traditionally associated with
women's work, 37; domestic architecture
courses, 41, 194n.45; empowerment of students, 41–42; and home economists' authority and control, 42; house design and
construction, 40; and "principles of clothing selection," 37–38; study of historic
clothing, 37, 38; and utility, 40–41,
194nn.42–43; and woman as spiritual
guardian of home and family, 39; and
women's role as textile consumer, 37,
193n.36
The Designer (magazine), 77
Dewey, Melvil, 9
Dewson, Molly, 34–35
Diggers movement, 151, 207n.13
Discovery Health Channel, 185
divorce rates, 103, 106, 110
domestic advice manuals, 3–4, 6–7
domestic advice media. See contemporary domestic advice media
"domestic feminists," 9, 194n.45

training for marriage, 44; as unlike real domestic situations, 48
primary schools. *See* home economics education (primary and secondary schools)
*Principles of Human Nutrition: A Study in Practical Dietetics* (Jordan), 23–24
professionalism: and anti-amateurism of late nineteenth century, 27; and emergence of academic field, 1–2, 52; kitchen laboratories and lab coats/uniforms, 23, *24, 25*; and renaming of academic departments, 166–72, 173–74; subverted by portrait of home economics as training for marriage/motherhood, 116
progressive movement and home economics, 9–13; bacteriology and sanitation courses, 21, 22; and industrial revolution, 7; and Lake Placid Conferences, 8–9; nostalgic modernism, 12; nutrition courses and social health, 28–29; overlap between settlement house movement, social work, and home economics, 12, 14; progressive reform model in higher education, 10–11; scientific management applied to domestic sphere, 11–12; social reform impulses, 11, 21, 22; and stigma of women's work, 8–9; World War I-era, 67, 197n.11

*Queer Eye for the Straight Guy* (television program), 186

radio: corporate sponsors, 73–77; non-corporate-sponsored shows, 77; post–World War I era (1920s), 73–77, 131; and professional authority, 77; university radio stations, 73; and virtual communities, 74–77; and World War II-era home economics message, 96
Raitt, Effie, 60, 61
Ray, Rachael, 182, 183, 186
*Real Simple* magazine, 176, 186
*Redbook* magazine, 162, 182
Reed, Hazel, 139
Reynolds Wrap, 173, 175
Rhodes, Opal T., 103
Richards, Ellen, 105, 152, 175, 184; advice pamphlets for Columbian Exposition, 7–8, 26; bacteriology and sanitation courses, 21; and FHA creed, 120; food science and nutrition courses, 23, 28–29; and home economics as early academic field, 11, 21, 23,

28–29; and *Laurel's Kitchen*, 154, 158, 159; at MIT, 11; model kitchen at Columbian Exposition, 7, 189n.8; on palatability, 26; portrayal as heroine for a new age, 13
Riis, Jacob, 28–29
Robertson, Laurel, 153–60
Roemer, John L., 65–66
*Rooms for Improvement* (television program), 132
Roosevelt, Eleanor: and aesthetic philosophy of home design, 40, 194n.42; feminism of, 90; friendships/alliances with home economists, 64, 159; public adoption of home economics philosophy, 88, 89–90, 194n.42
Roosevelt, Franklin, 64
Rose, Flora: alliances with state officials, 64; and the cabbage-eating legislator, 29–30; Cornell course on the study of women, 49–50; and Cornell's practice-house baby, 195n.50; and Depression-era low-cost menu, 90, 159; domestic partnership with Van Renssaeler, 50, 199n.35; establishing department at Cornell, 17, 19, 27–28; and writing for women's magazines, 199n.35
Rossiter, Margaret, 56, 129, 130, 167, 169
Rugg, Bertha Miller, 196n.64
Rumford Kitchen exhibit, Columbian Exposition, 7–8, 26, 189n.8

Sanitary Science Club, 21
sanitation courses, 20–22, 191n.4
*Saturday Evening Post*, 46
School Lunch Act (1946) and school lunch programs, 127
School of Domestic Arts and Sciences (Chicago), 14
School of Housekeeping (Boston), 34–35
*School Review*, 97
*Scientific American*, 42
scientific management, 11–12
Scott, Anna, 57–58
Scott, Elizabeth, 84
*Selling Mrs. Consumer* (Frederick), 84
*Semi-homemade* (television program), 182
separate-spheres gender ideology, 160, 162
settlement house movement, 12, 14
Shapiro, Laura, 192n.15
*Sharing Work at Home* (film), 107–8
Shaw, Byron, 129
Shaw, Pauline Agassiz, 28–29

# ACKNOWLEDGMENTS

MANY PEOPLE HAVE helped me through the stages of this project, and all deserve thanks. During the past four years I have enjoyed the support, through grants, of the Professional Staff Congress of the City University of New York and the anonymous reviewers who kept giving me the green light to continue working on this project. In addition, my colleagues at various campuses of the City University of New York have offered sustaining moral support.

I owe a great debt to David Nasaw, the Arthur M. Schlesinger, Jr. Professor of History at the City University of New York Graduate Center, for his continuing encouragement and example of prolific and significant scholarship. Alice Kessler-Harris, Thomas Kessner, Louis Menand, and Barbara Welter all also provided wise suggestions for improving this manuscript.

Kathy Feeley, Abigail Lewis, Cindy Lobel, and Delia Mellis all read or heard me ponder aloud parts of this work and responded with the kind of constructive criticism that makes scholarship a rewarding challenge. Annie Hauck-Lawson and Jonathan Deutsch gave me an opportunity to think more deeply about the culinary aesthetic of home economics. Conference participants in America, England, and Ireland asked useful questions as I presented pieces of this work, and I hope I was able to engage those questions successfully.

I have benefited immeasurably from working with Robert Lockhart at the University of Pennsylvania Press. He saw in my first proposal the different and more interesting book that it has been a pleasure to write. I am also grateful for the suggestions of Sarah Stage and an anonymous reader for the Press who helped me further refine my ideas.

Archivists across the country have kindly guided me through their collections, and I wish to thank in particular those of the National Archives and Records Administration in College Park, Maryland, who generously took time to think about where I might find the kinds of things I was looking for and then helped me find them. Susan Strange did me a great service in finding not only the particular image I was searching for in the National Archives but a far better one. The archivists of the Division of Rare and Manuscript Collections at Cornell University are also paragons of their profession, expressing genuine insight into the work of researchers who visit their institution.

Members of my family have been unfailingly supportive through this process, allowing me to ramble on about ideas and to serve them unfashionable foods. My father, Stephen Elias, asked vexing questions, which is his treasured talent. My aunt, Elizabeth Christenfeld, has been a particularly good friend to me and to this project. She and my uncle, Roger Christenfeld, and the extended Christenfeld, Cairns-Smith, Gordon, and Sanders families provided models of rigorous intellect and good cheer. My husband, Preston Johnson, who has been so generous with his confidence in me, continually demonstrates that equitable domestic partnership is not just possible but a pleasure.